A Programmer's Guide to C# 5.0

Eric Gunnerson

Apress®

A Programmer's Guide to C# 5.0

ISBN-13 (pbk): 978-1-4302-4593-3

ISBN-13 (electronic): 978-1-4302-4594-0

President and Publisher: Paul Manning
Lead Editor: Gwenan Spearing
Technical Reviewer: Jonathan Allen
Editorial Board: Steve Anglin, Ewan Buckingham, Gary Cornell, Louise Corrigan, Morgan Ertel, Jonathan Gennick, Jonathan Hassell, Robert Hutchinson, Michelle Lowman, James Markham, Matthew Moodie, Jeff Olson, Jeffrey Pepper, Douglas Pundick, Ben Renow-Clarke, Dominic Shakeshaft, Gwenan Spearing, Matt Wade, Tom Welsh
Coordinating Editor: Kevin Shea
Copy Editor: Kim Wimpsett
Compositor: SPi Global
Indexer: SPi Global
Artist: SPi Global
Cover Designer: Anna Ishchenko

Distributed to the book trade worldwide by Springer Science+Business Media New York, 233 Spring Street, 6th Floor, New York, NY 10013. Phone 1-800-SPRINGER, fax (201) 348-4505, e-mail orders-ny@springer-sbm.com, or visit www.springeronline.com.

For information on translations, please e-mail rights@apress.com, or visit www.apress.com.

Apress and friends of ED books may be purchased in bulk for academic, corporate, or promotional use. eBook versions and licenses are also available for most titles. For more information, reference our Special Bulk Sales–eBook Licensing web page at www.apress.com/bulk-sales.

Any source code or other supplementary materials referenced by the author in this text is available to readers at www.apress.com. For detailed information about how to locate your book's source code, go to www.apress.com/source-code.

To Tony Jongejan, for being ahead of his time and introducing me to programming.

—Eric Gunnerson

Contents at a Glance

Contents

Preface

It was January 4, 1999, and the Visual C++ team had just returned from our holiday break, ready to put the finishing touches on a new version of Visual C++.[1] We had a surprise group meeting and discovered that the entire developer division was switching gears; our release was canceled, and we were going to work on a new thing that would become the .NET managed environment, libraries, and compilers.

I transitioned from test lead on the C++ compiler parser to test lead on a new language that we were building—one that would be a natural fit with the new environment. At that point, the language spec was only in an embryonic stage, and to understand how this language was supposed to work, I joined the design team. That led to a very enjoyable period, working with a small group of very smart people. A few years later, we were releasing the first version of C# and .NET to the world, and from the response, it was clear that developing for Microsoft platforms would never be the same.

More than 12 years have passed since the day I first picked up the language spec. C# was the kind of language that I always wanted to use when it was first released, and innovations such as Linq have only made it better. I'm confident that recent additions such as asynchronous support and treating the compiler as a service will continue that tradition.

I hope you enjoy this look behind the language.

—Eric Gunnerson

---

[1] If I recall correctly, it would have been Visual C++ V6.5.

About the Author

After narrowly escaping the era of punch cards, **Eric Gunnerson** worked at various companies before landing at Microsoft, where he has worked on Visual C++, Visual C#, Windows DVD Maker, Microsoft HealthVault, and, most recently, internal tools in the Engineering Excellence group.

He was a member of the C# language design team through the development of the early versions of the language and was the author of a well-trafficked blog during that time.

In his spare time, he enjoys skiing and ski instruction, leading bicycle rides, doing home improvement, working on microcontroller projects, and writing about himself in the third person.

About the Technical Reviewer

Jonathan Allen is a lead editor for the news site InfoQ and a software developer for the consulting firm Cynergy. He got his start working on MIS projects for a health clinic in the late 1990s, bringing them up from Access and Excel to an enterprise solution by degrees. After spending five years writing automated trading systems for the financial sector, he decided to shift to high-end user interface development. In his free time he enjoys studying and writing about Western martial arts from the 15th through 17th centuries.

Acknowledgments

Thanks to all who helped me with this project over the years, including the team members who answered questions, the team at Apress, and the readers who sent in courteous notes when I made mistakes.

Special thanks to the spouse and offspring, who once again sacrificed family time for the latest version of this project.

—Eric Gunnerson

Introduction

When I started on the first edition of this book, I got some very sage advice. "Write the book that you wish existed."

This is not a book to teach you how to write code, nor is it a detailed language specification. It is designed to explain both how C# works and why it works that way—the kind of book that a professional developer who is going to be writing C# code would want.

Who This Book Is For

This book is for software developers who want to understand why C# is designed the way it is and how to use it effectively. The content assumes familiarity with object-oriented programming concepts.

How This Book Is Structured

After a couple of introductory chapters, the book progresses from the simpler C# features to the more complex ones. You can read the chapters in order, working your way through the entire language. Or you can choose an individual chapter to understand the details of a specific feature.

If you are new to C#, I suggest you start by reading the chapters on properties, generics, delegates and events, as well as the Linq chapters. These are the areas where C# is most different from other languages.

If you are more interested in the details of the language syntax, you may find it useful to download the C# Language Reference from MSDN.

Downloading the Code

The code for the examples shown in this book is available on the Apress web site, `www.apress.com`. You can find a link on the book's information page. Scroll down and click on the Source Code/Downloads tab.

Contacting the Author

One of the humbling parts of being an author is that despite the best efforts of the technical reviewer and copy editor, mistakes and poor explanations will show up in any book. If you have found such a mistake or have a comment, you can contact me at `csharpguide@outlook.com`.

CHAPTER 1

▪ ▪ ▪

C# and the .NET Runtime and Libraries

If you are reading this chapter, my guess is that you are interested in learning more about C#. Welcome.

This book is primarily about the C# language, but before diving into the details, it is important to understand the basics of the environment in which C# code is written.

The C# compiler will take C# programs and convert them into an intermediate language that can be executed only by the .NET Common Language Runtime (CLR). Languages that target a runtime are sometimes known as *managed languages*[1] and are contrasted with unmanaged languages such as C++ that do not require a runtime[2] and therefore run directly on the hardware.[3]

The .NET Runtime manages memory allocation, security, type safety, exception handling, and many other low-level concerns. There are several different variants of the .NET Runtime, running on everything from multiprocessor servers to smartphones to microcontrollers.

To perform useful tasks, your C# code will be using code in the .NET Base Class Library (BCL). The BCL contains classes that are likely to be useful to many programs and includes support for the following:

- Performing network operations

- Performing I/O operations

- Managing security

- Globalizing programs[4]

- Manipulating text

- Accessing a database

- Manipulating XML

- Interacting with event logging, tracing, and other diagnostic operations

- Using unmanaged code

- Creating and calling code dynamically

---

[1]Java is another managed language; it runs using the Java Virtual Machine (JVM), and Visual Basic is of course another language that runs on the CLR.
[2]Confusingly, C and C++ use the C Runtime, which is a collection of libraries and not a runtime like the .NET Runtime.
[3]Microsoft Visual C++ can be used as either a managed or unmanaged language (or both).
[4]Globalization helps developers write applications that can be used in different areas of the world. It helps the application support multiple languages, different date and number formats, and so on.

1

The BCL is big enough that it would be easy to get confused; the various capabilities are organized into *namespaces*. For example, the System.Globalization namespace is used to help with globalization, the System.XML namespace is used to manipulate XML, and so on.

Layered on top of the BCL are specialized libraries that are targeted to creating specific types of applications or services, including the following:

- Console applications
- Windows GUI applications, using either Windows Forms or the Windows Presentation Foundation (WPF)
- ASP.NET (web) applications
- Windows Services
- Service-oriented applications, using Windows Communication Foundation (WCF)
- Workflow-enabled applications, Windows Workflow Foundation (WF)
- Windows 8 applications
- Windows Phone applications

The Base Class Library and all of the other libraries are referred to collectively as the .NET Framework.

MANAGED VS. UNMANAGED CODE

If you are used to writing unmanaged code, writing C# code may be a bit unsettling. The runtime manages some things that you previously controlled yourself, which does reduce the flexibility you have. After you have explored the capabilities of the .NET Framework, I think you will find that in the vast majority of cases, you can write much more quickly and with higher quality using C#.

■ ■ ■

CHAPTER 2

C# QuickStart and Developing in C#

This chapter presents a quick overview of the C# language. It assumes a certain level of programming knowledge and therefore doesn't present very much detail. If the explanation here doesn't make sense, look for a more detailed explanation of the particular topic later in the book.

The second part of the chapter discusses how to obtain the C# compiler and the advantages of using Visual Studio to develop C# applications.

Hello, Universe

As a supporter of SETI,[1] I thought that it would be appropriate to do a "Hello, Universe" program rather than the canonical "Hello, World" program.

```
using System;
class Hello
{
    public static void Main(string[] args)
    {
        Console.WriteLine("Hello, Universe");

            // iterate over command-line arguments,
            // and print them out
        for (int arg = 0; arg < args.Length; arg++)
        {
            Console.WriteLine("Arg {0}: {1}", arg, args[arg]);
        }
    }
}
```

As discussed earlier, the .NET Runtime has a unified namespace for all program information (or metadata). The using System clause is a way of referencing the classes that are in the System namespace so they can be used without having to put System in front of the type name. The System namespace contains many useful classes, one of which is the Console class, which is used (not surprisingly) to communicate with the console (or DOS box, or command line, for those who have never seen a console).

Because there are no global functions in C#, the example declares a class called Hello that contains the static Main() function, which serves as the starting point for execution. Main() can be declared with no parameters or with a string array. Since it's the starting function, it must be a static function, which means it isn't associated with an instance of an object.

---

[1] Search for Extraterrestrial Intelligence. See http://www.teamseti.org for more information.

The first line of the function calls the `WriteLine()` function of the `Console` class, which will write "Hello, Universe" to the console. The `for` loop iterates over the parameters that are passed in and then writes out a line for each parameter on the command line.

Namespace and Using Statements

Namespaces in the .NET Runtime are used to organize classes and other types into a single hierarchical structure. The proper use of namespaces will make classes easy to use and prevent collisions with classes written by other authors.

Namespaces can also be thought of as a way to specify long and useful names for classes and other types without having to always type a full name.

Namespaces are defined using the `namespace` statement. For multiple levels of organization, namespaces can be nested:

```
namespace Outer
{
    namespace Inner
    {
        class MyClass
        {
            public static void Function() {}
        }
    }
}
```

That's a fair amount of typing and indenting, so it can be simplified by using the following instead:

```
namespace Outer.Inner
{
    class MyClass
    {
        public static void Function() {}
    }
}
```

A source file can define more than one namespace, but in the majority of cases, all the code within one file lives in a single namespace.

The fully qualified name of a class—the name of the namespace followed by the name of the class—can become quite long. The following is an example of such a class:

```
System.Xml.Serialization.Advanced.SchemaImporterExtension
```

It would be very tedious to have to write that full class name every time we wanted to use it, so we can add a `using` statement:

```
using System.Xml.Serialization.Advanced;
```

This statement says, "treat all of the types defined inside this namespace as if they don't have a namespace in front of them," which allows us to use

```
SchemaImporterExtension
```

instead of the full name. The using statement only works for types directly inside the namespace; if we had the following using statement:

```
using System.Xml.Serialization;
```

we would not be able to use the following name:

```
Advanced.SchemaImporterExtension
```

With a limited number of names in the world, there will sometimes be cases where the same name is used in two different namespaces. Collisions between types or namespaces that have the same name can always be resolved by using a type's fully qualified name. This could be a very long name if the class is deeply nested, so there is a variant of the using clause that allows an alias to be defined to a class:

```
using ThatConsoleClass = System.Console;
class Hello
{
    public static void Main()
    {
        ThatConsoleClass.WriteLine("Hello");
    }
}
```

To make the code more readable, the examples in this book rarely use namespaces, but they should be used in most real code.

Namespaces and Assemblies

An object can be used from within a C# source file only if that object can be located by the C# compiler. By default, the compiler will only open the single assembly known as mscorlib.dll, which contains the core functions for the Common Language Runtime.

To reference objects located in other assemblies, the name of the assembly file must be passed to the compiler. This can be done on the command line using the /r:<assembly> option or from within the Visual Studio IDE by adding a reference to the C# project.

Typically, there is a correlation between the namespace that an object is in and the name of the assembly in which it resides. For example, the types in the System.Net namespace and child namespaces reside in the System.Net.dll assembly. This may be revised based on the usage patterns of the objects in that assembly; a large or rarely used type in a namespace may reside in a separate assembly.

The exact name of the assembly that an object is contained in can be found in the online MSDN documentation for that object.

Basic Data Types

C# supports the usual set of data types. For each data type that C# supports, there is a corresponding underlying .NET Common Language Runtime type. For example, the int type in C# maps to the System.Int32 type in the runtime. System.Int32 can be used in most of the places where int is used, but that isn't recommended because it makes the code tougher to read.

The basic data types are described in Table 2-1. The runtime types can all be found in the System namespace of the .NET Common Language Runtime.

Table 2-1. *Basic Data Types in C#*

Type	Size in Bytes	Runtime Type	Description
byte	1	Byte	Unsigned byte
sbyte	1	SByte	Signed byte
short	2	Int16	Signed short
ushort	2	UInt16	Unsigned short
int	4	Int32	Signed integer
uint	4	UInt32	Unsigned int
long	8	Int64	Signed big integer
ulong	8	UInt64	Unsigned big integer
float	4	Single	Floating point number
double	8	Double	Double-precision floating point number
decimal	8	Decimal	Fixed-precision number
string	Variable	String	Unicode string
char	2	Char	Unicode character
bool	1	Boolean	Boolean value

The distinction between basic (or built-in) types and user-defined ones is largely an artificial one, as user-defined types can operate in the same manner as the built-in ones. In fact, the only real difference between the built-in data types and user-defined data types is that it is possible to write literal values for the built-in types.

Data types are separated into value types and reference types. *Value types* are either stack allocated or allocated inline in a structure. *Reference types* are heap allocated.

Both reference and value types are derived from the ultimate base class object. In cases where a value type needs to act like an object, a wrapper that makes the value type look like a reference object is allocated on the heap, and the value type's value is copied into it. This process is known as *boxing*, and the reverse process is known as *unboxing*. Boxing and unboxing let you treat *any* type as an object. That allows the following to be written:

```
using System;
class Hello
{
    public static void Main(string[] args)
    {
        Console.WriteLine("Value is: {0}", 3);
    }
}
```

In this case, the integer 3 is boxed, and the Int32.ToString() function is called on the boxed value.

C# arrays can be declared in either the multidimensional or jagged forms. More advanced data structures, such as stacks and hash tables, can be found in the System.Collections and System.Collections.Generic namespaces.

Classes, Structs, and Interfaces

In C#, the class keyword is used to declare a reference (a heap-allocated) type, and the struct keyword is used to declare a value type. Structs are used for lightweight objects that need to act like the built-in types, and classes are used in all other cases. For example, the int type is a value type, and the string type is a reference type. Figure 2-1 details how these work.

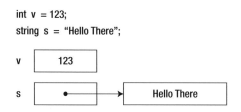

Figure 2-1. *Value and reference type allocation*

C# and the .NET Runtime do not support multiple inheritance for classes but do support multiple implementation of interfaces.

Statements

The statements in C# are similar to C++ statements, with a few modifications to make errors less likely,[2] and a few new statements. The foreach statement is used to iterate over arrays and collections, the lock statement is used for mutual exclusion in threading scenarios, and the checked and unchecked statements are used to control overflow checking in arithmetic operations and conversions.

Enums

Enumerations are used to declare a set of related constants—such as the colors that a control can take—in a clear and type-safe manner. For example:

```
enum Colors
{
    red,
    green,
    blue
}
```

Enumerations are covered in more detail in Chapter 20.

---

[2] In C#, the switch statement does not allow fall through, and it is not possible to accidentally write "if (x = 3)" instead of "if (x == 3)".

Delegates and Events

Delegates are a type-safe, object-oriented implementation of function pointers and are used in many situations where a component needs to call back to the component that is using it. They are used as the basis for events, which allows a delegate to easily be registered for an event. They are discussed in Chapter 22.

Properties and Indexers

C# supports properties and indexers, which are useful for separating the interface of an object from the implementation of the object. Rather than allowing a user to access a field or array directly, a property or indexer allows a code block to be specified to perform the access, while still allowing the field or array usage. Here's a simple example:

```
using System;
class Circle
{
    public int Radius
    {
        get
        {
            return(m_radius);
        }
        set
        {
            m_radius = value;
            Draw();
        }
    }
    public void Draw()
    {
        Console.WriteLine("Drawing circle of radius: {0}", radius);
    }
    int m_radius;
}
class Test
{
    public static void Main()
    {
        Circle c = new Circle();
        c.Radius = 35;
    }
}
```

The code in the get or set blocks (known as accessors) is called when the value of the Radius property is get or set.

Attributes

Attributes are used in C# and the .NET Frameworks to communicate declarative information from the writer of the code to other code that is interested in the information. They might be used to specify which fields of an object should be serialized, what transaction context to use when running an object, how to marshal fields to native functions, or how to display a class in a class browser.

Attributes are specified within square braces. A typical attribute usage might look like this:

```
[CodeReview("12/31/1999", Comment = "Well done")]
```

Attribute information is retrieved at runtime through a process known as *reflection*. New attributes can be easily written, applied to elements of the code (such as classes, members, or parameters), and retrieved through reflection.

Developing in C#

To program in C#, you're going to need a way to build C# programs. You can do this with a command-line compiler, Visual Studio, or a C# package for a programming editor.

Visual Studio provides a great environment in which to develop C# programs. If cost is an issue, the Visual Studio Express product covers most development scenarios, and the SharpDevelop IDE is also available. Both are available free of charge.

If you are targeting non-Microsoft platforms, the Mono project provides a C# environment that can target Linux, iOS, and Android.

Tools of Note

There are a number of tools that you may find useful when developing in C#. They are discussed in the following sections.

ILDASM

ILDASM (Intermediate Language [IL] Disassembler) is the most useful tool in the software development kit (SDK). It can open an assembly, show all the types in the assembly, what methods are defined for those types, and the IL that was generated for that method.

This is useful in a number of ways. Like the object browser, it can be used to find out what's present in an assembly, but it can also be used to find out how a specific method is implemented. This capability can be used to answer some questions about C#.

If, for example, you want to know whether C# will concatenate constant strings at compile time, it's easy to test. First, a short program is created:

```
using System;
class Test
{
    public static void Main()
    {
        Console.WriteLine("Hello " + "World");
    }
}
```

After the program is compiled, ILDASM can be used to view the IL for `Main()`:

```
.method public hidebysig static void Main() cil managed
{
  .entrypoint
  // Code size       11 (0xb)
```

```
  .maxstack  8
  IL_0000:  ldstr      "Hello World"
  IL_0005:  call       void [mscorlib]System.Console::WriteLine(string)
  IL_000a:  ret
} // end of method Test::Main
```

Even without knowing the details of the IL language, it's pretty clear that the two strings are concatenated into a single string.

Decompilers

The presence of metadata in .NET assemblies makes it feasible to decompile an assembly back to C# code.[3] There are a few decompilers available; I've been using DotPeek from JetBrains recently.

Obfuscators

If you are concerned about the IP in your code, you can use an obfuscator on your code to make it harder to understand when decompiled. A limited version of Dotfuscator ships with Visual Studio.

Spend some time understanding what a specific obfuscator can give you before decided to use it to obfuscate your code.

NGEN

NGEN (Native Image Generator) is a tool that performs the translation from IL to native processor code before the program is executed, rather than doing it on demand.

At first glance, this seems like a way to get around many of the disadvantages of the just-in-time (JIT) approach; simply pre-JIT the code, and performance will be better and nobody will be able to decode the IL.

Unfortunately, things don't work that way. Pre-JIT is only a way to store the results of the compilation, but the metadata is still required to do class layout and support reflection. Further, the generated native code is only valid for a specific environment, and if configuration settings (such as the machine security policy) change, the Runtime will switch back to the normal JIT.

Although pre-JIT does eliminate the overhead of the JIT process, it also produces code that runs slightly slower because it requires a level of indirection that isn't required with the normal JIT.

So, the real benefit of pre-JIT is to reduce the JIT overhead (and therefore the startup time) of a client application, and it isn't really very useful elsewhere.

---

[3] Or, at least, something that is good enough to understand.

CHAPTER 3

■ ■ ■

Classes 101

Classes are the heart of any application in an object-oriented language. This chapter is broken into several sections. The first section describes the parts of C# that will be used often, and the later sections describe things that won't be used as often, depending on what kind of code is being written.

A Simple Class

A C# class can be very simple:

```
class VerySimple
{
    int m_simpleValue = 0;
}
class Test
{
    public static void Main()
    {
        VerySimple vs = new VerySimple();
    }
}
```

This class is a container for a single integer. Because the integer is declared without specifying how accessible it is, it's private to the VerySimple class and can't be referenced outside the class. The private modifier could be specified to state this explicitly.

The integer m_simpleValue is a member of the class; there can be many different types of members, and a simple variable that is part of the class is known as a *field*.

In the Main() function, the system creates an instance of the class and returns a reference to the instance. A reference is simply a way to refer to an instance.[1]

There is no need to specify when an instance is no longer needed. In the preceding example, as soon as the Main() function completes, the reference to the instance will no longer exist. If the reference hasn't been stored elsewhere, the instance will then be available for reclamation by the garbage collector. The garbage collector will reclaim the memory that was allocated when necessary.[2]

---

[1] For those of you used to pointers, a reference is a pointer that you can only assign to and dereference.
[2] The garbage collector used in the .NET Runtime is discussed in Chapter 39. At this point it is reasonable to just assume that it handles all the memory for you.

C# FIELD NAMING CONVENTIONS

There are a few common choices for the naming of fields in C# classes:

- A bare name: "salary"

- A name preceded by an underscore: "_salary"

- A name preceded by "m_": "m_salary"

- An uppercase name preceded by "m_": "m_Salary"

In the early days of .NET and C#, there was a conscious decision to move far away from the Hungarian notation common in C/C++ code, the convention that gave us names such as lpszName. Most of the early code that I wrote[3] used the bare name syntax, but since then I've been in groups that have used the other syntaxes and have written a fair amount of code in all three.

While it is true that modern IDEs have made it much easier to understand the type of a variable with minimal effort, I still find it very useful to know which variables are instance variables and which ones are local variables or parameters. I am also not a fan of having to use "this." in constructors to disambiguate.

I preferred the second syntax for a while but have since converted to using the third syntax, which coincidentally (or perhaps not given the time I spent on the VC++ team) is the same syntax used by the Microsoft Foundation Class libraries.

This is all very nice, but this class doesn't do anything useful because the integer isn't accessible. Here's a more useful example:[4]

```
using System;
class Point
{
        // constructor
    public Point(int x, int y)
    {
        m_x = x;
        m_y = y;
    }

        // member fields
    public int m_x;
    public int m_y;
}

class Test
{
    public static void Main()
    {
        Point myPoint = new Point(10, 15);
```

---

[3] Including the code in earlier versions of this book.

[4] If you were really going to implement your own point class, you'd probably want it to be a value type (struct). We'll talk more about structs in Chapter 8.

```
        Console.WriteLine("myPoint.x {0}", myPoint.m_x);
        Console.WriteLine("myPoint.y {0}", myPoint.m_y);
    }
}
```

In this example, there is a class named Point, with two integers in the class named m_x and m_y. These members are public, which means that their values can be accessed by any code that uses the class.

In addition to the data members, there is a constructor for the class, which is a special function that is called to help construct an instance of the class. The constructor takes two integer parameters. It is called in the Main() method.

In addition to the Point class, there is a Test class that contains a Main function that is called to start the program. The Main function creates an instance of the Point class, which will allocate memory for the object and then call the constructor for the class. The constructor will set the values for m_x and m_y. The remainder of the lines of Main() print out the values of m_x and m_y.

In this example, the data fields are accessed directly. This is usually a bad idea, because it means that users of the class depend on the names of fields, which constrains the modifications that can be made later.

In C#, rather than writing a member function to access a private value, a property would be used, which gives the benefits of a member function while retaining the user model of a field. Chapter 16 discusses properties in more detail.

Member Functions

The constructor in the previous example is an example of a member function; a piece of code that is called on an instance of the object. Constructors can only be called automatically when an instance of an object is created with new.

Other member functions can be declared as follows:

```
using System;
class Point
{
    public Point(int x, int y)
    {
        m_x = x;
        m_y = y;
    }

        // accessor functions
    public int GetX() {return m_x;}
    public int GetY() {return m_y;}

        // variables now private
    int m_x;
    int m_y;
}

class Test
{
    public static void Main()
    {
        Point myPoint = new Point(10, 15);
        Console.WriteLine("myPoint.X {0}", myPoint.GetX());
        Console.WriteLine("myPoint.Y {0}", myPoint.GetY());
    }
}
```

ref and out Parameters

Having to call two member functions to get the values may not always be convenient, so it would be nice to be able to get both values with a single function call. There's only one return value, however.

One solution is to use reference (or ref) parameters, so that the values of the parameters passed into the member function can be modified:

```
using System;
class Point
{
    public Point(int x, int y)
    {
        m_x = x;
        m_y = y;
    }
        // get both values in one function call
    public void GetPoint(ref int x, ref int y)
    {
        x = m_x;
        y = m_y;
    }
    int m_x;
    int m_y;
}

class Test
{
    public static void Main()
    {
        Point myPoint = new Point(10, 15);
        int x;
        int y;

            // illegal
        myPoint.GetPoint(ref x, ref y);
        Console.WriteLine("myPoint({0}, {1})", x, y);
    }
}
```

In this code, the parameters have been declared using the ref keyword, as has the call to the function.

This code appears to be correct, but when compiled, it generates an error message that says that uninitialized values were used for the ref parameters x and y. This means that variables were passed into the function before having their values set, and the compiler won't allow the values of uninitialized variables to be exposed.

There are two ways around this. The first is to initialize the variables when they are declared:

```csharp
using System;
class Point
{
    public Point(int x, int y)
    {
        m_x = x;
        m_y = y;
    }

    public void GetPoint(ref int x, ref int y)
    {
        x = m_x;
        y = m_y;
    }

    int m_x;
    int m_y;
}

class Test
{
    public static void Main()
    {
        Point myPoint = new Point(10, 15);
        int x=0;
        int y=0;

        myPoint.GetPoint(ref x, ref y);
        Console.WriteLine("myPoint({0}, {1})", x, y);
    }
}
```

The code now compiles, but the variables are initialized to zero only to be overwritten in the call to GetPoint(). For C#, another option is to change the definition of the function GetPoint() to use an out parameter rather than a ref parameter:

```csharp
using System;
class Point
{
    public Point(int x, int y)
    {
        m_x = x;
        m_y = y;
    }

    public void GetPoint(out int x, out int y)
    {
        x = m_x;
        y = m_y;
    }
```

```
        int m_x;
        int m_y;
}

class Test
{
    public static void Main()
    {
        Point myPoint = new Point(10, 15);
        int x;
        int y;

        myPoint.GetPoint(out x, out y);
        Console.WriteLine("myPoint({0}, {1})", x, y);
    }
}
```

Out parameters are exactly like ref parameters except that an uninitialized variable can be passed to them, and the call is made with out rather than ref.[5]

■ **Note**   It's fairly uncommon to use ref or out parameters in C#. If you find yourself wanting to use them, I suggest taking a step back and seeing if there isn't a better solution.

Overloading

Sometimes it may be useful to have two functions that do the same thing but take different parameters. This is especially common for constructors, when there may be several ways to create a new instance.

```
class Point
{
        // create a new point from x and y values
    public Point(int x, int y)
    {
        m_x = x;
        m_y = y;
    }
        // create a point from an existing point
    public Point(Point p)
    {
        m_x = p.m_x;
        m_y = p.m_y;
    }

    int m_x;
    int m_y;
}
```

---

[5] From the perspective of other .NET languages, there is no difference between ref and out parameters. A C# program calling this function will see the parameters as out parameters, but other languages will see them as ref parameters.

```
class Test
{
    public static void Main()
    {
        Point myPoint = new Point(10, 15);
        Point mySecondPoint = new Point(myPoint);
    }
}
```

The class has two constructors: one that can be called with x and y values, and one that can be called with another point. The Main() function uses both constructors: one to create an instance from an x and y value, and another to create an instance from an already-existing instance.[6]

When an overloaded function is called, the compiler chooses the proper function by matching the parameters in the call to the parameters declared for the function.

---

[6]This function may look like a C++ copy constructor, but the C# language doesn't use such a concept. A constructor such as this must be called explicitly.

■ ■ ■

CHAPTER 4

Base Classes and Inheritance

Class inheritance is a commonly used construct[1] in object-oriented languages, and C# provides a full implementation.

The Engineer Class

The following class implements an Engineer class and methods to handle billing for that Engineer.

```
using System;
class Engineer
{
        // constructor
    public Engineer(string name, float billingRate)
    {
        m_name = name;
        m_billingRate = billingRate;
    }
        // figure out the charge based on engineer's rate
    public float CalculateCharge(float hours)
    {
        return(hours * m_billingRate);
    }
        // return the name of this type
    public string TypeName()
    {
        return("Engineer");
    }
    private string m_name;
    private float m_billingRate;
}
class Test
{
    public static void Main()
```

---

[1]Too commonly used, in my opinion, but that discussion would be another book.

```
    {
        Engineer engineer = new Engineer("Hank", 21.20F);
        Console.WriteLine("Name is: {0}", engineer.TypeName());
    }
}
```

Engineer will serve as a base class for this scenario. It contains private fields to store the name of the engineer and the engineer's billing rate, along with a member function that can be used to calculate the charge based on the number of hours of work done.

Simple Inheritance

A `CivilEngineer` is a type of engineer and therefore can be derived from the Engineer class:

```
using System;
class Engineer
{
    public Engineer(string name, float billingRate)
    {
        m_name = name;
        m_billingRate = billingRate;
    }

    public float CalculateCharge(float hours)
    {
        return(hours * m_billingRate);
    }

    public string TypeName()
    {
        return("Engineer");
    }

    private string m_name;
    protected float m_billingRate;
}
class CivilEngineer: Engineer
{
    public CivilEngineer(string name, float billingRate) :
        base(name, billingRate)
    {
    }
        // new function, because it's different than the
        // same as base version
    public new float CalculateCharge(float hours)
    {
        if (hours < 1.0F)
        {
            hours = 1.0F;          // minimum charge.
        }
```

```
            return(hours * m_billingRate);
        }
            // new function, because it's different than the
            // base version
        public new string TypeName()
        {
            return("Civil Engineer");
        }
    }
}
class Test
{
    public static void Main()
    {
        Engineer e = new Engineer("George", 15.50F);
        CivilEngineer c = new CivilEngineer("Sir John", 40F);

        Console.WriteLine("{0} charge = {1}",
                    e.TypeName(),
                    e.CalculateCharge(2F));
        Console.WriteLine("{0} charge = {1}",
                    c.TypeName(),
                    c.CalculateCharge(0.75F));
    }
}
```

Because the CivilEngineer class derives from Engineer, it inherits all the data members of the class, and it also inherits the CalculateCharge() member function.

Constructors can't be inherited, so a separate one is written for CivilEngineer. The constructor doesn't have anything special to do, so it calls the constructor for Engineer, using the base syntax. If the call to the base class constructor was omitted, the compiler would call the base class constructor with no parameters.

CivilEngineer has a different way to calculate charges; the minimum charge is for one hour of time, so there's a new version of CalculateCharge(). That exposes an issue; this new method needs to access the billing rate that is defined in the Engineer class, but the billing rate was defined as private and is therefore not accessible. To fix this, the billing rate is now declared to be protected. This change allows all derived classes to access the billing rate.

The example, when run, yields the following output:

```
Engineer Charge = 31
Civil Engineer Charge = 40
```

■ **Note**   The terms *inheritance* and *derivation* are fairly interchangeable in discussions such as this. My preference is to say that class CivilEngineer derives from class Engineer, and, because of that, it inherits certain things.

Arrays of Engineers

The code above works fine in the early years of a company, when there are only a few employees. As the company grows, it's easier to deal with an array of engineers.

Because CivilEngineer is derived from Engineer, an array of type Engineer can hold either type. This example has a different Main() function, putting the engineers into an array:

```csharp
using System;
class Engineer
{
    public Engineer(string name, float billingRate)
    {
        m_name = name;
        m_billingRate = billingRate;
    }

    public float CalculateCharge(float hours)
    {
        return(hours * m_billingRate);
    }

    public string TypeName()
    {
        return("Engineer");
    }

    private string m_name;
    protected float m_billingRate;
}
class CivilEngineer: Engineer
{
    public CivilEngineer(string name, float billingRate) :
        base(name, billingRate)
    {
    }

    public new float CalculateCharge(float hours)
    {
        if (hours < 1.0F)
        {
            hours = 1.0F;          // minimum charge.
        }
        return(hours * m_billingRate);
    }

    public new string TypeName()
    {
        return("Civil Engineer");
    }
}
class Test
{
    public static void Main()
    {
            // create an array of engineers
        Engineer[] engineers = new Engineer[2];
```

```
        engineers[0] = new Engineer("George", 15.50F);
        engineers[1] = new CivilEngineer("Sir John", 40F);

        Console.WriteLine("{0} charge = {1}",
                    engineers[0].TypeName(),
                    engineers[0].CalculateCharge(2F));
        Console.WriteLine("{0} charge = {1}",
                    engineers[1].TypeName(),
                    engineers[1].CalculateCharge(0.75F));
    }
}
```

This version yields the following output:

```
Engineer Charge = 31
Engineer Charge = 30
```

That's not right.

Because CivilEngineer is derived from Engineer, an instance of CivilEngineer can be used wherever an instance of Engineer is required.

When the engineers were placed into the array, the fact that the second engineer was really a CivilEngineer rather than an Engineer was lost. Because the array is an array of Engineer, when CalculateCharge() is called, the version from Engineer is called.

What is needed is a way to correctly identify the type of an engineer. This can be done by having a field in the Engineer class that denotes what type it is. In the following (contrived) example, the classes are rewritten with an enum field to denote the type of the engineer:

```
using System;
enum EngineerTypeEnum
{
    Engineer,
    CivilEngineer
}
class Engineer
{
    public Engineer(string name, float billingRate)
    {
        m_name = name;
        m_billingRate = billingRate;
        m_type = EngineerTypeEnum.Engineer;
    }

    public float CalculateCharge(float hours)
    {
        if (m_type == EngineerTypeEnum.CivilEngineer)
        {
            CivilEngineer c = (CivilEngineer) this;
            return(c.CalculateCharge(hours));
        }
        else if (m_type == EngineerTypeEnum.Engineer)
```

```
        {
            return(hours * m_billingRate);
        }
        return(0F);
    }

    public string TypeName()
    {
        if (m_type == EngineerTypeEnum.CivilEngineer)
        {
            CivilEngineer c = (CivilEngineer) this;
            return(c.TypeName());
        }
        else if (m_type == EngineerTypeEnum.Engineer)
        {
            return("Engineer");
        }
        return("No Type Matched");
    }

    private string m_name;
    protected float m_billingRate;
    protected EngineerTypeEnum m_type;
}

class CivilEngineer: Engineer
{
    public CivilEngineer(string name, float billingRate) :
        base(name, billingRate)
    {
        m_type = EngineerTypeEnum.CivilEngineer;
    }

    public new float CalculateCharge(float hours)
    {
        if (hours < 1.0F)
        {
            hours = 1.0F;          // minimum charge.
        }
        return(hours * m_billingRate);
    }

    public new string TypeName()
    {
        return("Civil Engineer");
    }
}
```

```
class Test
{
    public static void Main()
    {
        Engineer[] engineers = new Engineer[2];
        engineers[0] = new Engineer("George", 15.50F);
        engineers[1] = new CivilEngineer("Sir John", 40F);

        Console.WriteLine("{0} charge = {1}",
                    engineers[0].TypeName(),
                    engineers[0].CalculateCharge(2F));
        Console.WriteLine("{0} charge = {1}",
                    engineers[1].TypeName(),
                    engineers[1].CalculateCharge(0.75F));
    }
}
```

By looking at the type field, the functions in Engineer can determine the real type of the object and call the appropriate function.

The output of the code is as expected:

```
Engineer Charge = 31
Civil Engineer Charge = 40
```

Unfortunately, the base class has now become much more complicated; for every function that cares about the type of a class, there is code to check all the possible types and call the correct function. That's a lot of extra code, and it would be untenable if there were 50 kinds of engineers.

Worse is the fact that the base class needs to know the names of all the derived classes for it to work. If the owner of the code needs to add support for a new engineer, the base class must be modified. If a user who doesn't have access to the base class needs to add a new type of engineer, it won't work at all.

Virtual Functions

To make this work cleanly, object-oriented languages allow a function to be specified as virtual. *Virtual* means that when a call to a member function is made, the compiler should look at the real type of the object (not just the type of the reference) and call the appropriate function based on that type.

With that in mind, the example can be modified as follows:

```
using System;
class Engineer
{
    public Engineer(string name, float billingRate)
    {
        m_name = name;
        m_billingRate = billingRate;
    }

        // function now virtual
    virtual public float CalculateCharge(float hours)
    {
        return(hours * m_billingRate);
    }
```

```csharp
        // function now virtual
    virtual public string TypeName()
    {
        return("Engineer");
    }

    private string m_name;
    protected float m_billingRate;
}

class CivilEngineer: Engineer
{
    public CivilEngineer(string name, float billingRate) :
        base(name, billingRate)
    {
    }
        // overrides function in Engineer
    override public float CalculateCharge(float hours)
    {
        if (hours < 1.0F)
        {
            hours = 1.0F;          // minimum charge.
        }
        return(hours * m_billingRate);
    }
        // overrides function in Engineer
    override public string TypeName()
    {
        return("Civil Engineer");
    }
}
class Test
{
    public static void Main()
    {
        Engineer[] engineers = new Engineer[2];
        engineers[0] = new Engineer("George", 15.50F);
        engineers[1] = new CivilEngineer("Sir John", 40F);

        Console.WriteLine("{0} charge = {1}",
                    engineers[0].TypeName(),
                    engineers[0].CalculateCharge(2F));
        Console.WriteLine("{0} charge = {1}",
                    engineers[1].TypeName(),
                    engineers[1].CalculateCharge(0.75F));
    }
}
```

The CalculateCharge() and TypeName() functions are now declared with the virtual keyword in the base class, and that's all that the base class has to know. It needs no knowledge of the derived types, other than to know that each derived class can override CalculateCharge() and TypeName() if desired. In the derived class, the functions are declared with the override keyword, which means that they are the same function that was declared in the base class. If the override keyword is missing, the compiler will assume that the function is unrelated to the base class's function, and virtual dispatching won't function.[2]

Running this example leads to the expected output:

```
Engineer Charge = 31
Civil Engineer Charge = 40
```

When the compiler encounters a call to TypeName() or CalculateCharge(), it goes to the definition of the function and notes that it is a virtual function. Instead of generating code to call the function directly, it writes a bit of dispatch code that at runtime will look at the real type of the object and call the function associated with the real type, rather than just the type of the reference. This allows the correct function to be called even if the class wasn't implemented when the caller was compiled.

For example, if there was payroll processing code that stored an array of Engineer, a new class derived from Engineer could be added to the system without having to modify or recompile the payroll code.

VIRTUAL BY DEFAULT OR NOT?

In some languages, the use of "virtual" is required to make a method virtual, and in other languages all methods are virtual by default. VB, C++, and C# are in the "required" camp, and Java, Python, and Ruby are in the "default" camp.

The desirability of one behavior over the other has spawned numerous lengthy discussions. The default camp says "we don't know how users might use our classes, and if we restrict them, it just makes things harder for no good reason." The required camp say "if we don't know how users might use our classes, how can we make them predictable, and how can we guide users toward overriding the virtual methods we want them to use if all methods are virtual?"

My opinion has tended toward those who make it required, simply because if code can be extended in multiple ways, users will extend it in multiple ways, and I'm not a fan of the resultant mess and confusion. However, if you are writing unit tests, it's very inconvenient to have to write wrapper classes around existing classes merely so you can write your tests,[3] so I'm not as close to the required camp as I have been in the past.

Abstract Classes

There is a small problem with the approach used so far. A new class doesn't have to implement the "TypeName()" function, since it can inherit the implementation from Engineer. This makes it easy for a new class of engineer to have the wrong name associated with it.

---

[2] For a discussion of why this works this way, see Chapter 10.
[3] Yes, I know, there are some mocking technologies that can get around this limitation. I'm not sure, however, that you should; many times writing the wrapper gives some useful encapsulation.

If the ChemicalEngineer class is added, for example:

```
using System;
class Engineer
{
    public Engineer(string name, float billingRate)
    {
        m_name = name;
        m_billingRate = billingRate;
    }

    virtual public float CalculateCharge(float hours)
    {
        return(hours * m_billingRate);
    }

    virtual public string TypeName()
    {
        return("Engineer");
    }

    private string m_name;
    protected float m_billingRate;
}
class ChemicalEngineer: Engineer
{
    public ChemicalEngineer(string name, float billingRate) :
        base(name, billingRate)
    {
    }

    // overrides mistakenly omitted
}
class Test
{
    public static void Main()
    {
        Engineer[] engineers = new Engineer[2];
        engineers[0] = new Engineer("George", 15.50F);
        engineers[1] = new ChemicalEngineer("Dr. Curie", 45.50F);

        Console.WriteLine("{0} charge = {1}",
                    engineers[0].TypeName(),
                    engineers[0].CalculateCharge(2F));
        Console.WriteLine("{0} charge = {1}",
                    engineers[1].TypeName(),
                    engineers[1].CalculateCharge(0.75F));
    }
}
```

The ChemicalEngineer class will inherit the CalculateCharge() function from Engineer, which might be correct, but it will also inherit TypeName(), which is definitely wrong. What is needed is a way to force ChemicalEngineer to implement TypeName().

This can be done by changing Engineer from a normal class to an abstract class. In this abstract class, the TypeName() member function is marked as an abstract function, which means that all classes that derive from Engineer will be required to implement the TypeName() function.

An abstract class defines a contract that derived classes are expected to follow.[4] Because an abstract class is missing "required" functionality, it can't be instantiated, which for the example means that instances of the Engineer class cannot be created. So that there are still two distinct types of engineers, the ChemicalEngineer class has been added.

Abstract classes behave like normal classes except for one or more member functions that are marked as abstract:

```
using System;
abstract class Engineer
{
    public Engineer(string name, float billingRate)
    {
        m_name = name;
        m_billingRate = billingRate;
    }

    virtual public float CalculateCharge(float hours)
    {
        return(hours * m_billingRate);
    }

    abstract public string TypeName();

    private string m_name;
    protected float m_billingRate;
}

class CivilEngineer: Engineer
{
    public CivilEngineer(string name, float billingRate) :
        base(name, billingRate)
    {
    }

    override public float CalculateCharge(float hours)
    {
        if (hours < 1.0F)
        {
            hours = 1.0F;          // minimum charge.
        }
        return(hours * m_billingRate);
    }
```

---

[4]A similar effect can be achieved by using interfaces. See Chapter 9 for a comparison of the two techniques.

```
            // This override is required, or an error is generated.
        override public string TypeName()
        {
            return("Civil Engineer");
        }
}
class ChemicalEngineer: Engineer
{
    public ChemicalEngineer(string name, float billingRate) :
        base(name, billingRate)
    {
    }

    override public string TypeName()
    {
        return("Chemical Engineer");
    }
}
class Test
{
    public static void Main()
    {
        Engineer[] engineers = new Engineer[2];
        engineers[0] = new CivilEngineer("Sir John", 40.0F);
        engineers[1] = new ChemicalEngineer("Dr. Curie", 45.0F);

        Console.WriteLine("{0} charge = {1}",
                    engineers[0].TypeName(),
                    engineers[0].CalculateCharge(2F));
        Console.WriteLine("{0} charge = {1}",
                    engineers[1].TypeName(),
                    engineers[1].CalculateCharge(0.75F));
    }
}
```

The Engineer class has changed by the addition of abstract before the class, which indicates that the class is abstract (i.e., has one or more abstract functions), and the addition of abstract before the TypeName() virtual function. The use of abstract on the virtual function is the important one; the one before the name of the class makes it clear that the class is abstract, since the abstract function could easily be buried among the other functions.

The implementation of CivilEngineer is identical, except that now the compiler will check to make sure that TypeName() is implemented by both CivilEngineer and ChemicalEngineer.

In making the class abstract, we have also ensured that instances of the Engineer class cannot be created.

Sealed Classes and Methods

Sealed classes are used to prevent a class from being used as a base class. It is primarily useful to prevent unintended derivation:

```
// error
sealed class MyClass
{
    MyClass() {}
}
class MyNewClass : MyClass
{
}
```

This fails because MyNewClass can't use MyClass as a base class because MyClass is sealed.

Sealed classes are useful in cases where a class isn't designed with derivation in mind or where derivation could cause the class to break. The System.String class is sealed because there are strict requirements that define how the internal structure must operate, and a derived class could easily break those rules.

A sealed method lets a class override a virtual function and prevents a derived class from overriding that same function. In other words, placing sealed on a virtual method stops virtual dispatching. This is rarely useful, so sealed methods are rare.

CHAPTER 5

Exception Handling

In many programming books, exception handling warrants a chapter somewhat late in the book. In this book, however, it's near the front, for a few reasons.

The first reason is that exception handling is deeply ingrained in the .NET Runtime and is therefore very common in C# code. C++ code can be written without using exception handling, but that's not an option in C#.

The second reason is that it allows the code examples to be better. If exception handling is presented late in the book, early code samples can't use it, and that means the examples can't be written using good programming practices.

What's Wrong with Return Codes?

Most programmers have probably written code that looks like this:

```
bool success = CallFunction();
if (!success)
{
    // process the error
}
```

This works okay, but every return value has to be checked for an error. If the above was written as

```
CallFunction();
```

any error return would be thrown away. That's where bugs come from.

There are many different models for communicating status; some functions may return an HRESULT, some may return a Boolean value, and others may use some other mechanism.

In the .NET Runtime world, exceptions are the fundamental method of handling error conditions. Exceptions are nicer than return codes because they can't be silently ignored. Or, to put it another way, the error handling in the .NET world is correct by default; all exceptions are visible.

■ **Note**   In practice, this means that any exception code you write just gives you the opportunity to mess up that "correct-by-default" behavior. You should therefore be especially careful when writing exception handling code, and, more importantly, strive to write as little as possible.

Trying and Catching

To deal with exceptions, code needs to be organized a bit differently. The sections of code that might throw exceptions are placed in a try block, and the code to handle exceptions in the try block is placed in a catch block. Here's an example:

```
using System;
class Test
{
    static int Zero = 0;
    public static void Main()
    {
            // watch for exceptions here
        try
        {
            int j = 22 / Zero;
        }
            // exceptions that occur in try are transferred here
        catch (Exception e)
        {
            Console.WriteLine("Exception " + e.Message);
        }
        Console.WriteLine("After catch");
    }
}
```

The try block encloses an expression that will generate an exception. In this case, it will generate an exception known as DivideByZeroException. When the division takes place, the .NET Runtime stops executing code and searches for a try block surrounding the code in which the exception took place. It then looks for a catch block and writes out the exception message.

All C# exceptions inherit from a class named Exception. For example, the ArgumentException class inherits from the SystemException class, which inherits from Exception.

Choosing the Catch Block

When an exception occurs, the matching catch block is determined using the following approach:

1. The runtime searches for a try block that contains the code that caused the exception. If it does not find a try block in the current method, it searches the callers of the method.

2. After it finds a try block, it checks the catch blocks in order to see if the type of the exception that was thrown can be converted to the type of exception listed in the catch statement. If the conversion can be made, that catch block is a match.

3. If a matching catch block is found, the code in that block is executed.

4. If none of the catch blocks match, the search continues with step 1.

Returning to the example:

```
using System;
class Test
```

```csharp
{
    static int Zero = 0;
    public static void Main()
    {
        try
        {
            int j = 22 / Zero;
        }
        // catch a specific exception
        catch (DivideByZeroException e)
        {
            Console.WriteLine("DivideByZero {0}", e);
        }
        // catch any remaining exceptions
        catch (Exception e)
        {
            Console.WriteLine("Exception {0}", e);
        }
    }
}
```

The catch block that catches the DivideByZeroException is the first match and is therefore the one that is executed. Catch blocks always must be listed from most specific to least specific, so in this example, the two blocks couldn't be reversed.[1]

This example is a bit more complex:

```csharp
using System;
class Test
{
    static int Zero = 0;
    static void AFunction()
    {
        int j = 22 / Zero;
        // the following line is never executed.
        Console.WriteLine("In AFunction()");
    }
    public static void Main()
    {
        try
        {
            AFunction();
        }
        catch (DivideByZeroException e)
        {
            Console.WriteLine("DivideByZero {0}", e);
        }
    }
}
```

---

[1] More specifically, a clause catching a derived exception cannot be listed after a clause catching a base exception.

What happens here?

When the division is executed, an exception is generated. The runtime starts searching for a try block in AFunction(), but it doesn't find one, so it jumps out of AFunction() and checks for a try block in Main(). It finds one, and then looks for a catch block that matches. The catch block then executes.

Sometimes, there won't be any catch clauses that match.

```
using System;
class Test
{
    static int Zero = 0;
    static void AFunction()
    {
        try
        {
            int j = 22 / Zero;
        }
            // this exception doesn't match
        catch (ArgumentOutOfRangeException e)
        {
            Console.WriteLine("OutOfRangeException: {0}", e);
        }
        Console.WriteLine("In AFunction()");
    }
    public static void Main()
    {
        try
        {
            AFunction();
        }
            // this exception doesn't match
        catch (ArgumentException e)
        {
            Console.WriteLine("ArgumentException {0}", e);
        }
    }
}
```

Neither the catch block in AFunction() nor the catch block in Main() matches the exception that's thrown. When this happens, the exception is caught by the "last chance" exception handler. The action taken by this handler depends on how the runtime is configured, but it might write out the exception information before the program exits.[2]

Passing Exceptions on to the Caller

It's sometimes the case that there's not much that can be done when an exception occurs in a method; it really has to be handled by the calling function. There are three basic ways to deal with this, which are named based on their result in the caller: Caller Beware, Caller Confuse, and Caller Inform.

---

[2] This behavior can be changed by the application.

Caller Beware

The first way is to merely not catch the exception. This is usually the right design decision, but it could leave the object in an incorrect state, causing problems if the caller tries to use it later. It may also give insufficient information to the caller to know exactly what has happened.

Caller Confuse

The second way is to catch the exception, do some cleanup, and then rethrow the exception:

```
using System;
public class Summer
{
    int m_sum = 0;
    int m_count = 0;
    float m_average;
    public void DoAverage()
    {
        try
        {
            m_average = m_sum / m_count;
        }
        catch (DivideByZeroException e)
        {
            // do some cleanup here
            throw; //rethrow the exception
        }
    }
}
class Test
{
    public static void Main()
    {
        Summer summer = new Summer();
        try
        {
            summer.DoAverage();
        }
        catch (Exception e)
        {
            Console.WriteLine("Exception {0}", e);
        }
    }
}
```

This is usually the minimal bar for handling exceptions; an object should always maintain a valid state after an exception.

This is called Caller Confuse because while the object is in a valid state after the exception occurs, the caller often has little information to go on. In this case, the exception information says that a `DivideByZeroException` occurred somewhere in the called function, without giving any insight into the details of the exception or how it might be fixed.

If the information in the exception is sufficient for the caller to understand what has happened, this is the preferred behavior.

Caller Inform

In Caller Inform, additional information is returned for the user. The caught exception is wrapped in an exception that has additional information.

```
using System;
public class Summer
{
    int m_sum = 0;
    int m_count = 0;
    float m_average;
    public void DoAverage()
    {
        try
        {
            m_average = m_sum / m_count;
        }
        catch (DivideByZeroException e)
        {
                // wrap exception in another one,
                // adding additional context.
                throw (new DivideByZeroException(
                    "Count is zero in DoAverage()", e));
        }
    }
}
public class Test
{
    public static void Main()
    {
        Summer summer = new Summer();
        try
        {
            summer.DoAverage();
        }
        catch (Exception e)
        {
            Console.WriteLine("Exception: {0}", e);
        }
    }
}
```

When the DivideByZeroException is caught in the DoAverage() function, it is wrapped in a new exception that gives the user additional information about what caused the exception. Usually the wrapper exception is the same type as the caught exception, but this might change depending on the model presented to the caller.

This program generates the following output:

```
Exception: System.DivideByZeroException: Count is zero in DoAverage()
  ---> System.DivideByZeroException
  at Summer.DoAverage()
  at Test.Main()
```

If wrapping an exception can provide useful information to the user, it is generally a good idea. However, wrapping is a two-edged sword; done the wrong way, it can make things worse. See the "Design Guidelines" section later in this chapter for more information on how to wrap effectively.

User-Defined Exception Classes

One drawback of the last example is that the caller can't tell what exception happened in the call to DoAverage() by looking at the type of the exception. To know that the exception was caused because the count was zero, the expression message would have to be searched for using the string Count is zero.

That would be pretty bad, since the user wouldn't be able to trust that the text would remain the same in later versions of the class, and the class writer wouldn't be able to change the text. In this case, a new exception class can be created:

```
using System;
public class CountIsZeroException: Exception
{
    public CountIsZeroException()
    {
    }
    public CountIsZeroException(string message)
    : base(message)
    {
    }
    public CountIsZeroException(string message, Exception inner)
    : base(message, inner)
    {
    }
}
public class Summer
{
    int m_sum = 0;
    int m_count = 0;
    float m_average;
    public void DoAverage()
    {
        if (m_count == 0)
        {
            throw(new CountIsZeroException("Zero count in DoAverage()"));
        }
        else
        {
            m_average = m_sum / m_count;
        }
    }
}
```

```
class Test
{
    public static void Main()
    {
        Summer summer = new Summer();
        try
        {
            summer.DoAverage();
        }
        catch (CountIsZeroException e)
        {
            Console.WriteLine("CountIsZeroException: {0}", e);
        }
    }
}
```

DoAverage() now determines whether there would be an exception (whether count is zero), and if so, creates a CountIsZeroException and throws it.

In this example, the exception class has three constructors, which is the recommended design pattern. It is important to follow this design pattern because if the constructor that takes the inner exception is missing, it won't be possible to wrap the exception with the same exception type; it could only be wrapped in something more general. If, in the above example, our caller didn't have that constructor, a caught CountIsZeroException couldn't be wrapped in an exception of the same type, and the caller would have to choose between not catching the exception and wrapping it in a less-specific type.

In earlier days of .NET, it was recommended that all user-defined exceptions be derived from the ApplicationException class, but it is now recommended to simply use Exception as the base.[3]

Finally

Sometimes, when writing a function, there will be some cleanup that needs to be done before the function completes, such as closing a file. If an exception occurs, the cleanup could be skipped. The following code processes a file:

```
using System;
using System.IO;
class Processor
{
    int m_count;
    int m_sum;
    public int m_average;
    void CalculateAverage(int countAdd, int sumAdd)
    {
        m_count += countAdd;
        m_sum += sumAdd;
        m_average = m_sum / m_count;
    }
```

---

[3]If you are creating a library, it's a good idea to define a UnicornLibraryException class and then derive all your specific classes from that one.

```
    public void ProcessFile()
    {
        FileStream f = new FileStream("data.txt", FileMode.Open);
        try
        {
            StreamReader t = new StreamReader(f);
            string line;
            while ((line = t.ReadLine()) ! = null)
            {
                int count;
                int sum;
                count = Convert.ToInt32(line);
                line = t.ReadLine();
                sum = Convert.ToInt32(line);
                CalculateAverage(count, sum);
            }
        }
        // always executed before function exit, even if an
        // exception was thrown in the try.
        finally
        {
            f.Close();
        }
    }
}
class Test
{
    public static void Main()
    {
        Processor processor = new Processor();
        try
        {
            processor.ProcessFile();
        }
        catch (Exception e)
        {
            Console.WriteLine("Exception: {0}", e);
        }
    }
}
```

This example walks through a file, reading a count and sum from a file, and accumulates an average. What happens, however, if the first count read from the file is a zero?

If this happens, the division in CalculateAverage() will throw a DivideByZeroException, which will interrupt the file-reading loop. If the programmer had written the function without thinking about exceptions, the call to file.Close() would have been skipped and the file would have remained open.

The code inside the finally block is guaranteed to execute before the exit of the function, whether or not there is an exception. By placing the file.Close() call in the finally block, the file will always be closed.

The code in the previous example is a bit clunky. Chapter 7 covers the using statement, which is often used to make dealing with resource cleanup simpler.

Top-Level Exception Handlers

If our program encounters an exception and there is no code to catch the exception, the exception passes out of our code, and we depend on the behavior of the caller of our code. For console applications, the .NET Runtime will write the details of the exception out to the console window, but for other application types (ASP.NET, WPF, or Windows Forms), our program will just stop executing. The user will lose any unsaved work, and it will be difficult to track down the cause of the exception.

A top-level exception handler can be added to the catch the exception, perhaps allow the user to save his or her work,[4] and make the exception details available for troubleshooting.

The simplest top-level handler is a try-catch in the Main() method of the application:

```
static void Main(string[] args)
{
    try
    {
        Run();
    }
    catch (Exception e)
    {
        // log the exception, show a message to the user, etc.
    }
}
```

For a single-threaded program, this works fine, but many programs perform operations that do not occur on the main thread. It is possible to write exception handlers for each routine, but it's fairly easy to do it incorrectly, and other threads will probably want to communicate the exception back to the main program.

To make this easier, the .NET Runtime provides a central place where all threads go to die when an unhandled exception happens. We can write our top-level exception-handling code once and have it apply everywhere:

```
static void Main(string[] args)
{
    AppDomain.CurrentDomain.UnhandledException += UnhandledExceptionHandler;

    int i = 1;
    i--;

    int j = 12 / i;
}

static void UnhandledExceptionHandler (object sender, UnhandledExceptionEventArgs e)
{
    Exception exception = (Exception) e.ExceptionObject;

    Console.WriteLine(exception);
    System.Diagnostics.Debugger.Break();
}
```

---

[4]Saving their work can be problematic, as it's possible that the exception has left their work in an invalid state. If it has, saving it might be a bad thing to do. If you do decide to save their work, I suggest saving it as a copy.

The first line of Main() connects the event handler UnhandledExceptionHandler to the UnhandledException event on the current application domain.[5] Whenever there is an uncaught exception, the handler will be called.

The handler writes the message out to the console window (probably not the best thing to do in real code, especially code that does not have a console window), and then, if the debugger is attached, causes a breakpoint to be executed in the debugger.

Efficiency and Overhead

In languages without garbage collection, adding exception handling is expensive, since all objects within a function must be tracked to make sure they are properly destroyed at any time an exception could be thrown. The required tracking code adds both execution time and code size to a function.

In C#, however, objects are tracked by the garbage collector rather than the compiler, so exception handling is very inexpensive to implement and imposes little runtime overhead on the program when the exceptional case doesn't occur. It is, however, not cheap when exceptions are thrown.

Design Guidelines

The following are design guidelines for exception usage.

Exceptions Are Exceptional

Exceptions should be used to communicate exceptional conditions. Don't use them to communicate events that are expected, such as reaching the end of a file. In normal operation of a class, there should be no exceptions thrown.

■ **Tip** If you are writing C# using Visual Studio, the debugger exceptions window allows you to set up the debugger to break whenever an exception is thrown. Enabling this option is a great way to track whether your program is generating any unexpected exceptions.

Conversely, don't use return values to communicate information that would be better contained in an exception.

Choosing the Right Exception for Wrapping

It is very important to make the right choice when wrapping exceptions. Consider the following code:

```
try
{
    libraryDataValue.Process();
}
catch (Exception e)
{
```

---

[5]Which references two new concepts. For more on events, see Chapter 23. Application domains can be thought of as the overall context in which code executes.

```
    if (e.InnerException is FileNotFoundException)
    {
        Recover(); // Do appropriate recovery
    }
}
```

Look at that code for a minute and see if you can spot the bug. The problem is not with the code that is written; it is with the code that is missing. Correct code would look something like this:

```
try
{
    libraryDataValue.Process();
}
catch (Exception e)
{
    if (e.InnerException is FileNotFoundException)
    {
        Recover(); // Do appropriate recovery
    }
    else
    {
        throw;
    }
}
```

The lack of the `else` clause means that any exception thrown that does not have an inner exception of type `FileNotFoundException` will be swallowed, leaving the program in an unexpected state. In this case, we've written some code, and we've broken the "correct-by-default" behavior.

However, it's not really our fault. The fault lies in the author of the `Process()` method, who took a very useful and specific exception—`FileNotFoundException`—and wrapped it in the very generic `Exception` type, forcing us to dig into the inner code to find out what really happened. This is especially annoying because `FileNotFoundException` is a perfectly good exception and doesn't need to be wrapped in another type.

When considering wrapping exceptions, consider the following guidelines:

- *Evaluate how useful the additional information is going to be.* What information would the developer get if the exception wasn't wrapped, and would that be sufficient? Is the code going to be used by other developers on your team with access to the source (who can therefore just debug into it), or is it an API used by somebody else, where wrapping may be more useful?

- *Determine when this exception is likely to be thrown.* If it's in the "developer made a mistake" class, wrapping is probably less useful. If it's a runtime error, it's likely to be more useful.

- *Wrap exceptions at that same level of granularity that they are thrown.* Information in the inner exception is there to help debugging, nobody should ever have to write code that depends on it.

- *Wrapping an exception in the same type but with more information in the message is often a good choice.*

Exceptions Should be as Specific as Possible

If your code needs to throw exceptions, the exceptions that it throws should have as specific a type as possible. It's very tempting to just define a `SupportLibraryException` class and use it in multiple places, but that makes it much more likely that callers have to look inside that class, and they may even use text matching on the exception message text to get the desired behavior. Spend the extra time and give them a different exception for each discrete case. However, if you want to derive all of the specific exceptions from `SupportLibraryException`, that will make it easy for the caller to write general code if they want to.

Retry Logic

Some time ago, I came across a system that had retry logic at the low level; if it ran into an issue, it would retry ten times, with a few seconds' wait between each retry. If the retry logic failed, it would give up and throw the exception. And then the caller, which also implemented retry logic as well, would follow the same approach, as did the caller's caller.

When the system hit a missing file, it kept trying and trying, until it finally returned an exception to the caller, some 15 minutes later.

Retry logic is sometimes a necessary evil, but before you write it, spend some time thinking if there's a better way to structure your program. If you do write it, also write yourself a note to revisit the code in the future to make sure the retry logic is still useful and behaving the way you expect.

Rethrowing

Code that rethrows an exception that it caught is usually a sign that something is wrong, as noted in the guideline on wrapping exceptions. If you do need to rethrow, make sure you do this:

```
throw;
```

rather than this:

```
throw e;
```

The second option will throw away the stack trace that was originally generated with the exception, so the exception looks like it originated at the rethrow.

Catch Only if You Have Something Useful to Do

As noted at the beginning of the chapter, writing exception handling code is an opportunity to take a system that works just fine and turn it into one that doesn't work right. There are three definitions of useful that I've come across[6]:

---

[6]It is possible that I'm missing additional cases. Just be very thoughtful and deliberate before you conclude that what you want to do is, in fact, useful.

- *You are calling a method, it has a well-known exception case, and, most importantly, there is something you can do to recover from that case.* The canonical example is that you got a filename from a user and for some reason it wasn't appropriate (didn't exist, wrong format, couldn't be opened, etc.). In that case, the retry is to ask the user for another filename. In this case, "something" means "something different." Retry is almost never the right thing to do.[7]

- *The program would die if you didn't catch the exception, and there's nobody else above you.* At this point, there's nothing you can do except capture the exception information to a file or event log and perhaps tell the user that the program needs to exit, but those are important things to do.

- *You are at a point where catching and wrapping provide a real benefit to your caller.* In this case, you're going to catch the exception, wrap it, and then throw the wrapped exception.

---

[7]Say you are writing a mobile phone app that needs to be resilient if it loses network access. If you write logic to keep trying network operations, it will probably work, except that if you use polling you will run the battery down really quickly. The point here being that the correct retry behavior is typically something you need to design in architecturally, not handle at the low level.

■ ■ ■

CHAPTER 6

Member Accessibility and Overloading

One of the important decisions to make when designing an object is how accessible to make the members. In C#, accessibility can be controlled in several ways.

Class Accessibility

The coarsest level at which accessibility (also known as visibility) can be controlled is at the class. In most cases, the only valid modifiers on a class are public, which means that everybody can see the class, and internal. The exception to this is nesting classes inside of other classes, which is a bit more complicated and is covered in Chapter 7.

Internal is a way of granting access to a wider set of classes without granting access to everybody, and it is most often used when writing helper classes that should be hidden from the ultimate user of the class. In the .NET Runtime world, internal equates to allowing access to all classes that are in the same assembly as this class.

■ **Note**   In the C++ world, such accessibility is usually granted by the use of friends, which provides access to a specific class. The use of friends provides greater granularity in specifying who can access a class, but in practice the access provided by internal is sufficient. In general, all classes should be internal unless other assemblies need to be able to access them.

Using Internal on Members

The internal modifier can also be used on a member, which then allows that member to be accessible from classes in the same assembly as itself, but not from classes outside the assembly.

This is especially useful when several public classes need to cooperate, but some of the shared members shouldn't be exposed to the general public. Consider the following example:

```
public class DrawingObjectGroup
{
    public DrawingObjectGroup()
    {
        m_objects = new DrawingObject[10];
        m_objectCount = 0;
    }
```

```
    public void AddObject(DrawingObject obj)
    {
        if (m_objectCount < 10)
        {
            m_objects[m_objectCount] = obj;
            m_objectCount++;
        }
    }
    public void Render()
    {
        for (int i = 0; i < m_objectCount; i++)
        {
            m_objects[i].Render();
        }
    }

    DrawingObject[] m_objects;
    int m_objectCount;
}
public class DrawingObject
{
    internal void Render() {}
}
class Test
{
    public static void Main()
    {
        DrawingObjectGroup group = new DrawingObjectGroup();
        group.AddObject(new DrawingObject());
    }
}
```

Here, the DrawingObjectGroup object holds up to ten drawing objects. It's valid for the user to have a reference to a DrawingObject, but it would be invalid for the user to call Render() for that object, so this is prevented by making the Render() function internal.

■ **Tip**   This code doesn't make sense in a real program. The .NET Common Language Runtime has a number of collection classes that would make this sort of code much more straightforward and less error prone. See Chapter 33 for more information.

Expanding Internal Accessibility

In certain scenarios, it is useful to provide internal-level access to a class that is not in the same assembly. See the "Expanding Internal Accessibility" section in Chapter 31 for more information.

Protected

As noted in the chapter on inheritance, *protected* indicates that the member can also be accessed by classes that are derived from the class defining the member.

Internal Protected

To provide some extra flexibility in how a class is defined, the internal protected modifier can be used to indicate that a member can be accessed from either a class that could access it through the internal access path or a class that could access it through a protected access path. In other words, internal protected allows internal or protected access.

Note that there is no way to specify that a member can only be accessed through derived classes that live in the same assembly (the so-called internal **and** protected accessibility), although an internal class with a protected member will provide that level of access.[1]

The Interaction of Class and Member Accessibility

Class and member accessibility modifiers must both be satisfied for a member to be accessible. The accessibility of members is limited by the class so that it does not exceed the accessibility of the class.

Consider the following situation:

```
internal class MyHelperClass
{
    public void PublicFunction() {}
    internal void InternalFunction() {}
    protected void ProtectedFunction() {}
}
```

If this class were declared as a public class, the accessibility of the members would be the same as the stated accessibility; for example, PublicFunction() would be public, InternalFunction() would be internal, and ProtectedFunction() would be protected.

Because the class is internal, however, the public on PublicFunction() is reduced to internal.

Accessability Summary

The available accessability levels in C# are summarized in Table 6-1.

---

[1]During the design of C#, there was some discussion around whether it would make sense to provide an option that meant internal and protected. We elected not to provide it, partly because there wasn't a well-defined need for it, and partly because there was no obvious, nonconfusing way to express it syntactically.

Table 6-1. *Accessibility in C#*

Accessibility	Description
public	No restrictions on access.
protected	Can be accessed in the declaring class or derived classes.
internal	Can be accessed by all types in the same assembly of the declaring class and other assemblies specifically named using the InternalsVisibleTo attribute.
protected internal	Any access granted by protected or internal.
private	Only accessed by the declaring class.

Method Overloading

When there are several overloaded methods for a single named function, the C# compiler uses method overloading rules to determine which function to call.

In general, the rules are fairly straightforward, but the details can be somewhat complicated. Here's a simple example:

```
Console.WriteLine("Ummagumma");
```

To resolve this, the compiler will look at the Console class and find all methods that take a single parameter. It will then compare the type of the argument (string in this case) with the type of the parameter for each method, and if it finds a single match, that's the function to call. If it finds no matches, a compile-time error is generated. If it finds more than one match, things are a bit more complicated (see the "Better Conversions" section below).

For an argument to match a parameter, it must fit one of the following cases:

- The argument type and the parameter type are the same type.

- An implicit conversion exists from the argument type to the parameter type *and* the argument is not passed using ref or out.

Note that in the previous description, the return type of a function is not mentioned. That's because for C#—and for the .NET Common Language Runtime in general—overloading based on return type is not allowed.[2] Additionally, because out is a C#-only construct (it looks like ref to other languages), there cannot be a ref overload and an out overload that differ only in their ref and out-ness. There can, however, be a ref or out overload and a pass by value overload using the same type, although it is not recommended.

Method Hiding

When determining the set of methods to consider, the compiler will walk up the inheritance tree until it finds a method that is applicable and then perform overload resolution at that level in the inheritance hierarchy only; it will not consider functions declared at different levels of the hierarchy.[3] Consider the following example:

```
using System;
public class Base
```

---

[2]In other words, C++ covariant return types are not supported.
[3]See Chapter 10 for more discussion on this behavior.

```
{
    public void Process(short value)
    {
        Console.WriteLine("Base.Process(short): {0}", value);
    }
}
public class Derived: Base
{
    public void Process(int value)
    {
        Console.WriteLine("Derived.Process(int): {0}", value);
    }

    public void Process(string value)
    {
        Console.WriteLine("Derived.Process(string): {0}", value);
    }
}
class Test
{
    public static void Main()
    {
        Derived d = new Derived();
        short i = 12;
        d.Process(i);
        ((Base) d).Process(i);
    }
}
```

This example generates the following output:

```
Derived.Process(int): 12
Base.Process(short): 12
```

A quick look at this code might lead one to suspect that the d.Process(i) call would call the base class function because that version takes a short, which matches exactly. But according to the rules, once the compiler has determined that Derived.Process(int) is a match, it doesn't look any farther up the hierarchy; therefore, Derived.Process(int) is the function called.[4]

To call the base class function requires an explicit cast to the base class because the derived function hides the base class version.

---

[4]The reason for this behavior is fairly subtle. If the compiler kept walking up the tree to find the best match, adding a new method in a library base class could result in that method being called rather than the one in the user's derived class, which would be bad.

Better Conversions

In some situations there are multiple matches based on the simple rule mentioned previously. When this happens, a few rules determine which situation is considered better, and if there is a single one that is better than all the others, it is the one called.[5]

The three rules are as follows:

1. An exact match of type is preferred over one that requires a conversion.

2. If an implicit conversion exists from one type to another and there is no implicit conversion in the other direction, the type that has the implicit conversion is preferred.

3. If the argument is a signed integer type, a conversion to another signed integer type is preferred over one to an unsigned integer type.

Rules 1 and 3 don't require a lot of explanation. Rule 2, however, seems a bit more complex. An example should make it clearer:

```
using System;
public class MyClass
{
    public void Process(long value)
    {
        Console.WriteLine("Process(long): {0}", value);
    }
    public void Process(short value)
    {
        Console.WriteLine("Process(short): {0}", value);
    }
}

class Test
{
    public static void Main()
    {
        MyClass myClass = new MyClass();

        int i = 12;
        myClass.Process(i);

        sbyte s = 12;
        myClass.Process(s);
    }
}
```

This example generates the following output:

```
Process(long): 12
Process(short): 12
```

---

[5]The rules for this are detailed in section 7.4.2.3 of the C# Language Reference, which can be downloaded from MSDN.

In the first call to Process(), an int is passed as an argument. This matches the long version of the function because there's an implicit conversion from int to long and no implicit conversion from int to short.

In the second call, however, there are implicit conversions from sbyte to short or long. In this case, the second rule applies. There is an implicit conversion from short to long, and there isn't one from long to short; therefore, the version that takes a short is preferred.

Variable-Length Parameter Lists

It is sometimes useful to define a parameter to take a variable number of parameters (Console.WriteLine() is a good example). C# allows such support to be easily added:

```csharp
using System;
class Port
{
        // version with a single object parameter
    public void Write(string label, object arg)
    {
        WriteString(label);
        WriteString(arg.ToString());
    }
        // version with an array of object parameters
    public void Write(string label, params object[] args)
    {
        WriteString(label);
        foreach (object o in args)
        {
            WriteString(o.ToString());
        }
    }
    void WriteString(string str)
    {
            // writes string to the port here
        Console.WriteLine("Port debug: {0}", str);
    }
}

class Test
{
    public static void Main()
    {
        Port port = new Port();
        port.Write("Single Test", "Port ok");
        port.Write("Port Test: ", "a", "b", 12, 14.2);
        object[] arr = new object[4];
        arr[0] = "The";
        arr[1] = "answer";
        arr[2] = "is";
        arr[3] = 42;
        port.Write("What is the answer?", arr);
    }
}
```

The params keyword on the last parameter changes the way the compiler looks up functions. When it encounters a call to that function, it first checks to see if there is an exact match for the function. The first function call matches:

```
public void Write(string, object arg)
```

Similarly, the third function passes an object array, and it matches:

```
public void Write(string label, params object[] args)
```

Things get interesting for the second call. The definition with the object parameter doesn't match, but neither does the one with the object array.

When both of these matches fail, the compiler notices that the params keyword was specified, and it then tries to match the parameter list by removing the array part of the params parameter and duplicating that parameter until there are the same number of parameters.

If this results in a function that matches, it then writes the code to create the object array. In other words, the line

```
port.Write("Port Test: ", "a", "b", 12, 14.2);
```

is rewritten as:

```
object[] temp = new object[4];
temp[0] = "a";
temp[1] = "b";
temp[2] = 12;
temp[3] = 14.2;
port.Write("Port Test: ", temp);
```

In this example, the params parameter was an object array, but it can be an array of any type.

In addition to the version that takes the array, it usually makes sense to provide one or more specific versions of the function. This is useful both for efficiency (so the object array doesn't have to be created) and so languages that don't support the params syntax don't have to use the object array for all calls. Overloading a function with versions that take one, two, and three parameters, plus a version that takes an array, is a good rule of thumb.

Default Arguments

If a method has multiple parameters, some of them may be optional. Consider the following class:

```
public class Logger
{
    public void LogMessage(string message, string component)
    {
        Console.WriteLine("{0} {1}", component, message);
    }
}
```

To use that, we can write the following code:

```
logger.LogMessage("Started", "Main");
```

Looking at the usages of the LogMessage() method, we discover that many of them pass "Main" as the component. It would certainly be simpler if we could skip passing it when we didn't need it, so we add an overload:

```
public void LogMessage(string message)
{
    LogMessage(message, "Main");
}
```

which allows us to write:

```
logger.LogMessage("Started");
```

It would certainly be simpler if we could write that method once and not have to repeat ourselves simply to add a simpler overload. With default arguments,[6] we can do the following:

```
public void LogMessage(string message, string component = "Main")
{
    Console.WriteLine("{0} {1}", component, message);
}
```

This works pretty much the way you would expect it to; if you pass two arguments, it functions normally; but if you pass only one arguments, it will insert the value "Main" as the second arguments for the call.

There is one restriction to default arguments; the value that is specified has to be a compile-time constant value. If you want to use a value that is determined at runtime, you will have to use method overloading instead.

METHOD OVERLOADING VS DEFAULT ARGUMENTS

Method overloading and default arguments give the same result in most situations, so it's mostly a manner of choosing which one is more convenient. They do, however, differ in implementation.

In the overloaded case, the default values are contained within the assembly that contains the class with the method. In the default arguments case, the default values are stored where the method is called.

In many cases this is not significant. However, if the class ships as part of an assembly that might need to be versioned—for a security update, perhaps—then the defaults in the method case can be updated by shipping a new version of the assembly, while the default arguments case can only get updated defaults by recompiling the caller.

If you are in the business of shipping libraries, the difference may matter. Otherwise, it probably isn't significant.

---

[6]Wait, isn't this feature about default parameters? Why are you using the term "argument"? It's quite simple. A *parameter* is something you define as method declaration, so in this case component is a parameter. An argument is what you pass to a parameter, "Main", in this case.

Named Arguments

Named arguments allow us to specify a parameter by name instead of by position. For example, we could use it to specify the name of our component parameter:

```
logger.LogMessage("Started", component: "Main");
```

Named arguments can also be used to make code more readable. Consider the following logging class:

```
public class Logger
{
    public static void LogMessage(string message, bool includeDateAndTime)
    {
        if (includeDateAndTime)
        {
            Console.WriteLine(DateTime.Now);
        }
        Console.WriteLine(message);
    }
}
```

The class is used as follows:

```
Logger.LogMessage("Warp initiated", true);
```

If I don't know anything about the Logger class, I can probably guess that the first parameter is the message, but it's not clear what the second parameter is. I can, however, write it using a named argument:

```
Logger.LogMessage("Warp initiated", includeDateAndTime: true);
```

That is much clearer.[7]

■ **Tip** The named argument can also be used for the other arguments to methods, but my experience is that if you use well-named variables, it usually isn't an issue.

---

[7]Another option is to define an enum. The enum has the advantage of requiring the caller to specify the name, but it is much more work to set up.

CHAPTER 7

Other Class Details

This chapter discusses some of the miscellaneous issues of classes, including constructors, nesting, and overloading rules.

Nested Classes

Sometimes, it is convenient to nest classes within other classes, such as when a helper class is used by only one other class. The accessibility of the nested class follows similar rules to the ones outlined for the interaction of class and member modifiers. As with members, the accessibility modifier on a nested class defines what accessibility the nested class has outside of the nested class. Just as a private field is visible only within a class, a private nested class is visible only from within the class that contains it.

In the following example, the Parser class has a Token class that it uses internally. Without using a nested class, it might be written as follows:

```
public class Parser
{
    Token[] tokens;
}
public class Token
{
    string name;
}
```

In this example, both the Parser and Token classes are publicly accessible, which isn't optimal. Not only is the Token class one more class taking up space in the designers that list classes, but it isn't designed to be generally useful. It's therefore helpful to make Token a nested class, which will allow it to be declared with private accessibility, hiding it from all classes except Parser.

Here's the revised code:

```
public class Parser
{
    Token[] tokens;
    private class Token
    {
        string name;
    }
}
```

Now, nobody else can see Token. Another option would be to make Token an `Internal` class so that it wouldn't be visible outside the assembly, but with that solution, it would still be visible inside the assembly.

Making Token an internal class also misses out on an important benefit of using a nested class. A nested class makes it very clear to those reading the source code that the Token class can safely be ignored unless the internals for `Parser` are important. If this organization is applied across an entire assembly, it can help simplify the code considerably.

Nesting can also be used as an organizational feature. If the `Parser` class were within a namespace named Language, you might require a separate namespace named `Parser` to nicely organize the classes for `Parser` The `Parser` namespace would contain the Token class and a renamed `Parser` class. By using nested classes, the `Parser` class could be left in the Language namespace and contain the Token class.

Other Nesting

Classes aren't the only types that can be nested; interfaces, structs, delegates, and enums can also be nested within a class.

Anonymous Types

An anonymous type is a class that does not have a user-visible name. Here's an example:

```
var temporary = new { Name = "George", Charactistic = "Curious" };
```

Such a type can be used to hold temporary results within the scope of a single method. Because the type does not have a name, it cannot be used as a parameter type on a method or as a return value.[1]

Anonymous types are rarely used directly but are the result of the `Select()` Linq method. See Chapter 28 for more information.

Creation, Initialization, Destruction

In any object-oriented system, dealing with the creation, initialization, and destruction of objects is very important. In the .NET Runtime, the programmer can't control the destruction of objects, but it's helpful to know the other areas that can be controlled.

Constructors

If there are no constructors, the C# compiler will create a public parameter-less constructor.

A constructor can invoke a constructor of the base type by using the `base` syntax, like this:

```
using System;
public class BaseClass
```

---

[1] You can pass it to a method that takes the `type` object, though at that point there isn't a way to access the values directly without using reflection.

```
{
    public BaseClass(int x)
    {
        this.x = x;
    }
    public int X
    {
        get
        {
            return(x);
        }
    }
    int x;
}
public class Derived: BaseClass
{
    public Derived(int x): base(x)
    {
    }
}
class Test
{
    public static void Main()
    {
        Derived d = new Derived(15);
        Console.WriteLine("X = {0}", d.X);
    }
}
```

In this example, the constructor for the Derived class merely forwards the construction of the object to the BaseClass constructor.

Sometimes it's useful for a constructor to forward to another constructor in the same object, as in the following example:

```
using System;
class MyObject
{
    public MyObject(int x)
    {
        this.x = x;
    }
    public MyObject(int x, int y): this(x)
    {
        this.y = y;
    }
    public int X
    {
        get
        {
            return(x);
        }
    }
```

```
    public int Y
    {
        get
        {
            return(y);
        }
    }
    int x;
    int y;
}
class Test
{
    public static void Main()
    {
        MyObject my = new MyObject(10, 20);
        Console.WriteLine("x = {0}, y = {1}", my.X, my.Y);
    }
}
```

Private Constructors

Private constructors are—not surprisingly—usable only from within the class on which they're declared. If the only constructor on the class is private, this prevents any user from instantiating an instance of the class, which is useful for classes that are merely containers of static functions (such as System.Math, for example).

Private constructors are also used to implement the singleton pattern, when there should be only a single instance of a class within a program. This is usually done as follows:

```
public class SystemInfo
{
    static SystemInfo cache = null;
    static object cacheLock = new object();
    private SystemInfo()
    {
        // useful stuff here...
    }

    public static SystemInfo GetSystemInfo()
    {
        lock(cacheLock)
        {
            if (cache == null)
            {
                cache = new SystemInfo();
            }

            return(cache);
        }
    }
}
```

This example uses locking to make sure the code works correctly in a multithreaded environment. For more information on locking, see Chapter 31.

Initialization

If the default value of the field isn't what is desired, it can be set in the constructor. If there are multiple constructors for the object, it may be more convenient—and less error-prone—to set the value through an initializer rather than setting it in every constructor.

Here's an example of how initialization works:

```
public class Parser          // Support class
{
    public Parser(int number)
    {
        this.number = number;
    }
    int number;
}
class MyClass
{
    public int counter = 100;
    public string heading = "Top";
    private Parser parser = new Parser(100);
}
```

This is pretty convenient; the initial values can be set when a member is declared. It also makes class maintenance easier since it's clearer what the initial value of a member is.

To implement this, the compiler adds code to initialize these functions to the beginning of every constructor.

■ **Tip** As a general rule, if a member has differing values depending on the constructor used, the field value should be set in the constructor. If the value is set in the initializer, it may not be clear that the member may have a different value after a constructor call.

Destructors

Strictly speaking, C# doesn't have destructors, at least not in the way that most developers think of destructors, where the destructor is called when the object is deleted.

What is known as a *destructor* in C# is known as a *finalizer* in some other languages and is called by the garbage collector when an object is collected. The programmer doesn't have direct control over when the destructor is called, and it is therefore less useful than in languages such as C++. If cleanup is done in a destructor, there should also be another method that performs the same operation so that the user can control the process directly.

When a destructor is written in C#, the compiler will automatically add a call to the base class's finalizer (if present).

For more information on this, see the section on garbage collection in Chapter 38. If garbage collection is new to you, you'll probably want to read that chapter before delving into the following section.

Managing Nonmemory Resources

The garbage collector does a good job of managing memory resources, but it doesn't know anything about other resources, such as database handles, graphics handles, and so on. Because of this, classes that hold such resources will have to do the management themselves.

In many cases, this isn't a real problem; all that it takes is writing a destructor for the class that cleans up the resource.

```
using System;
using System.Runtime.InteropServices;

class ResourceWrapper
{
    int handle = 0;

    public ResourceWrapper()
    {
        handle = GetWindowsResource();
    }

    ~ResourceWrapper()
    {
        FreeWindowsResource(handle);
        handle = 0;
    }

    [DllImport("dll.dll")]
    static extern int GetWindowsResource();

    [DllImport("dll.dll")]
    static extern void FreeWindowsResource(int handle);
}
```

Some resources, however, are scarce and need to be cleaned up in a more timely manner than the next time a garbage collection occurs. Since there's no way to call finalizers automatically when an object is no longer needed,[2] it needs to be done manually.

In the .NET Framework, objects can indicate that they hold on to such resources by implementing the IDisposable interface, which has a single member named Dispose(). This member does the same cleanup as the finalizer, but it also needs to do some additional work. If either its base class or any of the other resources it holds implement IDisposable, it needs to call Dispose() on them so that they also get cleaned up at this time.[3] After it does this, it calls GC.SuppressFinalize() so that the garbage collector won't bother to finalize this object. Here's the modified code:

```
using System;
using System.Runtime.InteropServices;
```

---

[2]The discussion why this isn't possible is long and involved. In summary, lots of really smart people tried to make it work and couldn't.
[3]This is different from the finalizer. Finalizers are responsible only for their own resources, while Dispose() also deals with referenced resources.

```csharp
class ResourceWrapper: IDisposable
{
    int handle = 0;
    bool disposed;
    public ResourceWrapper()
    {
        handle = GetWindowsResource();
    }

    // does cleanup for this object only
    protected virtual void Dispose(bool disposing)
    {
        if (!disposed)
        {
            if (disposing)
            {
                // call Dispose() for any managed resources
            }

            //dispose unmanaged resources
            FreeWindowsResource(handle);
            handle = 0;
            disposed = true;
        }
        //if there was a base class you would use the following line
        //base.Dispose(disposing);
    }

    ~ResourceWrapper()
    {
        Dispose(false);
    }

    // dispose cleans up its object, and any objects it holds
    // that also implement IDisposable.
    public void Dispose()
    {
        Dispose(true);
        GC.SuppressFinalize(this);
    }

    [DllImport("dll.dll")]
    static extern int GetWindowsResource();

    [DllImport("dll.dll")]
    static extern void FreeWindowsResource(int handle);
}
```

If your object has semantics where another name is more appropriate than Dispose() (a file would have Close(), for example), then you should implement IDisposable using explicit interface implementation. You would then have the better-named function forward to Dispose().

This pattern is complex and easy to get wrong. If you are dealing with handle classes, you should instead use one of the handle classes defined in the `Microsoft.Win32.SafeHandles` namespace or one of the types derived from `System.Runtime.InteropServices.SafeHandle`.

IDisposable and the Using Statement

When using classes that implement `IDisposable`, it's important to make sure `Dispose()` gets called at the appropriate time. When a class is used locally, this is easily done by wrapping the usage in `try-finally`, such as in this example:

```
ResourceWrapper rw = new ResourceWrapper();
try
{
    // use rw here
}
finally
{
    if (rw != null)
    {
        ((IDisposable) rw).Dispose();
    }
}
```

The cast of the `rw` to `IDisposable` is required because `ResourceWrapper` could have implemented `Dispose()` with explicit interface implementation.[4] The `try-finally` *is* a bit ugly to write and remember, so C# provides the `using` statement to simplify the code, like this:

```
using (ResourceWrapper rw = new ResourceWrapper())
{
    // use rw here
}
```

The `using` variant is equivalent to the earlier example using `try-finally`. If two or more instances of a single class are used, the `using` statement can be written as follows:

```
using (ResourceWrapper rw = new ResourceWrapper(), rw2 = new ResourceWrapper())
```

For different classes, two `using` statements can be placed next to each other.

```
using (ResourceWrapper rw = new ResourceWrapper())
using (FileWrapper fw = new FileWrapper())
```

In either case, the compiler will generate the appropriate nested `try-finally` blocks.

IDisposable and Longer-Lived Objects

The `using` statement provides a nice way to deal with objects that are around for only a single function. For longer-lived objects, however, there's no automatic way to make sure `Dispose()` is called.

---

[4]See Chapter 10.

It's fairly easy to track this through the finalizer, however. If it's important that `Dispose()` is always called, it's possible to add some error checking to the finalizer to track any such cases. This could be done with a few changes to the `ResourceWrapper` class.

```
static int finalizeCount = 0;
~ResourceWrapper()
{
    finalizeCount++;
    Dispose(false);
}

[Conditional("DEBUG")]
static void CheckDisposeUsage(string location)
{
    GC.Collect();
    GC.WaitForPendingFinalizers();
    if (finalizeCount != 0)
    {
        finalizeCount = 0;
        throw new Exception("ResourceWrapper(" + location +
        ": Dispose() = " + finalizeCount);
    }
}
```

The finalizer increments a counter whenever it is called, and the `CheckDisposeUsage()` routine first makes sure that all objects are finalized and then checks to see whether there were any finalizations since the last check. If so, it throws an exception.[5]

Static Fields

It is sometimes useful to define members of an object that aren't associated with a specific instance of the class but rather with the class as a whole. Such members are known as *static* members.

A static field is the simplest type of static member; to declare a static field, simply place the `Static` modifier in front of the variable declaration. For example, the following could be used to track the number of instances of a class that were created:

```
using System;
class MyClass
{
    public MyClass()
    {
        instanceCount++;
    }
    public static int instanceCount = 0;
}
```

---

[5]It might make more sense to log this to a file, depending on the application.

```
class Test
{
    public static void Main()
    {
        MyClass my = new MyClass();
        Console.WriteLine(MyClass.instanceCount);
        MyClass my2 = new MyClass();
        Console.WriteLine(MyClass.instanceCount);
    }
}
```

The constructor for the object increments the instance count, and the instance count can be referenced to determine how many instances of the object have been created. A static field is accessed through the name of the class rather than through the instance of the class; this is true for all static members.

■ **Note** This is unlike the VB/C++ behavior where a static member can be accessed through either the class name or the instance name. In VB and C++, this leads to some readability problems, because it's sometimes not clear from the code whether an access is static or through an instance.

Static Member Functions

The previous example exposes an internal field, which is usually something to be avoided. It can be restructured to use a static member function instead of a static field, like in the following example:

```
using System;
class MyClass
{
    public MyClass()
    {
        instanceCount++;
    }
    public static int GetInstanceCount()
    {
        return instanceCount;
    }
    static int instanceCount = 0;
}
class Test
{
    public static void Main()
    {
        MyClass my = new MyClass();
        Console.WriteLine(MyClass.GetInstanceCount());
    }
}
```

This now uses a static member function and no longer exposes the field to users of the class, which increases future flexibility. Because it is a static member function, it is called using the name of the class rather than the name of an instance of the class.

In the real world, this example would probably be better written using a static property, which is discussed Chapter 19.

Static Constructors

Just as there can be other static members, there can also be static constructors. A static constructor will be called before the first instance of an object is created. It is useful to do setup work that needs to be done only once.

■ **Note**   Like many other things in the .NET Runtime world, the user has no control over when the static constructor is called; the runtime guarantees only that it is called sometime after the start of the program and before the first instance of an object is created. Therefore, it can't be determined in the static constructor that an instance is about to be created.

A static constructor is declared simply by adding the `static` modifier in front of the constructor definition. A static constructor cannot have any parameters.

```
using System;
class MyClass
{
    static MyClass()
    {
        Console.WriteLine("MyClass is initializing");
    }
}
```

There is no static analog of a destructor.

Constants

C# allows values to be defined as constants. For a value to be a constant, its value must be something that can be written as a constant. This limits the types of constants to the built-in types that can be written as literal values.

Not surprisingly, putting `const` in front of a variable means that its value cannot be changed. Here's an example of some constants:

```
using System;
enum MyEnum
{
    Jet
}
class LotsOLiterals
{
        // const items can't be changed.
        // const implies static.
    public const int value1 = 33;
    public const string value2 = "Hello";
    public const MyEnum value3 = MyEnum.Jet;
}
```

```
class Test
{
    public static void Main()
    {
        Console.WriteLine("{0} {1} {2}",
                LotsOLiterals.value1,
                LotsOLiterals.value2,
                LotsOLiterals.value3);
    }
}
```

Read-Only Fields

Because of the restriction on constant types being knowable at compile time, const cannot be used in many situations.

In a Color class, it can be useful to have constants as part of the class for the common colors. If there were no restrictions on const, the following would work:

```
// error
class Color
{
    public Color(int red, int green, int blue)
    {
        m_red = red;
        m_green = green;
        m_blue = blue;
    }

    int m_red;
    int m_green;
    int m_blue;
        // call to new can't be used with static
    public const Color Red = new Color(255, 0, 0);
    public const Color Green = new Color(0, 255, 0);
    public const Color Blue = new Color(0, 0, 255);
}
class Test
{
    static void Main()
    {
        Color background = Color.Red;
    }
}
```

This clearly doesn't work because the static members Red, Green, and Blue can't be calculated at compile time. But making them normal public members doesn't work either; anybody could change the red value to olive drab or puce.

The readonly modifier is designed for exactly that situation. By applying readonly, the value can be set in the constructor or in an initializer, but it can't be modified later.

Because the color values belong to the class and not a specific instance of the class, they'll be initialized in the static constructor, like so:

```
class Color
{
    public Color(int red, int green, int blue)
    {
        m_red = red;
        m_green = green;
        m_blue = blue;
    }

    int m_red;
    int m_green;
    int m_blue;

    public static readonly Color Red;
    public static readonly Color Green;
    public static readonly Color Blue;

        // static constructor
    static Color()
    {
        Red = new Color(255, 0, 0);
        Green = new Color(0, 255, 0);
        Blue = new Color(0, 0, 255);
    }
}
class Test
{
    static void Main()
    {
        Color background = Color.Red;
    }
}
```

This provides the correct behavior.

If the number of static members were high or creating the members was was expensive (in either time or memory), it might make more sense to declare them as readonly properties so that members could be constructed on the fly as needed.

On the other hand, it might be easier to define an enumeration with the different color names and return instances of the values as needed.

```
class Color
{
    public Color(int red, int green, int blue)
    {
        m_red = red;
        m_green = green;
        m_blue = blue;
    }
```

```csharp
    public enum PredefinedEnum
    {
        Red,
        Blue,
        Green
    }
    public static Color GetPredefinedColor(
    PredefinedEnum pre)
    {
        switch (pre)
        {
            case PredefinedEnum.Red:
                return new Color(255, 0, 0);

            case PredefinedEnum.Green:
                return new Color(0, 255, 0);

            case PredefinedEnum.Blue:
                return new Color(0, 0, 255);

            default:
                return new Color(0, 0, 0);
        }
    }
    int m_red;
    int m_blue;
    int m_green;
}
class Test
{
    static void Main()
    {
        Color background =
            Color.GetPredefinedColor(Color.PredefinedEnum.Blue);
    }
}
```

This requires a little more typing, but there isn't a start-up penalty or lots of objects taking up space. It also keeps the class interface simple; if there were 30 members for predefined colors, the class would be much harder to understand.[6]

■ **Note**   Experienced C++ programmers are probably cringing at the previous code example. It embodies one of the classic problems with the way C++ deals with memory management. Passing back an allocated object means the caller has to free it. It's pretty easy for the user of the class to either forget to free the object or lose the pointer to the object, which leads to a memory leak. In C#, however, this isn't an issue, because the runtime handles memory allocation. In the preceding example, the object created in the Color.GetPredefinedColor() function gets copied immediately to the background variable and then is available for collection when background goes out of scope.

---

[6]For an explanation on why a default case is important, see Chapter 20.

Extension Methods

Consider the following scenario. Your company has some files to process and in them are some strangely formatted headers.

#Name#,#Date#,#Age#,#Salary#

You need to extract the list of headers and therefore add a method to the class.

```
static List<string> ExtractFields(string fieldString)
{
    string[] fieldArray = fieldString.Split(',');

    List<string> fields = new List<string>();

    foreach (string field in fieldArray)
    {
        fields.Add(field.Replace("#", ""));
    }

    return fields;
}
```

This then allows you to write the following code:

```
string test = "#Name#,#Date#,#Age#,#Salary#";

List<string> fields = ExtractFields(test);

foreach (string field in fields)
{
    Console.WriteLine(field);
}
```

It turns out that you need to perform this operation in other places in your code, and you therefore move it to a utility class and write the following code to use it:

```
List<string> fields = StringHelper.ExtractFields(test);
```

This works but is more than a bit clunky. What you want is a way to make ExtractFields() look like it is defined on the String class, which is exactly what extension methods allow you to do.

```
public static List<string> ExtractFields(this string fieldString) {}
```

Putting this in front of the first parameter of a static method in a static class converts that method into an extension method, allowing the methods to be called using the same syntax as the methods defined on the class.

```
List<string> fields = test.ExtractFields();
```

This gives a nice simplification.

Usage Guidelines

Extension methods are a very powerful feature and are a requirement for advanced features such as Linq,[7] but it can also make code less clear. Before using an extension method, the following questions should be asked:

- Is this method a general-purpose operation on the class?

- Will it be used often enough for developers to remember that it is there?

- Can it be named in a way that makes its function clear, and does that name fit well with the existing methods on the class?

The answers depend on context; a method that is general-purpose in one scenario may not be general-purpose in others.

My advice is not to implement extension methods right away; write them as helpers, and after you have used them for a while, it will be obvious whether they make sense as extension methods.

Object Initializers

Object initializers can be used in place of constructor parameters. Consider the following class:

```
public class Employee
{
    public string Name;
    public int Age;
    public decimal Salary
}
```

Using the class is quite simple.

```
Employee employee = new Employee();
employee.Name = "Fred";
employee.Age = 35;
employee.Salary = 13233m;
```

But it does take a lot of code to set the items. The traditional way of dealing with this is to write a constructor.

```
public Employee(string name, int age, decimal salary)
{
    Name = name;
    Age = age;
    Salary = salary;
}
```

That changes the creation to the following:

```
Employee emp = new Employee("Fred", 35, 13233m);
```

---

[7]Take a Linq expression with three clauses, and try writing it without using extension methods, and you'll see what I mean. The syntax is much more confusing, and the operations have to be written in reverse order.

C# supports an alternate syntax that removes the constructor and allows the properties to be mentioned by name.

```
Employee employee = new Employee() { Name = "Fred", Age = 35, Salary = 13233m };
```

This appears to be a nice shortcut; instead of having to create a constructor, you just allow the user to set the properties they want to set, and everybody is happy. Unfortunately, this construct also allows code such as this:

```
Employee employee = new Employee() { Age = 35};
```

which sets the Age while leaving the Name and Salary with their default values, which is clearly a nonsensical state for the object.

Basically, you have lost control about the possible states of the Employee object; instead of one state where the name, age, and salary are all set, you now have eight separate states, defined by all the possible combinations of each property being set or not.[8]

That puts you out of the realm of good object-oriented design.[9] It would be much better to have constructors enforce a specific contract around the creation of the object, change the properties to be read-only, and end up with an immutable object that is much easier to understand.

WHY DOES C# ALLOW OBJECT INITIALIZERS?

If object initializers allow developers to write code that is less good than the constructor alternative, why are they allowed in the language?

One of the big features in C# is the Linq syntax (see Chapter 29), and the Linq syntax requires a way of automatically creating a temporary type known as an *anonymous type*. The creation of an instance of an anonymous type requires a way of defining both the fields of the anonymous types and setting the values of each field, and that is where the object initializer syntax came from.

At that point, there was a choice. C# either could allow object initializers to be used for other classes or could impose an arbitrary restriction[10] where object initializers were allowed for anonymous classes but not for other classes, which would make the language a little more complicated.

Static Classes

Some classes—System.Environment is a good example—are just containers for a bunch of static methods and properties. It would be of no use to ever create an instance of such a class, and this can easily be accomplished by making the constructor of the class private.

This does not, however, make it easy to know the reason that there are no visible constructors; other classes have instances that can be created only through factory methods. Users may try to look for such factory methods, and maintainers of such a class may not realize they cannot be instantiated and accidentally add instance methods to the class, or they may intend to make a class static and forget to do so.

---

[8]Each property can be set or unset, and 2 cubed is equal to 8.
[9]I was tempted to use the word *travesty* in reference to this approach.
[10]Which would have to be designed, coded, tested, documented, and so on.

Static classes prevent this from happening. When the static keyword is added to a class:

```
static class Utilities
{
    static void LogMessage(string message) {}
}
```

it is easy for the user of the class to see that it is static, and the compiler will generate an error if instance methods are added.

Partial Classes and Methods

Code generators (which are programs that generate code, often from a UI design program) have a problem.

They need a place for the user to write the code that will extend the generated code to do something useful. There are two way this has traditionally been done. The first is to structure the generated code into sections; one section says "put your code here," and the other section says "generated code; do not touch."[11] This solution is unsatisfying; what should be implementation details are in the user's face, and the files are much bigger than they need to be, not to mention that the user can accidentally modify that code.

The second solution is based on inheritance; the user class is either the base class or the derived class of the generated class. This solves the "ugly code in my face" issue, at the cost of added complexity of base methods, derived methods, virtual methods that are virtual only because of this schema, and how everything fits together.

C# provides a third solution: partial classes and partial methods. A partial class is simply a class that is written in two (or more) separate parts. Consider the following:

```
partial class Saluter
{
    int m_saluteCount;

    public Saluter(int saluteCount)
    {
        m_saluteCount = saluteCount;
    }

    public void Ready()
    {
        Console.WriteLine("Ready");
    }
}
partial class Saluter
{
    public void Aim()
    {
        Console.WriteLine("Aim");
    }
}
```

---

[11] Or the somewhat less descriptive but ever-so-enjoyable "Here be dragons!"

```
partial class Saluter
{
    public void Fire(int count)
    {
        for (int i = 0; i < m_saluteCount; i++)
        {
            Console.WriteLine("Fire");
        }
    }
}
```

Here are three different partial classes of the Saluter class (in real partial class scenarios, they would be in three separate files). At compilation time, the compiler will glue all of the partial classes together and generate a single Saluter class, which can then be used as expected.

```
Saluter saluter = new Saluter(21);
saluter.Ready();
saluter.Aim();
saluter.Fire();
```

▨ **Note**   Since partial classes are a compiler feature, all partial parts of a class must be compiled at the same time.

Partial classes solve most of the issues with code generation; you can sequester the generated code into a separate file[12] so it's not annoying while still keeping the approach clean and simple. There is, however, one more issue. Consider the following:

```
// EmployeeForm.Designer.cs
partial class EmployeeForm
{
    public void Initialize()
    {
        StartInitialization();
        FormSpecificInitialization();
        FinishInitialization();
    }

    void StartInitialization() { }
    void FinishInitialization() { }
}
// EmployeeForm.cs
partial class EmployeeForm
{
    void FormSpecificInitialization()
    {
        // add form-specific initialization code here.
    }
}
```

---

[12]These are typically named something like file.designer.cs.

In this situation, the form needs to give the user the opportunity to perform operations before the form is fully initialized, so it calls FormSpecificInitialization(). Unfortunately, if the user doesn't need to do anything, the empty method is still present in the user's code. What is needed is a way to make this call only if the user wants. That way is through partial methods, by adding a partial method to the generated class.

```
partial void FormSpecificInitialization();
```

The compiler now knows that if there is no implementation at compilation time, the method should be removed from the source.[13] There are a few restrictions; because the method might not be there, it can't communicate anything back to the caller, which means no return values (it must be a void method) and no out parameters.

PARTIAL CLASSES AND BIG FILES

It has been suggested that partial classes are useful to break big classes down into smaller, more manageable chunks. While this is a possible use of partial classes, it is trading one kind of complexity (too many lines in the file) for a different kind of complexity (a class implementation spread across multiple files). In the vast majority of cases, it's far better to refactor the class that is too big into several smaller classes that do less.[14]

---

[13]Partial methods use the same infrastructure as conditional methods, which will be discussed in Chapter 41.
[14]If you are building a library where you've measured the performance cost of multiple classes and can't afford it, then you have my blessing to use partial classes to make your life a bit easier.

CHAPTER 8

■ ■ ■

Structs (Value Types)

Classes are used to implement most objects. Sometimes, however, it may be desirable to create an object that behaves like one of the built-in types (such as int, float, or bool)—one that is cheap and fast to allocate and doesn't have the overhead of references. In that case, you can use a value type, which is done by declaring a struct in C#.

Structs act similarly to classes, but with a few added restrictions. They can't inherit from any other type (though they implicitly inherit from object), and other classes can't inherit from them.[1]

A Point Struct

In a graphics system, a value class can be used to encapsulate a point. Here's how to declare it:

```
using System;
struct Point
{
    public Point(int x, int y)
    {
        m_x = x;
        m_y = y;
    }
    public override string ToString()
    {
        return String.Format("({0}, {1})", m_x, m_y);
    }

    public int m_x;
    public int m_y;
}
class Test
{
    public static void Main()
    {
        Point start = new Point(5, 5);
        Console.WriteLine("Start: {0}", start);
    }
}
```

---

[1]Technically, structs are derived from System.ValueType, but that's only an implementation detail. From a language perspective, they act like they're derived from System.Object.

The m_x and m_y components of the Point can be accessed. In the Main() function, a Point is created using the new keyword. For value types, new creates an object on the stack and then calls the appropriate constructor.

The call to Console.WriteLine() is a bit mysterious. If Point is allocated on the stack, how does that call work?

Boxing and Unboxing

In C# and the .NET Runtime world, a little bit of magic happens to make value types look like reference types, and that magic is called *boxing*. As magic goes, it's pretty simple. In the call to Console.WriteLine(), the compiler is looking for a way to convert start to an object, because the type of the second parameter to WriteLine() is object. For a reference type (in other words, a class), this is easy, because object is the base class of all classes. The compiler merely passes an object reference that refers to the class instance.

There's no reference-based instance for a value class, however, so the C# compiler allocates a reference type "box" for the Point, marks the box as containing a Point, and copies the value of the Point into the box. It is now a reference type, and you can treat it as if it were an object.

This reference is then passed to the WriteLine() function, which calls the ToString() function on the boxed Point, which gets dispatched to the ToString() function, and the code writes the following:

```
Start: (5, 5)
```

Boxing happens automatically whenever a value type is used in a location that requires (or could use) an object.

The boxed value is retrieved into a value type by unboxing it.

```
int v = 123;
object o = v;          // box the int 123
int v2 = (int) o;      // unbox it back to an integer
```

Assigning the object o the value 123 boxes the integer, which is then extracted back on the next line. That cast to int is required, because the object o could be any type of object, and the cast could fail.

This code can be represented by Figure 8-1. Assigning the int to the object variable results in the box being allocated on the heap and the value being copied into the box. The box is then labeled with the type it contains so the runtime knows the type of the boxed object.

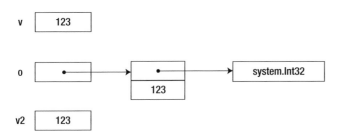

Figure 8-1. *Boxing and unboxing a value type*

During the unboxing conversion, the type must match exactly; a boxed value type can't be unboxed to a compatible type.

```
object o = 15;
short s = (short) o;        // fails, o doesn't contain a short
short t = (short)(int) o;   // this works
```

It's fairly rare to write code that does boxing explicitly. It's much more common to write code where the boxing happens because the value type is passed to a function that expects a parameter of type object, like the following code:

```
int value = 15;
DateTime date = new DateTime();
Console.WriteLine("Value, Date: {0} {1}", value, date);
```

In this case, both value and date will be boxed when WriteLine() is called.

Structs and Constructors

Structs and constructors behave a bit differently from classes. In classes, an instance must be created by calling new before the object is used; if new isn't called, there will be no created instance, and the reference will be null.

There is no reference associated with a struct, however. If new isn't called on the struct, an instance that has all of its fields zeroed is created. In some cases, a user can then use the instance without further initialization. Here's an example:

```
using System;
struct Point
{
    int m_x;
    int m_y;

    Point(int x, int y)
    {
        m_x = x;
        m_y = y;
    }
    public override string ToString()
    {
        return String.Format("({0}, {1})", m_x, m_y);
    }
}
class Test
{
    public static void Main()
    {
        Point[] points = new Point[5];
        Console.WriteLine("[2] = {0}", points[2]);
    }
}
```

Although this struct has no default constructor, it's still easy to get an instance that didn't come through the right constructor.

It is therefore important to make sure that the all-zeroed state is a valid initial state for all value types.

A default (parameterless) constructor for a struct could set different values than the all-zeroed state, which would be unexpected behavior. The .NET Runtime therefore prohibits default constructors for structs.

Mutable Structs

The Point class is an example of an immutable struct, which is when the value cannot be changed after it is created. Consider this mutable version of the Point struct and a PointHolder class that uses it:

```
struct Point
{
    public int m_x;
    public int m_y;

    public Point(int x, int y)
    {
        m_x = x;
        m_y = y;
    }
    public override string ToString()
    {
        return String.Format("({0}, {1})", m_x, m_y);
    }
}
class PointHolder
{
    public PointHolder(Point point)
    {
        Current = point;
    }

    public Point Current;
}
```

The PointHolder class is then used by the main program.

```
static void Example()
{
    Point point = new Point(10, 15);
    PointHolder pointHolder = new PointHolder(point);

    Console.WriteLine(pointHolder.Current);

    Point current = pointHolder.Current;
    current.m_x = 500;

    Console.WriteLine(pointHolder.Current);
}
```

Study this code, and determine what it will print. The answer is as follows:

```
(10, 15)
(10, 15)
```

Because Point is defined as a struct, when it is assigned into the Current variable, the whole value is copied, and any changes to Current do not change pointHolder.Current. If Point were a class, changing the Current value would change pointHolder.Current.

Because of this behavior, it is recommended that all structs be made immutable.

Design Guidelines

There are likely a few of you who are now wringing your hands and saying, "Finally, finally I can get the speed I want from C#."[2] But it's not that simple.

Structs should be used only for types that are really just a piece of data—in other words, for types that could be used in a similar way to the built-in types. An example is the built-in type decimal, which is implemented as a value type.

Even if more complex types *can* be implemented as value types, they probably shouldn't be, since the value type semantics will probably not be expected by the user. The user will expect that a variable of the type could be null, which is not possible with value types.

The performance benefits of using a struct versus using a class aren't always clear-cut; they depend on the following:

- The size of the struct, which impacts how much it costs to pass instances of the struct as parameters (for a struct, you pass the whole struct to a method, while with a class, you pass only a reference to the struct)

- Whether the code is running on a 32- or a 64-bit operating system[3]

- How often instances are created

- How often instance are passed as parameters

My recommendation is to understand the scenarios that are important to you, build both struct and class versions, and measure the performance.

■ **Note**   The framework design guidelines say that structs shouldn't be bigger than 16 bytes. Some other sources say 64 bytes. There are various justifications for both of these numbers, but neither is particularly strict. Measure the performance in your scenario, and then decide whether the performance difference makes using a struct a good or bad idea.

Immutable Classes

Value types nicely result in value semantics, which is great for types that "feel like data." But what if it's a type that needs to be a class type for implementation reasons but is still a data type, such as the string type?

To get a class to behave as if it were a value type, the class needs to be written as an immutable type. Basically, an immutable type is one designed so that it's not possible to tell that it has reference semantics for assignment.

---

[2]I was thinking of C. Montgomery Burns when I wrote this.
[3]References are 4 bytes on a 32-bit system and 8 bytes on a 64-bit system.

Consider the following example, with `string` written as a normal class:

```
string s = "Hello There";
string s2 = s;
s.Replace("Hello", "Goodbye");
```

Because `string` is a reference type, both `s` and `s2` will end up referring to the same string instance. When that instance is modified through `s`, the views through both variables will be changed.

The way to get around this problem is simply to prohibit any member functions that change the value of the class instance. In the case of `string`, member functions that look like they would change the value of the string instead return a new string with the modified value.

A class where there are no member functions that can change—or mutate—the value of an instance is called an *immutable class*. The revised example looks like this:

```
string s = "Hello There";
string s2 = s;
s = s.Replace("Hello", "Goodbye");
```

After the third line has been executed, `s2` still points to the original instance of the string, and `s` now points to a new instance containing the modified value.

CHAPTER 9

■ ■ ■

Interfaces

If multiple classes need to share behavior, they can all use the same base class, and that base class may be abstract. But there can be only one base class in C#, and it is often preferable to share behavior without using a base class.

This can be done by defining an interface, which is similar to an abstract class where all methods are abstract.

A Simple Example

The following code defines the interface IScalable and the class TextObject, which implements the interface, meaning that it contains implementations of all the methods defined in the interface.

```csharp
public class DiagramObject
{
    public DiagramObject() {}
}

interface IScalable
{
    void ScaleX(float factor);
    void ScaleY(float factor);
}
    // A diagram object that also implements IScalable
public class TextObject: DiagramObject, IScalable
{
    public TextObject(string text)
    {
        m_text = text;
    }
        // implementing IScalable.ScaleX()
    public void ScaleX(float factor)
    {
        // scale the object here.
    }

        // implementing IScalable.ScaleY()
    public void ScaleY(float factor)
```

```
    {
        // scale the object here.
    }

    private string m_text;
}

class Test
{
    public static void Main()
    {
        TextObject text = new TextObject("Hello");

        IScalable scalable = (IScalable) text;
        scalable.ScaleX(0.5F);
        scalable.ScaleY(0.5F);
    }
}
```

This code implements a system for drawing diagrams. All of the objects derive from DiagramObject so that they can implement common virtual functions (not shown in this example). Some of the objects can also be scaled, and this is expressed by the presence of an implementation of the IScalable interface.

Listing the interface name with the base class name for TextObject indicates that TextObject implements the interface. This means that TextObject must have methods that match every method in the interface. Interface members have no access modifiers, and the class members that implement the interface members must be publicly accessible.

When an object implements an interface, a reference to the interface can be obtained by casting to the interface. This can then be used to call the functions on the interface.

This example could have been done with abstract methods by moving the ScaleX() and ScaleY() methods to DiagramObject and making them virtual. The "Design Guidelines" section later in this chapter will discuss when to use an abstract method and when to use an interface.

Working with Interfaces

Typically, code doesn't know whether an object supports an interface, so it needs to check whether the object implements the interface before doing the cast.

```
using System;
interface IScalable
{
    void ScaleX(float factor);
    void ScaleY(float factor);
}
public class DiagramObject
{
    public DiagramObject() {}
}
public class TextObject: DiagramObject, IScalable
{
    public TextObject(string text)
```

```
    {
        m_text = text;
    }
        // implementing ISclalable.ScaleX()
    public void ScaleX(float factor)
    {
        Console.WriteLine("ScaleX: {0} {1}", m_text, factor);
        // scale the object here.
    }

        // implementing IScalable.ScaleY()
    public void ScaleY(float factor)
    {
        Console.WriteLine("ScaleY: {0} {1}", m_text, factor);
        // scale the object here.
    }

    private string m_text;
}
class Test
{
    public static void Main()
    {
        DiagramObject[] diagrams = new DiagramObject[100];

        diagrams[0] = new DiagramObject();
        diagrams[1] = new TextObject("Text Dude");
        diagrams[2] = new TextObject("Text Backup");

        // array gets initialized here, with classes that
        // derive from DiagramObject. Some of them implement
        // IScalable.

        foreach (DiagramObject diagram in diagrams)
        {
            if (diagram is IScalable)
            {
                IScalable scalable = (IScalable) diagram;
                scalable.ScaleX(0.1F);
                scalable.ScaleY(10.0F);
            }
        }
    }
}
```

Before the cast is done, it is checked to make sure that the cast will succeed. If it will succeed, the object is cast to the interface, and the scale functions are called.

This construct unfortunately checks the type of the object twice—once as part of the is operator and once as part of the cast. This is wasteful, since the cast can never fail.

One way around this would be to restructure the code with exception handling, but that's not a great idea, because it would make the code more complex, and exception handling should generally be reserved for exceptional conditions. It's also not clear whether it would be faster, since exception handling has some overhead.

The as Operator

C# provides a special operator for this situation, the as operator. Using the as operator, the loop can be rewritten as follows:

```
class Test
{
    public static void Main()
    {
        DiagramObject[] diagrams = new DiagramObject[100];

        diagrams[0] = new DiagramObject();
        diagrams[1] = new TextObject("Text Dude");
        diagrams[2] = new TextObject("Text Backup");

        // array gets initialized here, with classes that
        // derive from DiagramObject. Some of them implement
        // IScalable.

        foreach (DiagramObject diagram in diagrams)
        {
            IScalable scalable = diagram as IScalable;
            if (scalable != null)
            {
                scalable.ScaleX(0.1F);
                scalable.ScaleY(10.0F);
            }
        }
    }
}
```

The as operator checks the type of the left operand, and if it can be converted explicitly to the right operand, the result of the operator is the object converted to the right operand. If the conversion would fail, the operator returns null.

Both the is and as operators can also be used with classes.

Interfaces and Inheritance

When converting from an object to an interface, the inheritance hierarchy is searched until it finds a class that lists the interface on its base list. Having the right functions alone is not enough.

```
using System;
interface IHelper
{
    void HelpMeNow();
}
public class Base: IHelper
{
    public void HelpMeNow()
```

```
    {
        Console.WriteLine("Base.HelpMeNow()");
    }
}
    // Does not implement IHelper, though it has the right
    // form.
public class Derived: Base
{
    public new void HelpMeNow()
    {
        Console.WriteLine("Derived.HelpMeNow()");
    }
}
class Test
{
    public static void Main()
    {
        Derived der = new Derived();
        der.HelpMeNow();
        IHelper helper = (IHelper) der;
        helper.HelpMeNow();
    }
}
```

This code gives the following output:

```
Derived.HelpMeNow()
Base.HelpMeNow()
```

It doesn't call the Derived version of HelpMeNow() when calling through the interface, even though Derived does have a function of the correct form, because Derived doesn't implement the interface.

Design Guidelines

Both interfaces and abstract classes have similar behaviors and can be used in similar situations. Because of how they work, however, interfaces make sense in some situations, and abstract classes make sense in others. Here are a few guidelines to determine whether a capability should be expressed as an interface or an abstract class.

The first thing to check is whether the object would be properly expressed using the "is-a" relationship. In other words, what is the capability an object, and would the derived classes be examples of that object?

Another way of looking at this is to list what kind of objects would want to use this capability. If the capability would be useful across a range of different objects that aren't really related to each other, an interface is the proper choice.

■ **Caution** Because there can be only one base class in the .NET Runtime world, this decision is pretty important. If a base class is required, users will be very disappointed if they already have a base class and are unable to use the feature.

When using interfaces, remember that there is no versioning support for an interface. If a function is added to an interface after users are already using it, their code will break at runtime, and their classes will not properly implement the interface until the appropriate modifications are made.

Multiple Implementation

Unlike object inheritance, a class can implement more than one interface.

```
interface IFoo
{
    void ExecuteFoo();
}

interface IBar
{
    void ExecuteBar();
}

class Tester: IFoo, IBar
{
    public void ExecuteFoo() {}
    public void ExecuteBar() {}
}
```

That works fine if there are no name collisions between the functions in the interfaces. But if the example were just a bit different, there might be a problem.

```
// error
interface IFoo
{
    void Execute();
}

interface IBar
{
    void Execute();
}

class Tester: IFoo, IBar
{
        // IFoo or IBar implementation?
    public void Execute() {}
}
```

Does Tester.Execute() implement IFoo.Execute() or IBar.Execute()?

In this example, IFoo.Execute() and IBar.Execute() are implemented by the same function. If they are supposed to be separate, one of the member names could be changed, but that's not a very good solution in most cases.

More seriously, if IFoo and IBar came from different companies, they couldn't be changed.

The .NET Runtime and C# support a technique known as *explicit interface implementation*, which allows a function to specify which interface member it's implementing.

Explicit Interface Implementation

To specify which interface a member function is implementing, qualify the member function by putting the interface name in front of the member name.

Here's the previous example, revised to use explicit interface implementation:

```
using System;
interface IFoo
{
    void Execute();
}

interface IBar
{
    void Execute();
}

class Tester: IFoo, IBar
{
    void IFoo.Execute()
    {
        Console.WriteLine("IFoo.Execute implementation");
    }
    void IBar.Execute()
    {
        Console.WriteLine("IBar.Execute implementation");
    }
}

class Test
{
    public static void Main()
    {
        Tester tester = new Tester();

        IFoo iFoo = (IFoo) tester;
        iFoo.Execute();

        IBar iBar = (IBar) tester;
        iBar.Execute();
    }
}
```

This prints the following:

```
IFoo.Execute implementation
IBar.Execute implementation
```

This is what is expected. But what does the following test class do?

```
// error
using System;
interface IFoo
{
    void Execute();
}

interface IBar
{
    void Execute();
}

class Tester: IFoo, IBar
{
    void IFoo.Execute()
    {
        Console.WriteLine("IFoo.Execute implementation");
    }
    void IBar.Execute()
    {
        Console.WriteLine("IBar.Execute implementation");
    }
}
class Test
{
    public static void Main()
    {
        Tester tester = new Tester();

        tester.Execute();
    }
}
```

Is IFoo.Execute() called, or is IBar.Execute() called?

The answer is that neither is called. There is no access modifier on the implementations of IFoo.Execute() and IBar.Execute() in the Tester class, and therefore the functions are private and can't be called.

In this case, this behavior isn't because the public modifier wasn't used on the function; it's because access modifiers are prohibited on explicit interface implementations so that the only way the interface can be accessed is by casting the object to the appropriate interface.

To expose one of the functions, a forwarding function is added to Tester.

```
using System;
interface IFoo
{
    void Execute();
}

interface IBar
{
    void Execute();
}
```

```
class Tester: IFoo, IBar
{
    void IFoo.Execute()
    {
        Console.WriteLine("IFoo.Execute implementation");
    }
    void IBar.Execute()
    {
        Console.WriteLine("IBar.Execute implementation");
    }

    public void Execute()
    {
        ((IFoo) this).Execute();
    }
}
class Test
{
    public static void Main()
    {
        Tester tester = new Tester();

        tester.Execute();
    }
}
```

Now, calling the Execute() function on an instance of Tester will forward to Tester.IFoo.Execute().
This hiding can be used for other purposes, as detailed in the next section.

Implementation Hiding

There may be cases where it makes sense to hide the implementation of an interface from the users of a class,
either because it's not generally useful or just to reduce the member clutter. Doing so can make an object much
easier to use. Here's an example:

```
using System;
class DrawingSurface
{
}
interface IRenderIcon
{
    void DrawIcon(DrawingSurface surface, int x, int y);
    void DragIcon(DrawingSurface surface, int x, int y, int x2, int y2);
    void ResizeIcon(DrawingSurface surface, int xsize, int ysize);
}
class Employee: IRenderIcon
{
    public Employee(int id, string name)
    {
        m_id = id;
        m_name = name;
    }
```

```
    void IRenderIcon.DrawIcon(DrawingSurface surface, int x, int y)
    {
    }
    void IRenderIcon.DragIcon(DrawingSurface surface, int x, int y,
                                                int x2, int y2)
    {
    }
    void IRenderIcon.ResizeIcon(DrawingSurface surface, int xsize, int ysize)
    {
    }
    int m_id;
    string m_name;
}
```

If the interface had been implemented normally, the DrawIcon(), DragIcon(), and ResizeIcon() member functions would be visible as part of the public interface of the Employee class, which might be distracting to users of the class. By implementing them through explicit implementation, they are visible only through the IRenderIcon interface, and the Employee class is cleaner.

■ **Tip**   Ask yourself if the implementation of the interface is the main reason that the class exists. If it is not the main reason, implement the interface explicitly.

Interfaces Based on Interfaces

Interfaces can also be combined to form new interfaces. The ISortable and ISerializable interfaces can be combined, and new interface members can be added.

```
using System.Runtime.Serialization;
using System;
interface IComparableSerializable : IComparable, ISerializable
{
    string GetStatusString();
}
```

A class that implements IComparableSerializable would need to implement all the members in IComparable, all the members of ISerializable, and the GetStatusString() function introduced in IComparableSerializable.

Interfaces and Structs

Like classes, structs can also implement interfaces. Here's a short example:

```
using System;
struct Number: IComparable
{
    int m_value;
```

```
    public Number(int value)
    {
        m_value = value;
    }
    public int CompareTo(object object2)
    {
        Number number2 = (Number) object2;
        if (m_value < number2.m_value)
        {
            return(-1);
        }
        else if (m_value > number2.m_value)
        {
            return(1);
        }
        else
        {
            return(0);
        }
    }
}
class Test
{
    public static void Main()
    {
        Number x = new Number(33);
        Number y = new Number(34);

        IComparable Ic = (IComparable) x;
        Console.WriteLine("x compared to y = {0}", Ic.CompareTo(y));
    }
}
```

This struct implements the IComparable interface, which is used to compare the values of two elements for sorting or searching operations.

Like classes, interfaces are reference types, so there's a boxing operation involved here. When a value type is cast to an interface, the value type is boxed, and the interface pointer is to the boxed value type.

CHAPTER 10

■ ■ ■

Versioning and Aliases

Software projects rarely exist as a single version of code that is never revised, unless the software never sees the light of day. In most cases, the software library writer is going to want to change some things, and the client will need to adapt to such changes.

Dealing with such issues is known as *versioning* , and it's one of the harder things to do in software. One reason why it's tough is that it requires a bit of planning and foresight; the areas that might change have to be determined, and the design must be modified to allow change.

Another reason why versioning is tough is that most execution environments don't provide much help to the programmer. For example, in C++, compiled code has internal knowledge of the size and layout of all classes burned into it. With care, some revisions can be made to the class without forcing all users to recompile, but the restrictions are fairly severe. When compatibility is broken, all users need to recompile to use the new version. This may not be that bad, though installing a new version of a library may cause other applications that use an older version of the library to cease functioning.

While it is still possible to write code that has versioning problems, .NET makes versioning easier by deferring the physical layout of classes and members in memory until JIT compilation time. Rather than providing physical layout data, metadata is provided that allows a type to be laid out and accessed in a manner that makes sense for a particular process architecture.

■ **Note**   Versioning is most important when assemblies are replaced without recompiling the source code that uses them, such as when a vendor ships a security update, for example.

A Versioning Example

The following code presents a simple versioning scenario and explains why C# has new and override keywords. The program uses a class named Control, which is provided by another company.

```
public class Control
{
}
public class MyControl: Control
{
}
```

During the implementation of MyControl, the virtual function Foo() is added.

```
public class Control
{
}
public class MyControl: Control
{
    public virtual void Foo() {}
}
```

This works well, until an upgrade notice arrives from the suppliers of the Control object. The new library includes a virtual Foo() function on the Control object.

```
public class Control
{
        // newly added virtual
    public virtual void Foo() {}
}
public class MyControl: Control
{
    public virtual void Foo() {}
}
```

That Control uses Foo() as the name of the function is only a coincidence. In the C++ world, the compiler will assume that the version of Foo() in MyControl does what a virtual override of the Foo() in Control should do and will blindly call the version in MyControl. This is bad.

In the Java world, this will also happen, but things can be a fair bit worse; if the virtual function doesn't have the same return type, the class loader will consider the Foo() in MyControl to be an invalid override of the Foo() in Control, and the class will fail to load at runtime.

In C# and the .NET Runtime, a function defined with virtual is always considered to be the root of a virtual dispatch. If a function is introduced into a base class that could be considered a base virtual function of an existing function, the runtime behavior is unchanged. When the class is next compiled, however, the compiler will generate a warning, requesting that the programmer specify their versioning intent. Returning to the example, to continue the default behavior of not considering the function to be an override, the new modifier is added in front of the function.

```
class Control
{
    public virtual void Foo() {}
}
class MyControl: Control
{
        // not an override
    public new virtual void Foo() {}
}
```

The presence of new will suppress the warning.

If, on the other hand, the derived version is an override of the function in the base class, the override modifier is used.

```
class Control
{
    public virtual void Foo() {}
}
```

```
class MyControl: Control
{
        // an override for Control.Foo()
    public override void Foo() {}
}
```

This tells the compiler that the function really is an override.

■ **Caution**   About this time, you may be thinking, "I'll just put new on all of my virtual functions, and then I'll never have to deal with the situation again." However, doing so reduces the value that the new annotation has to somebody reading the code. If new is used only when it is required, the reader can find the base class and understand what function isn't being overridden. If new is used indiscriminately, the user will have to refer to the base class every time to see whether new has meaning.

Coding for Versioning

The C# language provides some assistance in writing code that versions well. Here are two examples:

- Methods aren't virtual by default. This helps limits the areas where versioning is constrained to those areas that were intended by the designer of the class and prevents "stray virtuals" that constrain future changes to the class.

- The C# lookup rules are designed to aid in versioning. Adding a new function with a more specific overload (in other words, one that matches a parameter better) to a base class won't prevent a less specific function in a derived class from being called,[1] so a change to the base class won't break existing behavior.

A language can do only so much. That's why versioning is something to keep in mind when doing class design. One specific area that has some versioning trade-offs is the choice between classes and interfaces.

The choice between class and interface should be fairly straightforward. Classes are appropriate only for "is-a" relationships (where the derived class is really an instance of the base class), and interfaces are appropriate for all others. If an interface is chosen, however, good design becomes more important because interfaces simply don't version; when a class implements an interface, it needs to implement the interface *exactly*, and adding another method at a later time will mean that classes that thought they implemented the interface no longer do.

Type Aliases

Sometimes you end up wanting to use two identically named classes in the same program. Consider the following two classes:

```
namespace MyCompany.HumanResources.Application.DataModel
{
    class Employee
    {
        public string Name { get; set; }
    }
}
```

---

[1] See Chapter 6 for just such an example.

```
namespace MyCompany.Computer.Network.Model.Classes
{
    class Employee
    {
        public string Name { get; set; }
    }
}
```

I need to write a method that will take an Employee instance of the first class's type to an Employee instance of the second class's type. Here's the first attempt:

```
public MyCompany.Computer.Network.Model.Classes.Employee
    CopyEmployeeData(
        MyCompany.HumanResources.Application.DataModel.Employee hrEmployee)
{
    MyCompany.Computer.Network.Model.Classes.Employee networkEmployee =
        new MyCompany.Computer.Network.Model.Classes.Employee();

    networkEmployee.Name = hrEmployee.Name;

    return networkEmployee;
}
```

That's really bad. What I need is a way to give different names so the compiler can tell which Employee I mean in a specific situation.

```
using NetworkEmployee = MyCompany.Computer.Network.Model.Classes.Employee;
using HREmployee = MyCompany.HumanResources.Application.DataModel.Employee;

public NetworkEmployee CopyEmployeeData(HREmployee hrEmployee)
{
    NetworkEmployee networkEmployee = new NetworkEmployee();
    networkEmployee.Name = hrEmployee.Name;

    return networkEmployee;
}
```

That's quite a bit nicer.

External Assembly Aliases

Sometimes it's worse than the previous situation; not only are the two classes named the same, but they are in the same namespace. If two groups ship the same class, the source file may be the same, but if they are in separate assemblies, they are considered different types by the compiler and runtime.[2]

Type aliases don't help here, since the full names (in other words, namespace + class name) of the two classes are identical. What is needed is a way to give them different names at the assembly level. This can be done on the command line by using the alias form of the /reference qualifier or by setting the alias property on the reference in Visual Studio, as shown in Figure 10-1.

```
csc /reference:HR = HRDataModel.dll /reference:Network = NetworkDataModel ...
```

---

[2]In other words, types have assembly identity.

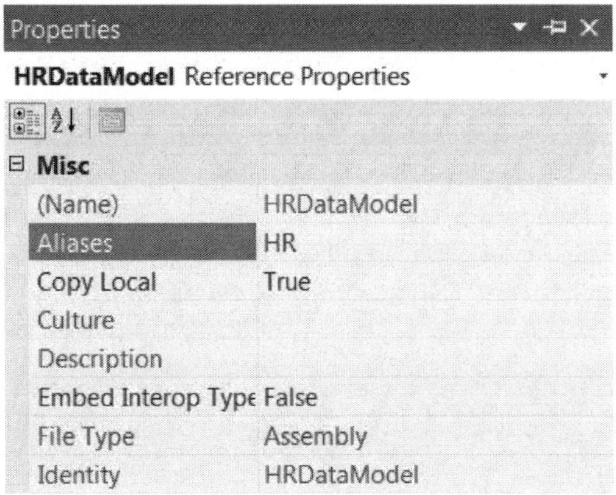

Figure 10-1. *Defining aliases in the Visual Studio project properties*

To use those aliases within code, first they must be defined.

```
extern alias HR;
extern alias Network;
using NetworkEmployee = Network::MyCompany.DataModel.Employee;
using HREmployee = HR::MyCompany.DataModel.Employee;
```

Then they can be used in code as before.

■ ■ ■

CHAPTER 11

Statements and Flow of Execution

The following sections detail the different statements that are available within the C# language.

Selection Statements

The selection statements are used to perform operations based on the value of an expression.

If

The if statement in C# requires that the condition inside the if statement evaluate to an expression of type bool. In other words, the following is illegal:[1]

```
// error
using System;
class Test
{
    public static void Main()
    {
        int value = 0;

        if (value)          // invalid
        {
            System.Console.WriteLine("true");
        }

        if (value == 0)     // must use this
        {
            System.Console.WriteLine("true");
        }
    }
}
```

---

[1] In C and C++, it is possible to accidentally write if (x = 1), which is an assignment rather than a conditional and therefore is always true. The C# behavior eliminates this issue.

Switch

Switch statements have often been error-prone; it is just too easy to inadvertently omit a break statement at the end of a case or, more likely, not to notice that there is fall-through when reading code.

C# gets rid of this possibility by requiring a flow-of-control statement (such as a break or goto, another case label) at the end of every case block.

```
using System;
class Test
{
    public void Process(int i)
    {
        switch (i)
        {
            case 1:
            case 2:
                // code here handles both 1 and 2
                Console.WriteLine("Low Number");
                break;

            case 3:
                Console.WriteLine("3");
                goto case 4;

            case 4:
                Console.WriteLine("Middle Number");
                break;

            default:
                Console.WriteLine("Default Number");
                break;
        }
    }
}
```

C# also allows the switch statement to be used with string variables.

```
using System;
class Test
{
    public void Process(string htmlTag)
    {
        switch (htmlTag)
        {
            case "P":
                Console.WriteLine("Paragraph start");
                break;
            case "DIV":
                Console.WriteLine("Division");
                break;
```

```
        case "FORM":
            Console.WriteLine("Form Tag");
            break;
        default:
            Console.WriteLine("Unrecognized tag");
            break;
        }
    }
}
```

Not only is it easier to write a switch statement than a series of if statements, but it's also more efficient, because the compiler uses an efficient algorithm to perform the comparison.

For small numbers of entries[2] in the switch, the compiler uses a feature in the .NET Runtime known as *string interning*. The runtime maintains an internal table of all constant strings so that all occurrences of that string in a single program will have the same object. In the switch, the compiler looks up the switch string in the runtime table. If it isn't there, the string can't be one of the cases, so the default case is called. If it is found, a sequential search is done of the interned case strings to find a match.

For larger numbers of entries in the case, the compiler generates a hash function and hash table and uses the hash table to efficiently look up the string.[3]

Iteration Statements

Iteration statements are often known as *looping statements*, and they are used to perform operations while a specific condition is true.

While

The while loop functions as expected: while the condition is true, the loop is executed. Like the if statement, the while requires a Boolean condition.

```
using System;
class Test
{
    public static void Main()
    {
        int n=0;
        while (n<10)
        {
            Console.WriteLine("Number is {0}", n);
            n++;
        }
    }
}
```

The break statement can be used to exit the while loop, and the continue statement can be used to skip to the closing brace of the while block for this iteration and then continue with the next iteration.

---

[2]The actual number is determined based upon the performance trade-offs of each method.
[3]If you're unfamiliar with hashing, consider looking at the System.Collections.HashTable class or a good algorithms book.

```
using System;
class Test
{
    public static void Main()
    {
        int n=0;
        while (n<10)
        {
            if (n == 3)
            {
                n++;
                continue; //don't print 3
            }
            if (n == 8)
            {
                break;
            }
            Console.WriteLine("Number is {0}", n);
            n++;
        }
    }
}
```

This code will generate the following output:

```
0
1
2
4
5
6
7
```

Do

A do loop functions just like a while loop, except the condition is evaluated at the end of the loop rather than the beginning of the loop.

```
using System;
class Test
{
    public static void Main()
    {
        int n=0;
        do
        {
            Console.WriteLine("Number is {0}", n);
            n++;
        } while (n<10);
    }
}
```

Like the while loop, the break and continue statements can be used to control the flow of execution in the loop.

For

A for loop is used to iterate over several values. The loop variable may be declared as part of the for statement.

```
using System;
class Test
{
    public static void Main()
    {
        for (int n=0; n<10; n++)
        {
            Console.WriteLine("Number is {0}", n);
        }
    }
}
```

The scope of the loop variable in a for loop is the scope of the statement or statement block that follows the for. It cannot be accessed outside of the loop structure.

```
// error
using System;
class Test
{
    public static void Main()
    {
        for (int n=0; n<10; n++)
        {
            if (n == 8)
            {
                break;
            }
            Console.WriteLine("Number is {0}", n);
        }
            // error; n is out of scope
        Console.WriteLine("Last Number is {0}", n);
    }
}
```

As with the while loop, the break and continue statements can be used to control the flow of execution in the loop.

Foreach

This is a very common looping idiom:

```
using System;
using System.Collections.Generic;
```

```
class MyObject
{
}
class Test
{
    public static void Process(List<MyObject> items)
    {
        for (int nIndex=0; nIndex<items.Count; nIndex++)
        {
            MyObject current=items[nIndex];
            Console.WriteLine("Item: {0}", current);
        }
    }
}
```

This works fine, but it requires the programmer to ensure that the array in the for statement matches the array that is used in the indexing operation. If they don't match, it can sometimes be difficult to track down the bug. It also requires declaring a separate index variable, which could accidentally be used elsewhere.

It's also a lot of typing.

Some languages[4] provide a different construct for dealing with this problem, and C# also provides such a construct. The preceding example can be rewritten as follows:

```
using System;
using System.Collections.Generic;
class MyObject
{
}
class Test
{
    public static void Process(List<MyObject> items)
    {
        foreach (MyObject current in items)
        {
            Console.WriteLine("Item: {0}", current);
        }
    }
}
```

Foreach works for any object that implements the proper interfaces. It can, for example, be used to iterate over the keys of a hash table.

```
using System;
using System.Collections;
class Test
{
    public static void Main()
    {
        Hashtable hash=new Hashtable();
        hash.Add("Fred", "Flintstone");
```

---

[4]Depending on your language background, this might be Perl or Visual Basic.

```
        hash.Add("Barney", "Rubble");
        hash.Add("Mr.", "Slate");
        hash.Add("Wilma", "Flintstone");
        hash.Add("Betty", "Rubble");

        foreach (string firstName in hash.Keys)
        {
            Console.WriteLine("{0} {1}", firstName, hash[firstName]);
        }
    }
}
```

User-defined objects can be implemented so that they can be iterated over using foreach; see the "Indexers and Foreach" section in Chapter 20 for more information.

The one thing that can't be done in a foreach loop is changing the contents of the container. In other words, in the previous example, the firstName variable can't be modified. If the container supports indexing, the contents could be changed through that route, though many containers that enable use by foreach don't provide indexing. Another thing to watch is to make sure the container isn't modified during the foreach; the behavior in such situations is undefined.[5]

As with other looping constructs, break and continue can be used with the foreach statement.

Jump Statements

Jump statements are used to do just that—jump from one statement to another.

Break

The break statement is used to break out of the current iteration or switch statement and continue execution after that statement.

Continue

The continue statement skips all of the later lines in the current iteration statement and then continues executing the iteration statement.

Goto

The goto statement can be used to jump directly to a label. Because the use of goto statements is widely considered to be harmful,[6] C# prohibits some of their worst abuses. A goto cannot be used to jump into a statement block, for example. The only place where their use is recommended is in switch statements or to transfer control to outside a nested loop,[7] though they can be used elsewhere.

---

[5]It is recommended that a container throw an exception in this case, though it may be expensive to detect the condition.
[6]See "GO TO considered harmful" by Edsger W. Dijkstra.
[7]I've written a lot of C# code in the past few years, and never once have I been tempted to use a goto.

Return

The `return` statement returns to the calling function and optionally returns a value.

Other Statements

The following statements are covered in other chapters.

lock

The `lock` statement is used to provide exclusive access to a thread. See the section on threads in Chapter 35.

using

The `using` statement is used in two ways. The first is to specify namespaces, which is covered in Chapter 2. The second use is to ensure that `Dispose()` is called at the end of a block, which is covered in detail in Chapter 7.

try, catch, and finally

The `try`, `catch`, and `finally` statements are used to control exception handling and are covered in Chapter 3.

checked and unchecked

The `checked` and `unchecked` statements control whether exceptions are thrown if conversions or expressions overflow and are covered in Chapter 13.

yield

The `yield` statement is used to implement iterators, covered in Chapter 19.

CHAPTER 12

■ ■ ■

Variable Scoping and Definite Assignment

In C#, local variables must be given names that allow all variables to be uniquely identified throughout the method. Consider the following:

```
using System;
class MyObject
{
    public MyObject(int x)
    {
        x = x;
    }
    int x;
}
```

Since the compiler looks up parameters before it looks up member variables, the constructor in this example does not do anything useful; it copies the value of parameter x to parameter x.[1] You can fix this by adding this. to the front of the name that you want to refer to the member variable.[2]

```
using System;
class MyObject
{
    public MyObject(int x)
    {
        this.x = x;
    }
    int x;
}
```

In the following situation, it's unclear what x means inside the for loop, and there's no way to make the meaning clear. It is therefore an error.

---

[1]The C# compiler will flag this and ask you whether you wanted to do something different.
[2]My preference is never to use a different name for the member variable so that there is no possibility for confusion.

```
// error
using System;
class MyObject
{
    public void Process()
    {
        int x = 12;
        for (int y = 1; y < 10; y++)
        {
            int x = 14;
                // which x do we mean?
            Console.WriteLine("x={0}", x);
        }
    }
}
```

C# has this restriction to improve code readability and maintainability. It is possible to use the same variable multiple times in different scopes.

```
using System;
class MyObject
{
    public void Process()
    {
        for (int y = 1; y < 10; y++)
        {
            int x = 14;
            Console.WriteLine("x={0}", x);
        }

        for (int y = 1; y < 10; y++)
        {
            int x = 21;
            Console.WriteLine("x={0}", x);
        }
    }
}
```

This is allowed because there is no ambiguity present; it is always clear which x is being used.

Definite Assignment

Definite assignment rules prevent the value of an unassigned variable from being observed. Suppose the following is written:

```
// error
using System;
class Test
{
    public static void Main()
```

```
    {
        int n;
        Console.WriteLine("Value of n is {0}", n);
    }
}
```

When this is compiled, the compiler will report an error because the value of n is used before it has been initialized.

Similarly, operations cannot be done with a class variable before the variable is initialized.

```
// error
using System;
class MyClass
{
    public MyClass(int value)
    {
        m_value = value;
    }
    public int Calculate()
    {
        return m_value * 10;
    }
    public int m_value;
}
class Test
{
    public static void Main()
    {
        MyClass mine;

        Console.WriteLine("{0}", mine.m_value);        // error
        Console.WriteLine("{0}", mine.Calculate());    // error
        mine = new MyClass(12);
        Console.WriteLine("{0}", mine.m_value);        // okay now...
    }
}
```

Structs work slightly differently when definite assignment is considered. The runtime will always make sure they're zeroed out, but the compiler will still check to make sure they're initialized to a value before they're used.

A struct is initialized either through a call to a constructor or by setting all the members of an instance before it is used.

```
using System;
struct Complex
{
    public Complex(float real, float imaginary)
    {
        m_real = real;
        m_imaginary = imaginary;
    }
    public override string ToString()
```

```
    {
        return String.Format("({0}, {1})", m_real, m_imaginary);
    }

    public float m_real;
    public float m_imaginary;
}

class Test
{
    public static void Main()
    {
        Complex myNumber1;
        Complex myNumber2;
        Complex myNumber3;

        myNumber1 = new Complex();
        Console.WriteLine("Number 1: {0}", myNumber1);

        myNumber2 = new Complex(5.0F, 4.0F);
        Console.WriteLine("Number 2: {0}", myNumber2);

        myNumber3.m_real = 1.5F;
        myNumber3.m_imaginary = 15F;
        Console.WriteLine("Number 3: {0}", myNumber3);
    }
}
```

In the first section, myNumber1 is initialized by the call to new. Remember that for structs, there is no default constructor, so this call doesn't do anything; it merely has the side effect of marking the instance as initialized.

In the second section, myNumber2 is initialized by a normal call to a constructor.

In the third section, myNumber3 is initialized by assigning values to all members of the instance. Obviously, this can be done only if the members are accessible.

Definite Assignment and Class Members

C# does not require definite assignment of class members before use. Consider the following:

```
class AlwaysNullName
{
    string m_name;

    string GetName()
    {
        return m_name;
    }
}
```

The value of m_name will be null when GetName() is called. The compiler will provide a helpful warning in this situation, but there are other situations that it cannot detect.

Definite Assignment and Arrays

Arrays work a bit differently for definite assignment. For arrays of both reference and value types (classes and structs), an element of an array *can* be accessed, even if it hasn't been initialized with a value.

For example, suppose there is an array of Complex.

```
using System;
struct Complex
{
    public Complex(float real, float imaginary)
    {
        m_real = real;
        m_imaginary = imaginary;
    }
    public override string ToString()
    {
        return(String.Format("({0}, {1})", m_real, m_imaginary));
    }

    public float m_real;
    public float m_imaginary;
}

class Test
{
    public static void Main()
    {
        Complex[] arr = new Complex[10];
        Console.WriteLine("Element 5: {0}", arr[5]);        // legal
    }
}
```

Because of the operations that might be performed on an array—such as Reverse()—the compiler can't track definite assignment in all situations, and it could lead to spurious errors. It therefore doesn't try.

CHAPTER 13

■ ■ ■

Operators and Expressions

The C# expression syntax is very similar to the C/C++ expression syntax.

Operator Precedence

When an expression contains multiple operators, the precedence of the operators controls the order in which the elements of the expression are evaluated. The default precedence can be changed by grouping elements with parentheses.

```
int value1 = 1 + 2 * 3;      // 1 + (2 * 3) = 7
int value2 = (1 + 2) * 3;    // (1 + 2) * 3 = 9
```

In C#, all binary operators are left-associative, which means that operations are performed left to right, except for the assignment and conditional (?:) operators, which are performed right to left.

Table 13-1 summarizes all operators in precedence from highest to lowest.

Table 13-1. *Operators in Precedence Order*

Category	Operators
Primary	`(x)  x.y  f(x)  a[x]  x++  x--  new  typeof  sizeof  checked unchecked default delegate`
Unary	`+  -  !  ~  ++x  --x (T)x`
Multiplicative	`*  /  %`
Additive	`+  -`
Shift	`<<  >>`
Relational	`<  >  <=  >=  is  as`
Equality	`==  !=`
Logical AND	`&`
Logical XOR	`^`
Logical OR	`|`
Conditional AND	`&&`

(continued)

Table 13-1. (*continued*)

Category	Operators
Conditional OR	||
Null coalescing	??
Conditional	?:
Assignment	= *= /= %= += -= <<= >>= &= ^= |=
Anonymous function/lambda	(T x) => y

Built-in Operators

For numeric operations in C#, there are typically built-in operators for the int, uint, long, ulong, float, double, and decimal types. Because there aren't built-in operators for other types, expressions must first be converted to one of the types for which there is an operator before the operation is performed.

A good way to think about this is to consider that an operator (+ in this case)[1] has the following built-in overloads:

```
int operator+(int x, int y);
uint operator+(uint x, uint y);
long operator+(long x, long y);
ulong operator+(ulong x, ulong y);
float operator+(float x, float y);
double operator+(double x, double y);
```

Notice that these operations all take two parameters of the same type and return that type. For the compiler to perform an addition, it can use only one of these functions. This means that smaller sizes (such as two short values) cannot be added without them being converted to int, and such an operation will return an int.

The result is that when operations are done with numeric types that can be converted implicitly to int (those types that are "smaller" than int), the result will have to be cast to store it in the smaller type.[2]

```
// error
class Test
{
    public static void Main()
    {
        short s1 = 15;
        short s2 = 16;
        short ssum = (short) (s1+s2);    // cast is required

        int i1 = 15;
        int i2 = 16;
        int isum = i1+i2;                // no cast required
    }
}
```

---

[1]There are also overloads for string, but that's outside the scope of this example.
[2]You may object to this, but you really wouldn't like the type system of C# if it didn't work this way. It is, however, a considerable departure from C++.

User-Defined Operators

User-defined operators may be declared for classes or structs, and they function in the same manner in which the built-in operators function. In other words, the + operator can be defined on a class or struct so that an expression like a + b is valid. In the following sections, the operators that can be overloaded are marked with "over" in subscript. See Chapter 26 for more information.

Numeric Promotions

Numeric promotions occur when a variable is converted from a smaller type (such as a 2-byte short integer) to a larger type (such as a 4-byte int integer). See Chapter 15 for information on the rules for numeric promotion.

Arithmetic Operators

The following sections summarize the arithmetic operations that can be performed in C#. The floating-point types have very specific rules that they follow.[3] For full details, see the CLR. If executed in a checked context, arithmetic expressions on nonfloating types may throw exceptions.

Unary Plus (+)

For unary plus, the result is simply the value of the operand.

Unary Minus (−)

Unary minus works only on types for which there is a valid negative representation, and it returns the value of the operand subtracted from zero.

Bitwise Complement (~)

The ~ operator is used to return the bitwise complement of a value.

Addition (+)

In C#, the + sign is used both for addition and for string concatenation.

Numeric Addition

The two operands are added together.

---

[3]They conform to IEEE 754 arithmetic.

String Concatenation

String concatenation can be performed between two strings or between a string and an operand of type object.[4] If either operand is null, an empty string is substituted for that operand.

Operands that are not of type string will be automatically converted to a string by calling the virtual ToString() method on the object.

Subtraction (–)

The second operand is subtracted from the first operand. If the expression is evaluated in a checked context and the difference is outside the range of the result type, an OverflowException is thrown.

Multiplication (*)

The two operands are multiplied together. If the expression is evaluated in a checked context and the result is outside the range of the result type, an OverflowException is thrown.

Division (/)

The first operand is divided by the second operand. If the second operand is zero, a DivideByZero exception is thrown.

Remainder (%)

The result x % y is computed as x - (x / y) * y using integer operations. If y is zero, a DivideByZero exception is thrown.

Shift (<< and >>)

For left shifts, the high-order bits are discarded, and the low-order empty bit positions are set to zero.

For right shifts with uint or ulong, the low-order bits are discarded, and the high-order empty bit positions are set to zero.

For right shifts with int or long, the low-order bits are discarded, and the high-order empty bit positions are set to zero if x is non-negative and are set to 1 if x is negative.

Increment and Decrement (++ and ——)

The increment operator increases the value of a variable by 1, and the decrement operator decreases the value of the variable by 1.[5]

Increment and decrement can be used either as a prefix operator, where the variable is modified before it is read, or as a postfix operator, where the value is returned before it is modified.

---

[4]Since any type can convert to object, this means any type.
[5]In unsafe mode, pointers increment and decrement by the size of the pointed-to object. See Chapter 40 for more details.

Here's an example:

```
int k = 5;
int value = k++;    // value is 5
value = --k;    // value is still 5
value = ++k;    // value is 6
```

Note that increment and decrement are exceptions to the rule about smaller types requiring casts to function. A cast is required when adding two shorts and assigning them to another short.

```
short s = (short) a+b;
```

Such a cast is not required for an increment of a short.[6]

```
s++;
```

Relational and Logical Operators

Relational operators are used to compare two values, and logical operators are used to perform bitwise operations on values.

Logical Negation (!)

The ! operator is used to return the negation of a Boolean value.

Relational Operators _{over}

C# defines the following relational operations, shown in Table 13-2.

Table 13-2. *C# Relational Operators*

Operation	Description
a == b	Returns true if a is equal to b
a != b	Returns true if a is not equal to b
a < b	Returns true if a is less than b
a <= b	Returns true if a is less than or equal to b
a > b	Returns true if a is greater than b
a >= b	Returns true if a is greater than or equal to b

---

[6]In other words, there are predefined increment and decrement functions for the types smaller than int and uint.

These operators return a result of type `bool`.

When performing a comparison between two reference-type objects, the compiler will first look for user-defined relational operators defined on the objects (or base classes of the objects). If it finds no applicable operator and the relational is == or !=, the appropriate relational operator will be called from the `object` class. This operator compares whether the two operands reference the same instance, not whether they have the same value.

For value types, the process is the same if the operators == and != are overloaded. If they aren't overloaded, there is no default implementation for value types, and an error is generated.

The overloaded versions of == and != are closely related to the `Object.Equals()` member. See Chapter 32 for more information.

For the `string` type, the relational operators are overloaded so that == and != compare the values of the strings, not the references.

To compare references of two instances that have overloaded relational operators, cast the operators to object.

```
if ((object) string1 == (object) string 2) // reference comparison
```

Logical Operators

C# defines the following logical operators, as listed in Table 13-3.

Table 13-3. *C# Logical Operators*

Operator	Description
&	Bitwise AND of the two operands
|	Bitwise OR of the two operands
^	Bitwise exclusive OR (XOR) of the two operands
&&	Logical AND of the two operands
||	Logical OR of the two operands

The operators &, |, and ^ are usually used on integer data types, though they can also be applied to the `bool` type.

The operators && and || differ from the single-character versions in that they perform short-circuit evaluation. In the expression

```
a && b
```

b is evaluated only if a is true. In the expression

```
a || b
```

b is evaluated only if a is false.

Conditional Operator (?:)

Sometimes called the *ternary* or *question* operator, the conditional operator selects from two expressions based on a Boolean expression.

```
int value = (x<10) ? 15 : 5;
```

This is equivalent to the following:

```
int value;
if (x<10)
{
    value = 15;
}
else
{
    value = 5;
}
```

■ **Tip** The conditional operator is great for examples like this; it saves lines and is easier to read. Be careful with complex statements that include method calls or calculations; they are often much clearer with a traditional if/else statement.

Null Coalescing Operator (??)

The null coalescing operator is used to provide a default value for a null value. This example

```
string s = name ?? "<unknown>";
```

is equivalent to the following:

```
string s;
if (name != null)
{
    s = name;
}
else
{
    s = "<unknown>";
}
```

For more on nullable types, see Chapter 27.

Assignment Operators

Assignment operators are used to assign a value to a variable. There are two forms: the simple assignment and the compound assignment.

Simple Assignment

Simple assignment is done in C# using the single equal (=) sign. For the assignment to succeed, the right side of the assignment must be a type that can be implicitly converted to the type of the variable on the left side of the assignment.

Compound Assignment

Compound assignment operators perform some operation in addition to simple assignment. The compound operators are the following:

```
+=    -=    *=    /=    %=    &=    |=    ^=    <<=    >>=
```

The compound operator

```
x <op>= y
```

is evaluated exactly as if it were written as

```
x = x <op> y
```

with these two exceptions:

- x is evaluated only once, and that evaluation is used for both the operation and the assignment.
- If x contains a function call or array reference, it is performed only once.

Under normal conversion rules, if x and y are both short integers, then evaluating

```
x = x + 3;
```

would produce a compile-time error, because addition is performed on int values, and the int result is not implicitly converted to a short. In this case, because short can be implicitly converted to int, it is possible to write the following:

```
x = 3;
```

Type Operators

Rather than dealing with the values of an object, the type operators are used to deal with the type of an object.

typeof

The typeof operator returns the type of the object, which is an instance of the System.Type class. The typeof operator is useful to avoid having to create an instance of an object just to obtain the type object. If an instance already exists, a type object can be obtained by calling the GetType() function on the instance.

Once the type object is obtained for a type, it can be queried using reflection to obtain information about the type. See the "Deeper Reflection" section in Chapter 40 for more information.

is

The is operator is used to determine whether an object reference can be converted to a specific type or interface. The most common use of this operator is to determine whether an object supports a specific interface.

```
using System;
interface IAnnoy
{
    void PokeSister(string name);
}
class Brother: IAnnoy
{
    public void PokeSister(string name)
    {
        Console.WriteLine("Poking {0}", name);
    }
}
class BabyBrother
{
}
class Test
{
    public static void AnnoyHer(string sister, params object[] annoyers)
    {
        foreach (object o in annoyers)
        {
            if (o is IAnnoy)
            {
                IAnnoy annoyer = (IAnnoy) o;
                annoyer.PokeSister(sister);
            }
        }
    }
    public static void Main()
    {
        Test.AnnoyHer("Jane", new Brother(), new BabyBrother());
    }
}
```

This code produces the following output:

```
Poking: Jane
```

In this example, the Brother class implements the IAnnoy interface, and the BabyBrother class doesn't. The AnnoyHer() function walks through all the objects that are passed to it, checks to see whether an object supports IAnnoy, and then calls the PokeSister() function if the object supports the interface.

as

The as operator is very similar to the is operator, but instead of just determining whether an object is a specific type or interface, it also performs the explicit conversion to that type. If the object can't be converted to that type, the operator returns null. Using as is more efficient than the is operator, since the as operator needs to check the type of the object only once, while the example using is checks the type when the operator is used and again when the conversion is performed.

In the previous example, this code

```
if (o is IAnnoy)
{
    IAnnoy annoyer = (IAnnoy) o;
    annoyer.PokeSister(sister);
}
```

can be replaced with this:

```
IAnnoy annoyer = o as IAnnoy;
if (annoyer != null)
{
    annoyer.PokeSister(sister);
}
```

Note that the as operator can't be used with boxed value types. This example

```
int value = o as int;
```

doesn't work, because there's no way to get a null value of a value type.

Checked and Unchecked Expressions

When dealing with expressions, it's often difficult to strike the right balance between the performance of expression evaluation and the detection of overflow in expressions or conversions. Some languages choose performance and can't detect overflow, and other languages put up with reduced performance and always detect overflow.

In C#, the programmer is able to choose the appropriate behavior for a specific situation. This is done using the checked and unchecked keywords.

Code that depends upon the detection of overflow can be wrapped in a checked block.

```
using System;

class Test
{
    public static void Main()
    {
        checked
        {
            byte a = 55;
            byte b = 210;
            byte c = (byte) (a+b);
        }
    }
}
```

When this code is compiled and executed, it will generate an `OverflowException`.

Similarly, if the code depends on the truncation behavior, the code can be wrapped in an unchecked block.

```
using System;

class Test
{
    public static void Main()
    {
        unchecked
        {
            byte a = 55;
            byte b = 210;
            byte c = (byte) (a+b);
        }
    }
}
```

For the remainder of the code, the behavior can be controlled with the /checked + compiler switch. Usually, /checked + is turned on for debug builds to catch possible problems and then turned off in retail builds to improve performance.

Type Inference (var)

C# allows method variables that are initialized to be declared using var instead of the type of the expression. Here's an example:

```
int age = 33;
var height = 72;
```

Both age and height are of type int; in the first case, the type is set explicitly, and in the second case, the type is inferred from the type of the expression.

Type inference was added to C# because it is not possible to specify the name of an anonymous type, and therefore there needed to be some way to declare a variable of such a type. Type inference is often used in Linq; see Chapter 28 for more information.

Best Practices

There is a tension in the use of var between the simplicity of expression that it allows and the ambiguity that it can create. I recommend using var only with Linq and in cases where its use would prevent saying the same thing twice. This example

```
Dictionary<string, Guid> personIds = new Dictionary<string,Guid> ();
```

lists the same type twice, and this alternative

```
var personIds = new Dictionary<string,Guid> ();
```

is shorter and easier to type, and it is still very clear what the type of personIds is. However, the use of var is not recommended in other situations. This example

```
var personIds = CreateIdLookup();
```

does not provide any clue about what the type of personIds is, and the code is therefore harder to understand.

CHAPTER 14

■ ■ ■

Conversions

In C#, conversions are divided into implicit and explicit conversions. Implicit conversions are those that will always succeed; the conversion can always be performed without data loss. For numeric types, this means the destination type can fully represent the range of the source type. For example, a short can be converted implicitly to an int, because the short range is a subset of the int range. Explicit conversions may result in data loss and therefore must be specified directly.

Numeric Types

For the numeric types, there are widening implicit conversions for all the signed and unsigned numeric types. Figure 14-1 shows the conversion hierarchy. If a path of arrows can be followed from a source type to a destination type, there is an implicit conversion from the source to the destination. For example, there are implicit conversions from sbyte to short, from byte to decimal, and from ushort to long.

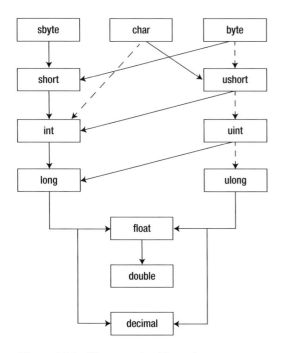

Figure 14-1. C# conversion hierarchy

Note that the path taken from a source type to a destination type in the figure does not represent how the conversion is done; it merely indicates that it can be done. In other words, the conversion from byte to long is done in a single operation, not by converting through ushort and uint. The dotted lines represent implicit conversions paths that are less preferred; this will be discussed more in the following section.

The following code shows a few conversions:

```
class Test
{
    public static void Main()
    {
            // all implicit
        sbyte v = 55;
        short v2 = v;
        int v3 = v2;
        long v4 = v3;

            // explicit to "smaller" types
        v3 = (int) v4;
        v2 = (short) v3;
        v = (sbyte) v2;
    }
}
```

Conversions and Member Lookup

When considering overloaded members, the compiler may have to choose between several functions. Consider the following:

```
using System;
class Conv
{
    public static void Process(sbyte value)
    {
        Console.WriteLine("sbyte {0}", value);
    }
    public static void Process(short value)
    {
        Console.WriteLine("short {0}", value);
    }
    public static void Process(int value)
    {
        Console.WriteLine("int {0}", value);
    }
}
class Test
{
    public static void Main()
    {
        int value1 = 2;
        sbyte value2 = 1;
```

```
        Conv.Process(value1);
        Conv.Process(value2);
    }
}
```

The preceding code produces the following output:

```
int 2
sbyte 1
```

In the first call to `Process()`, the compiler could match the `int` parameter to only one of the functions, the one that took an `int` parameter.

In the second call, however, the compiler had three versions to choose from, taking `sbyte`, `short`, or `int`. To select one version, it first tries to match the type exactly. In this case, it can match `sbyte`, so that's the version that gets called. If the `sbyte` version wasn't there, it would select the `short` version, because a `short` can be converted implicitly to an `int`. In other words, `short` is "closer to" `sbyte` in the conversion hierarchy and is therefore preferred.

The preceding rule handles many cases, but it doesn't handle the following one:

```
using System;
class Conv
{
    public static void Process(short value)
    {
        Console.WriteLine("short {0}", value);
    }
    public static void Process(ushort value)
    {
        Console.WriteLine("ushort {0}", value);
    }
}
class Test
{
    public static void Main()
    {
        byte value = 3;
        Conv.Process(value);
    }
}
```

Here, the earlier rule doesn't allow the compiler to choose one function over the other, because there are no implicit conversions in either direction between `ushort` and `short`.

In this case, there's another rule that kicks in, which says that if there is a single-arrow implicit conversion to a signed type, it will be preferred over all conversions to unsigned types. This is graphically represented in Figure 14-1 by the dotted arrows; the compiler will choose a single solid arrow over any number of dotted arrows.

Explicit Numeric Conversions

Explicit conversions—those using the cast syntax—are the conversions that operate in the opposite direction from the implicit conversions. Converting from `short` to `long` is implicit, and therefore converting from `long` to `short` is an explicit conversion.

Viewed another way, an explicit numeric conversion may result in a value that is different from the original.[1]

```
using System;
class Test
{
    public static void Main()
    {
        uint value1 = 312;
        byte value2 = (byte) value1;
        Console.WriteLine("Value2: {0}", value2);
    }
}
```

The preceding code results in the following output:

56

In the conversion to byte, the least-significant (lowest-valued) part of the uint is put into the byte value. In many cases, the programmer either knows that the conversion will succeed or is depending on this behavior.

Checked Conversions

In other cases, it may be useful to check whether the conversion succeeded. This is done by executing the conversion in a checked context.

```
using System;
class Test
{
    public static void Main()
    {
        checked
        {
            uint value1 = 312;
            byte value2 = (byte) value1;
            Console.WriteLine("Value: {0}", value2);
        }
    }
}
```

When an explicit numeric conversion is done in a checked context, if the source value will not fit in the destination data type, an exception will be thrown.

The checked statement creates a block in which conversions are checked for success. Whether a conversion is checked is determined at compile time, and the checked state does not apply to code in functions called from within the checked block.

---

[1] Conversions from int, uint, or long to float and from long to double may result in a loss of precision but will not result in a loss of magnitude. These conversions are therefore defined as implicit ones (even though the conversion isn't quite exact), because they are closer to exact than the ones in the opposite direction.

Checking conversions for success does have a small performance penalty and therefore may not be appropriate for all software. It can, however, be useful to check all explicit numeric conversions when developing software. The C# compiler provides a /checked compiler option that will generate checked conversions for all explicit numeric conversions. This option can be used while developing software and then can be turned off to improve performance for released software if desired.

If the programmer is depending upon the unchecked behavior, turning on /checked could cause problems. In this case, the unchecked statement can be used to indicate that none of the conversions in a block should ever be checked for conversions.

It is sometimes useful to be able to specify the checked state for a single statement; in this case, the checked or unchecked operator can be specified at the beginning of an expression.

```
using System;
class Test
{
    public static void Main()
    {
        uint value1 = 312;
        byte value2;

        value2 = unchecked((byte) value1);    // never checked
        value2 = (byte) value1;               // checked if /checked
        value2 = checked((byte) value1);      // always checked
    }
}
```

In this example, the first conversion will never be checked, the second conversion will be checked if the /checked statement is present, and the third conversion will always be checked.

Conversions of Classes (Reference Types)

Conversions involving classes are similar to those involving numeric values, except that object conversions deal with casts up and down the object inheritance hierarchy instead of conversions up and down the numeric type hierarchy.

C# also allows conversion between unrelated classes (or structs) to be overloaded. This is discussed in Chapter 25.

As with numeric conversions, implicit conversions are those that will always succeed, and explicit conversions are those that may fail.

From an Object to the Base Class of an Object

A reference to an object can be converted implicitly to a reference to the base class of an object. Note that this does *not* convert the object to the type of the base class; only the reference is to the base class type. The following example illustrates this:

```
using System;
public class Base
{
    public virtual void WhoAmI()
    {
        Console.WriteLine("Base");
    }
}
```

```
public class Derived: Base
{
    public override void WhoAmI()
    {
        Console.WriteLine("Derived");
    }
}
public class Test
{
    public static void Main()
    {
        Derived d = new Derived();
        Base b = d;

        b.WhoAmI();
        Derived d2 = (Derived) b;

        object o = d;
        Derived d3 = (Derived) o;
    }
}
```

This code produces the following output:

```
Derived
```

Initially, a new instance of Derived is created, and the variable d contains a reference to that object. The reference d is then converted to a reference to the base type Base. The object referenced by both variables, however, is still a Derived; this is shown because when the virtual function WhoAmI() is called, the version from Derived is called.[2] It is also possible to convert the Base reference b back to a reference of type Derived or to convert the Derived reference to an object reference and back.

Converting to the base type is an implicit conversion because a derived class *is* always an example of the base class. In other words, Derived has an "is-a" relationship to Base.

Explicit conversions can be written between classes when there is a "could-be" relationship. Because Derived is derived from Base, any reference to Base could really be a Base reference to a Derived object, and therefore the conversion can be attempted. At runtime, the actual type of the object referenced by the Base reference (b in the previous example) will be checked to see whether it is really a reference to Derived. If it isn't, an exception will be thrown on the conversion.

Because object is the ultimate base type, any reference to a class can be implicitly converted to a reference to object, and a reference to object may be explicitly converted to a reference to any class type.

Figure 14-2 shows the previous example pictorially.

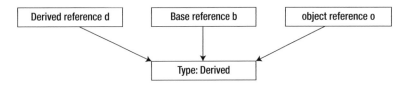

Figure 14-2. *Different references to the same instance*

---

[2] Similarly, Type.GetType(), is, and as would also show it to be a derived instance.

From an Object to an Interface the Object Implements

Interface implementation is somewhat like class inheritance. If a class implements an interface, an implicit conversion can be used to convert from a reference to an instance of the class to the interface. This conversion is implicit because it is known at compile time that it works.

Once again, the conversion to an interface does not change the underlying type of an object. A reference to an interface can therefore be converted explicitly back to a reference to an object that implements the interface, since the interface reference "could-be" referencing an instance of the specified object.

In practice, converting back from the interface to an object is an operation that is rarely, if ever, used.

From an Object to an Interface the Object Might Implement

The implicit conversion from an object reference to an interface reference discussed in the previous section isn't the common case. An interface is especially useful in situations where it isn't known whether an object implements an interface. The following example implements a debug trace routine that uses an interface if it's available:

```
using System;
interface IDebugDump
{
    string DumpObject();
}
class Simple
{
    public Simple(int value)
    {
        m_value = value;
    }
    public override string ToString()
    {
        return(m_value.ToString());
    }
    int m_value;
}
class Complicated: IDebugDump
{
    public Complicated(string name)
    {
        m_name = name;
    }
    public override string ToString()
    {
        return(m_name);
    }
    string IDebugDump.DumpObject()
    {
        return(String.Format(
            "{0}\nLatency: {1}\nRequests: {2}\nFailures: {3}\n",
            new object[] { m_name, m_latency, m_requestCount, m_failedCount} ));
    }
```

```
    string m_name;
    int m_latency = 0;
    int m_requestCount = 0;
    int m_failedCount = 0;
}
class Test
{
    public static void DoConsoleDump(params object[] arr)
    {
        foreach (object o in arr)
        {
            IDebugDump dumper = o as IDebugDump;
            if (dumper !=null)
            {
                Console.WriteLine("{0}", dumper.DumpObject());
            }
            else
            {
                Console.WriteLine("{0}", o);
            }
        }
    }
    public static void Main()
    {
        Simple s = new Simple(13);
        Complicated c = new Complicated("Tracking Test");
        DoConsoleDump(s, c);
    }
}
```

This produces the following output:

```
13
Tracking Test
Latency: 0
Requests: 0
Failures: 0
```

In this example, there are dumping functions that can list objects and their internal state. Some objects have a complicated internal state and need to pass back some rich information, while others can get by with the information returned by their ToString() functions.

This is nicely expressed by the IDebugDump interface, which is used to generate the output if an implementation of the interface is present.

This example uses the as operator, which will return the interface if the object implements it and will return null if it doesn't.

From One Interface Type to Another

A reference to an interface can be converted implicitly to a reference to an interface that it is based upon. It can be converted explicitly to a reference to any interface that it isn't based upon. Such a conversion would be successful only if the interface reference was a reference to an object that implemented the other interface as well.

Conversions of Structs (Value Types)

The only built-in conversion dealing with structs is an implicit conversion from a struct to an interface that it implements. The instance of the struct will be boxed to a reference and then converted to the appropriate interface reference. There are no implicit or explicit conversions from an interface to a struct.

CHAPTER 15

■ ■ ■

Arrays

Arrays in C# are reference objects; they are allocated out of heap space rather than on the stack. The elements of an array are stored as dictated by the element type; if the element type is a reference type (such as string), the array will store references to strings. If the element type is a value type (such as a numeric type or a struct type), the elements are stored directly within the array.

Arrays are declared using the following syntax:

```
<type>[] identifier;
```

The initial value of an array is null. An array object is created using new.

```
int[] store = new int[50];
string[] names = new string[50];
```

When an array is created, it initially contains the default values for the types that are in the array. For the store array, each element is an int with the value 0. For the names array, each element is a string reference with the value null.

Array Initialization

Arrays can be initialized at the same time as they are created. During initialization, the new int[x] can be omitted, and the compiler will determine the size of the array to allocate from the number of items in the initialization list.

```
int[] store = {0, 1, 2, 3, 10, 12};
```

The preceding line is equivalent to this:

```
int[] store = new int[6] {0, 1, 2, 3, 10, 12};
```

Multidimensional and Jagged Arrays

To index elements in more than one dimension, either a multidimensional or jagged array can be used.

Multidimensional Arrays

Multidimensional arrays have more than one dimension.

```
int[,] matrix = new int[4, 2];
matrix[0, 0] = 5;
matrix[3, 1] = 10;
```

The `matrix` array has a first dimension of 5 and a second dimension of 2. This array could be initialized using the following statement:

```
int[,] matrix = { {1, 1}, {2, 2}, {3, 5}, {4, 5} };
```

The `matrix` array has a first dimension of 4 and a second dimension of 2.

Multidimensional arrays are sometimes called *rectangular arrays* because the elements can be written in a rectangular table (for dimensions <= 2). When the matrix array is allocated, a single chunk is obtained from the heap to store the entire array. It can be represented by Figure 15-1.

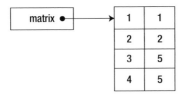

Figure 15-1. *Storage in a multidimensional array*

The following is an example of using a multidimensional array:

```
using System;
class Test
{
    public static void Main()
    {
        int[,] matrix = { {1, 1}, {2, 2}, {3, 5}, {4, 5}, {134, 44} };

        for (int i = 0; i < matrix.GetLength(0); i++)
        {
            for (int j = 0; j < matrix.GetLength(1); j++)
            {
                Console.WriteLine("matrix[{0}, {1}] = {2}", i, j, matrix[i, j]);
            }
        }
    }
}
```

The GetLength() member of an array will return the length of that dimension. This example produces the following output:

```
matrix[0, 0] = 1
matrix[0, 1] = 1
matrix[1, 0] = 2
matrix[1, 1] = 2
matrix[2, 0] = 3
matrix[2, 1] = 5
matrix[3, 0] = 4
matrix[3, 1] = 5
matrix[4, 0] = 134
matrix[4, 1] = 44
```

Jagged Arrays

A jagged array is merely an array of arrays and is called a *jagged* array because it doesn't have to be rectangular. Here's an example:

```
int[][] matrix = new int[3][];
matrix[0] = new int[5];
matrix[1] = new int[4];
matrix[2] = new int[2];
matrix[0][3] = 4;
matrix[1][1] = 8;
matrix[2][0] = 5;
```

The matrix array here has only a single dimension of three elements. Its elements are integer arrays. The first element is an array of five integers, the second is an array of four integers, and the third is an array of two integers.

This array could be represented by Figure 15-2. The matrix variable is a reference to an array of three references to arrays of integers. Four heap allocations were required for this array.

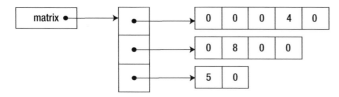

Figure 15-2. *Storage in a jagged array*

Using the initialization syntax for arrays, a full example can be written as follows:

```
using System;
class Test
{
    public static void Main()
    {
        int[][] matrix = {new int[5], new int[4], new int[2] };
        matrix[0][3] = 4;
        matrix[1][1] = 8;
        matrix[2][0] = 5;
```

```
        for (int i = 0; i < matrix.Length; i++)
        {
            for (int j = 0; j < matrix[i].Length; j++)
            {
                Console.WriteLine("matrix[{0}, {1}] = {2}", i, j, matrix[i][j]);
            }
        }
    }
}
```

Note that the traversal code is different from the multidimensional case. Because matrix is an array of arrays, a nested single-dimensional traverse is used.

Arrays of Reference Types

Arrays of reference types can be somewhat confusing, because the elements of the array are initialized to null rather than to the element type. Here's an example:

```
class Employee
{
    public void LoadFromDatabase(int employeeID)
    {
        // load code here
    }
}
class Test
{
    public static void Main()
    {
        Employee[] emps = new Employee[3];
        emps[0].LoadFromDatabase(15);
        emps[1].LoadFromDatabase(35);
        emps[2].LoadFromDatabase(255);
    }
}
```

When LoadFromDatabase() is called, a null exception will be generated because the elements referenced have never been set and are therefore still null.

The class can be rewritten as follows:

```
class Employee
{
    public static Employee LoadFromDatabase(int employeeID)
    {
        Employee emp = new Employee();
        // load code here
        return(emp);
    }
}
```

```
class Test
{
    public static void Main()
    {
        Employee[] emps = new Employee[3];
        emps[0] = Employee.LoadFromDatabase(15);
        emps[1] = Employee.LoadFromDatabase(35);
        emps[2] = Employee.LoadFromDatabase(255);
    }
}
```

This allows you to create an instance and load it and then save it into the array.

The reason that arrays aren't initialized is for performance. If the compiler did do the initialization, it would need to do the same initialization for each element, and if that wasn't the right initialization, all of those initializations would be wasted.

Array Conversions

Conversions are allowed between arrays based on the number of dimensions and the conversions available between the element types.

An implicit conversion is permitted from array S to array T if the following are all true:

- the arrays have the same number of dimensions,

- the elements of S have an implicit reference conversion to the element type of T,

- both S and T are reference types.

In other words, if there is an array of class references, it can be converted to an array of a base type of the class.

Explicit conversions have the same requirements, except that the elements of Σ must be explicitly convertible to the element type of T.

```
using System;
class Test
{
    public static void PrintArray(object[] arr)
    {
        foreach (object obj in arr)
        {
            Console.WriteLine("Word: {0}", obj);
        }
    }
    public static void Main()
    {
        string s = "I will not buy this record, it is scratched.";
        char[] separators = {' '};
        string[] words = s.Split(separators);
        PrintArray(words);
    }
}
```

In this example, the `string` array of words can be passed as an `object` array, because each `string` element can be converted to `object` through a reference conversion. This is not possible, for example, if there is a user-defined implicit conversion.

The System.Array Type

Because arrays in C# are based on the .NET Runtime `System.Array` type, several operations can be done with them that aren't traditionally supported by array types.

Sorting and Searching

The ability to do sorting and searching is built into the `System.Array` type. The `Sort()` function will sort the items of an array, and the `IndexOf()`, `LastIndexOf()`, and `BinarySearch()` functions are used to search for items in the array. For more information, see Chapter 33.

Reverse

Calling `Reverse()` simply reverses all the elements of the array.

```
using System;
class Test
{
    public static void Main()
    {
        int[] arr = {5, 6, 7};
        Array.Reverse(arr);
        foreach (int value in arr)
        {
            Console.WriteLine("Value: {0}", value);
        }
    }
}
```

This produces the following output:

```
7
6
5
```

CHAPTER 16

■ ■ ■

Properties

Most object-oriented languages support fields and methods. Fields are used to store data, and methods are used to perform operations. This distinction is very useful in organizing classes and making them easy to understand.

Assume that your code needs to fetch the current date and time. It could call a method to perform the operation.

```
DateTime now = DateTime.GetCurrent();
```

Since the current time is conceptually a single value, it maps well to a field. It would be much nicer if you could write the following:

```
DateTime now = DateTime.Current;
```

But to write that, you would need to have a construct that looks like a field but instead calls a method. That construct is known as a *property* in C# and is one of the core building blocks in C# classes.

Accessors

A property consists of a property declaration and either one or two blocks of code—known as *accessors*[1]—that handle getting or setting the property. Here's a simple example:

```
class Test
{
    private string m_name;

    public string Name
    {
        get { return m_name; }
        set { m_name = value; }
    }
}
```

This class declares a property called Name and defines both a getter and a setter for that property. The getter merely returns the value of the private variable, and the setter updates the internal variable through a special

---

[1]In some languages/idioms, a set accessor is also known as a *mutator*.

parameter named value. Whenever the setter is called, the variable value contains the value that the property should be set to. The type of value is the same as the type of the property.

Properties can have a getter, a setter, or both. A property that has only a getter is called a *read-only property*, and a property that has only a setter is called a *write-only property*.[2]

Properties and Inheritance

Like member functions, properties can also be declared using the virtual, override, or abstract modifiers. These modifiers are placed on the property and affect both accessors.

When a derived class declares a property with the same name as in the base class, it hides the entire property; it is not possible to hide only a getter or setter.

Using Properties

Properties separate the interface of a class from the implementation of a class. This is useful in cases where the property is derived from other fields and also to do lazy initialization and fetch a value only if the user really needs it.

Suppose that a car maker wanted to be able to produce a report that listed some current information about the production of cars, but fetching that information was an expensive operation. The information can be fetched once and cached by the property.

```
using System;
class Auto
{
    public Auto(int id, string name)
    {
        m_id = id;
        m_name = name;
    }

        // query to find # produced
    public int ProductionCount
    {
        get
        {
            if (m_productionCount == -1)
            {
                // fetch count from database here.
            }
            return(m_productionCount);
        }
    }
    public int SalesCount
    {
        get
        {
            if (m_salesCount == -1)
```

---

[2]Write-only properties are rare—rare enough that you should consider whether what you are defining is really a property.

```
        {
            // query each dealership for data
        }
        return(m_salesCount);
    }
}
string m_name;
int m_id;
int m_productionCount = -1;
int m_salesCount = -1;
}
```

Both the ProductionCount and SalesCount properties are initialized to –1, and the expensive operation of calculating them is deferred until it is actually needed.[3]

Side Effects When Setting Values

Properties are also very useful to do something beyond merely setting a value when the setter is called. A shopping basket could update the total when the user changed an item count, for example.

```
using System;
using System.Collections;
class Basket
{
    internal void UpdateTotal()
    {
        m_total = 0;
        foreach (BasketItem item in m_items)
        {
            m_total += item.Total;
        }
    }

    ArrayList m_items = new ArrayList();
    Decimal m_total;
}
class BasketItem
{
    BasketItem(Basket basket)
    {
        m_basket = basket;
    }
    public int Quantity
    {
        get { return(m_quantity); }
        set
        {
            m_quantity = value;
```

---

[3]Another option is to use a nullable type (see Chapter 27). I think using –1 as a sentinel value is a bit cleaner in this case.

```
            m_basket.UpdateTotal();
        }
    }
    public Decimal Price
    {
        get { return(m_price); }
        set
        {
            m_price = value;
            m_basket.UpdateTotal();
        }
    }
    public Decimal Total
    {
        get
        {
                // volume discount; 10% if 10 or more are purchased
            if (m_quantity >= 10)
            {
                return(m_quantity * m_price * 0.90m);
            }
            else
            {
                return(m_quantity * m_price);
            }
        }
    }

    int m_quantity;        // count of the item
    Decimal m_price;       // price of the item
    Basket m_basket;       // reference back to the basket
}
```

In this example, the Basket class contains an array of BasketItem. When the price or quantity of an item is updated, an update is fired back to the Basket class, and the basket walks through all the items to update the total for the basket.

This interaction could also be implemented more generally using events, which are covered in Chapter 23.

Static Properties

In addition to member properties, C# also allows the definition of static properties, which belong to the whole class rather than to a specific instance of the class. Like static member functions, static properties cannot be declared with the virtual, abstract, or override modifiers.

When readonly fields were discussed Chapter 7, there was a case that initialized some static read-only fields. The same thing can be done with static properties without having to initialize the fields until necessary. The value can also be fabricated when needed and not stored. If creating the field is costly and it will likely be used again, then the value should be cached in a private field. If it is cheap to create or it is unlikely to be used again, it can be created as needed.

```
class Color
{
    public Color(int red, int green, int blue)
    {
        m_red = red;
        m_green = green;
        m_blue = blue;
    }

    int m_red;
    int m_green;
    int m_blue;

    public static Color Red
    {
        get
        {
            return(new Color(255, 0, 0));
        }
    }
    public static Color Green
    {
        get
        {
            return(new Color(0, 255, 0));
        }
    }
    public static Color Blue
    {
        get
        {
            return(new Color(0, 0, 255));
        }
    }
}
class Test
{
    static void Main()
    {
        Color background = Color.Red;
    }
}
```

When the user wants one of the predefined color values, the getter in the property creates an instance with the proper color on the fly and returns that instance.

Property Efficiency

Let's consider the efficiency of a very simple property.

```
class Test
{
    private string m_name;

    public string Name
    {
        get { return m_name; }
        set { m_name = value; }
    }
}
```

This may seem to be an inefficient design, because a member function call is added where there would normally be a field access. However, there is no reason that the underlying runtime environment can't inline the accessors as it would any other simple function, so there is often[4] no performance penalty in choosing a property instead of a simple field. The opportunity to be able to revise the implementation at a later time without changing the interface can be invaluable, so properties are usually a better choice than fields for public members.

Property Accessibility

It is common to want to expose a read-only property to a user of a class and also provide a way to allow derived classes to set the value of the property. One option is the following:

```
class Test
{
    private string m_name;
    public string Name
    {
        get { return m_name; }
    }
    protected void SetName(string name)
    {
        m_name = name;
    }
}
```

This works but is a bit clunky, and therefore C# provides the following alternative:

```
class Test
{
    private string m_name;
    public string Name
    {
        get { return m_name; }
        protected set { m_name = value; }
    }
}
```

---

[4]The Windows version of the .NET Runtime does perform the inlining of trivial accessors, though other environments wouldn't have to.

An accessibility modifier has been added to change the visibility of the set accessor to protected. Accessibility modifiers can be used only to reduce the visibility of an accessor and can be applied to the get or set but not both.[5]

THE EVOLUTION OF MIXED-ACCESSIBILITY

In early versions of C#, this feature (or the lack thereof) likely generated more discussion than any other design decision. Allowing two different levels of accessibility breaks the simplicity of the property model; instead of having a single property, you have one model for public users of the class (typically read-only) and another model for the protected users of the class (typically read-write).

It is certainly true, however, that the workaround is both ugly and confusing and that allowing mixed accessibility makes the code easier to write and understand, regardless of the cleanliness of the underlying model.

With the introduction of automatic properties (introduced later in this chapter), mixed accessibility becomes a requirement.

Virtual Properties

If a property makes sense as part of base class, it may make sense to make the property virtual. Virtual properties follow the same rules as other virtual entities. Here's a quick example of a virtual property:

```
using System;

public abstract class DrawingObject
{
    public abstract string Name { get; }
}
class Circle: DrawingObject
{
    string m_name = "Circle";

    public override string Name
    {
        get { return m_name; }
    }
}
class Test
{
    public static void Main()
    {
        DrawingObject drawing = new Circle();
        Console.WriteLine("Name: {0}", drawing.Name);
    }
}
```

The abstract property Name is declared in the DrawingObject class, with an abstract get accessor. This accessor must then be overridden in the derived class.

---

[5]I've never come across a case where I wanted the get accessor to be less visible than the set accessor.

When the Name property is accessed through a reference to the base class, the overridden property in the derived class is called.

Automatic Properties

In early versions of C#, there were a lot of properties that looked like the first example.

```
string m_name;
public string Name
{
    get { return m_name; }
    set { name = m_value; }
}
```

This sort of boilerplate code is annoying; it's easy to write, but you have to do it for every property that you write, and it makes your class look more complex. C# therefore provides automatic properties,[6] where the compiler will do this for you.

```
public string Name { get; set; }
```

The compiler will declare a backing variable of type string and separate get and set accessors. In this case, there is no way to name the backing variable and access it directly, so it's common to see the following:

```
public string Name { get; private set; }
```

where the property is initialized in the class constructor.

PROPERTY FORMATTING

I recommend the following rules for property formatting:

- A getter or setter with a single return or assignment statement should be written on a single line.
- A more complex getter or setter should always be expanded into method formatting, even if it is only a single statement.
- Automatic properties should be written on a single line.

Properties vs. Fields

Properties are great for code that has to be versioned; you can change the code underneath without users of the code needing to recompile. This is wonderful for companies that may need to ship updates to their customers, and that is why the base class library—and the framework design guidelines that are published for libraries— highly encourage the use of properties.

---

[6]These are technically known as *automatically implemented properties*, but most people just call them *automatic properties*.

In the early days of C#, those were the only design guidelines available; most C# developers used properties everywhere, whether they were building libraries or client applications that never had the requirement to ship updates.[7] They did this despite having to write the following:

```
string m_name;
public string Name
{
    get { return m_name; }
    set { m_name = value; }
}
```

instead of just writing this:

```
public string Name;
```

There were a few attempts to discuss whether public fields might be OK, but they were not successful,[8] and developers kept writing properties that they didn't really need and requesting that the language make it easier to write such properties. This eventually happened as automatic properties made such properties almost as easy to write as public fields, relegating the discussion to books such as this.

There is still no reason to prefer automatic properties over public fields in many cases, but since there is no real downside (except for a small increase in metadata and one usage restriction[9]), there's no reason to avoid automatic properties either. And you'll spend less time in long discussions about whether public fields are OK.

---

[7]This is a great example of unintended consequences; the combination of the advocacy around properties and the lack of nonframework design guidelines led to this situation.
[8]I tried a couple of times, and IIRC there was at least one occasion when Anders expressed the same sentiment, but it was pretty clear that the ship had already sailed.
[9]Properties cannot be passed as arguments to ref or out parameters.

■ ■ ■

CHAPTER 17

Generic Types

It is sometimes useful to separate the implementation of a class—the members and methods that it exposes—from the type it is using. A list of items, for example, behaves in the same way whether it is a list of Decimal items or a list of Employee items.

A generic type is used to create such an implementation. The word *generic* refers to the implementation being written using a generic type rather than a specific one.

A List of Integers

Consider the following class that stores integer values:

```
public class IntList
{
    int m_count = 0;
    int[] m_values;

    public IntList(int capacity)
    {
        m_values = new int[capacity];
    }
    public void Add(int value)
    {
        m_values[m_count] = value;
        m_count++;
    }
    public int this[int index]
    {
        get { return m_values[index];}
        set { m_values[index] = value; }
    }
    public int Count { get { return m_count; } }
}
```

This class deals with only int values, so if you want to store a list of other types, you need to create a separate list class for each type of data (ShortList, FloatList, and so on). That doesn't make much sense, so you can look for alternatives.

One alternative is to note that all types in C# derive from the object base class, and if you make a list that can store objects (ObjectList), you can use it with any type. This approach works and is in fact the approach taken with C# 1.0, but it has a few disadvantages.

- It's not typesafe at compile time; you can add a `string` and an `Employee` to an `ObjectList` instance, and everything works fine. When you access an item in the list, you have to specify which type you are expecting, and you will get an exception if the type isn't the one you expect.

- Any value types that you insert into the list have to be boxed into object instances to be added and unboxed when you pull them out again.

- The resulting code is ugly.

It works, but it's not really what you want.

WHY WERE GENERICS MISSING IN C# 1.0?

The preceding approach is exactly the approach that was used in C# 1.0.

The answer is pretty simple; because of the way that generics are implemented (more on that in the near future), they required a considerable amount of work, both in the C# language and the .NET Runtime. As a work item, it just didn't fit in the schedule, and it was decided that it was better to ship a version of the .NET stack (C#, VB, libraries, and so on) that didn't have generics than to wait for generics to be done. Given the amount of time it took to get C# 2.0 out the door, this seems to have been an excellent choice.

A close examination of the `IntList` class shows that there isn't anything special about the fact that the class stores integer values; the class code would be identical if it stored floats. What you need is a way to generate different implementations for each specific type from one standard implementation. You can start by modifying the class so that all of the instances of `int` are replaced with a placeholder.

```
class MyList
{
    int m_count = 0;
    T[] m_values;

    public MyList(int capacity)
    {
        m_values = new T[capacity];
    }
    public void Add(T value)
    {
        m_values[m_count] = value;
        m_count++;
    }
    public T this[int index]
    {
        get { return m_values[index]; }
        set { m_values[index] = value; }
    }
    public int Count { get { return m_count; } }
}
```

This placeholder is known as a *type parameter*.[1] Now, you just need a way to replace those instances of T with the real type you want. That's a bit complicated; the code doesn't show you what placeholder to replace, and it's valid to have a type named T. You need a way to tell which identifiers in the code are type parameters. You'll do this by adding a decoration to the class name.

```
class MyList<T>
```

Now it is simple to find the T in the class name, and when somebody writes this:

```
MyList<int>
```

you know that you can create the class you want by just substituting all instances of T with int and compiling the resulting code. The type MyList <T> is known as a *generic type*, while the use of MyList <int> is known as a *constructed type*. The use of int is known as a *type argument*.[2]

There are two different ways in which the transformation from generic type to constructed type can be architected.

The first is to do it in a single step. When compiling code with a use of a generic type:

```
MyList<int>
```

you can find the definition of MyList <T>, do the substitution, and compile the resulting code. This is the approach that C++ templates use; templates are purely a compiler feature, and in this example, the MyList <int> class is what gets compiled.

C# and .NET use a two-step approach. In the first step, the generic type (in this case, MyList <T>) is compiled, just like any nongeneric type. When you want to create the constructed type MyList <int>, the compiled definition of MyList <T> is referenced, and the constructed type is created from that.

C++ TEMPLATES VS. C# GENERICS

When the .NET teams were designing generics, there were two important requirements.

- A generic type written in one language has to be consumable in any other .NET language[3] that supports generics.

- Generic types must work as expected when accessed at runtime. Among other things, that means being able to tell that a type is a generic type and being able to construct instances of generic types from their names.

Neither of these would make sense in the C++ world, since C++ doesn't interoperate with other languages and doesn't work in a managed environment.[4]

Supporting generics through the two-step approach has one big disadvantage. When compiling a type such as MyList <T>, the C# compiler does not know what type will ultimately be used instead of T, and therefore it can generate code based only on what it does know.

In many cases, if you have questions about why generics look the way they do in C# or why they can't do something that C++ can do, it will help to ask yourself what the compiler knows at the time the generic type is compiled.

---

[1]Technically, a *generic* type parameter.
[2]This is symmetrical with how methods work; methods define parameters and are called with arguments.
[3]There are the "big 3" Microsoft .NET languages (Visual Basic .NET, C#, and C++), but there are also numerous less common languages, and giving them access to generic types was an important goal.
[4]I'm talking about standard C++, not the Microsoft version that includes .NET support.

Constraints

As described in the previous section, generics are quite limited. Returning to the example, perhaps you want to create the MyConstructedList <T> class, which will initialize each element when the class is created. In this class, you write the following constructor:

```
public MyConstructedList(int capacity)
{
    m_values = new T[capacity];
    for (int i = 0; i < capacity; i++)
    {
        m_values[i] = new T();
    }
}
```

That doesn't compile. The type T could be any type in .NET, which means that all the compiler knows is that type T can do what type object can. It does not know that it has a parameterless constructor, so trying to write this:

```
new T();
```

is illegal. What is needed is a way to specify that MyConstructedList <T> can be used for only those types that have such a constructor. This is done by introducing a constraint[5] on the declaration of the generic type.

```
class MyConstructedList<T> where T : new()
```

At this point, the compiler knows that a parameterless constructor will always be there for type T.

Interface Constraints

You now want to extend your list so that it is sortable. To do so, you're going to have to write code that compares two values.

```
if (m_values[x].CompareTo(m_values[y]) > 0)
```

This is, of course, illegal, because the compiler doesn't know if there is a way to compare two T values. You can address this by adding an interface constraint.

```
class MySortedList<T> where T: IComparable
```

The compiler will now require that T implements the IComparable interface. Since a class can implement more than one interface, a generic class can specify more than one interface constraint.

Base Class Constraints

It is also possible to specify that a type parameter be a specific class or a class derived from that class.

```
class Processor<T>where T: Employee
```

---

[5]This use of the term *constraint* is a bit odd; you add a constraint so that your generic code can do more than it could before, and generally, the tighter the constraint, the more you can do. If you look at it from the perspective of the generic type argument, it makes more sense.

Any instance method that is defined on Employee can now be used through T.

■ **Note**   I'm not a big fan of base class constraints. The point of creating a generic class is to write code that is generic, and tying that to a specific class seems to make things less generic. I think that constraints on interfaces are generally a better idea.

Class and Struct Constraints

If you want to constrain your class so that the type parameter is only a class or only a struct, a class or struct constraint can be used.

```
class Processor<T> where T: class
class Executor<T> where T: struct
```

Multiple Constraints

It is possible to put multiple constraints on a single type parameter or to add constraints to more than one type parameter.

```
class Storer<T, U>
    where T: IComparable, IEnumerable
    where U: class
```

The contraints for a given type parameter are listed in a comma-separated list, and each type parameter has a separate where clause.

The Default Value of a Type

It is sometimes necessary to write code that initializes a variable. If the generic type is unconstrained, the type argument could be either a struct or a class, and you therefore need a way to do the appropriate thing. You can write the following:

```
value = default(T);
```

which will set the value to null if the generic type is a class and zero it out if the type is a struct.

Generic Interfaces and Inheritance

Since classes can be generic, interfaces can also be generic. Here's an example:

```
interface IMyList<T>
{
    void Add(T value);
}
```

Specifying the generic interface imposes a requirement that classes that implement the interface contain an appropriate method. For example, a generic class would be a match.

```
class MyList<T>: IMyList<T>
{
    public void Add(T value) {...}
}
```

You can also match with a nongeneric class.

```
class NewIntList : IMyList<int>
{
    public void Add(int value) { }
}
```

Here's another example:

```
class NewIntList : MyList<int>, IMyList<int>{}
```

Generic Methods

Generic methods are used when the thing you want to make generic is an algorithm rather than a class. Consider the following simple method in the Shuffle class:

```
public static List<string> Shuffle(List<string> list1, List<string> list2)
{
    List<string> shuffled = new List<string>();

    for (int i = 0; i < list1.Count; i++)
    {
        shuffled.Add(list1[i]);
        shuffled.Add(list2[i]);
    }

    return shuffled;
}
```

This method is called as follows:

```
List<string> shuffledList = Shuffler.Shuffle(list1, list2);
```

The method that is used to perform the shuffle is not dependent on the type being string, so it can easily be made generic by replacing all the instances of string with T.

```
public static List<T> Shuffle<T>(List<T> list1, List<T> list2)
{
    List<T> shuffled = new List<T>();

    for (int i = 0; i<list1.Count; i++)
```

```
    {
        shuffled.Add(list1[i]);
        shuffled.Add(list2[i]);
    }

    return shuffled;
}
```

This method is called as follows:

```
List<string> shuffledList = Shuffler.Shuffle<string>(list1, list2);
```

The use of <string> tells the compiler what type to use to replace T in the generic method. If the generic type parameter (T in this case) is used in the arguments, the compiler is able to infer the generic type argument, and the call can be simplified to the following:

```
List<string> shuffledList = Shuffler.Shuffle(list1, list2);
```

The first parameter of the Shuffle() method is a List<T>, and you are passing a List<string>, so T must be string in this call.

Generic Delegates

For an introduction to delegates, see Chapter 22.

Generic delegates can be declared in a way similar to generic methods. In a generic class, the generic type parameter can be used in the declaration of a delegate.

```
public class Stack<T>
{
    public delegate void ItemAdded(T newItem);
}
```

A delegate can also be declared with its own type parameters. For example, the base class library contains the following delegate:

```
public delegate void EventHandler<TEventArgs>(object sender, TEventArgs e)
                                        where TEventArgs : EventArgs
```

This delegate requires that the second argument must be a class derived from the EventArgs class. It is now simple to declare events that follow the .NET convention without having to define your own type-specific delegate.

```
public event EventHandler<StackChangeEventArgs> StackChanged;
```

Covariance and Contravariance

Covariance and contravariance are big terms that describe how conversions are performed between types.[6]

---

[6]The information in this section may make your head hurt. This is perfectly normal; it makes my head hurt as well.

Consider the following:

```
class Auto
{
}
class Sedan: Auto
{
}
void ReferenceCovariance()
{
    Sedan dodgeDart = new Sedan();
    Auto currentCar = dodgeDart;
}
```

This works exactly as you would expect; because Sedan is derived from Auto, every Sedan is an Auto, and therefore you can safely make this assignment.

When you extend this to arrays of reference types, it gets more interesting.

```
void ArrayCovariance()
{
    Sedan[] sedans = new Sedan[1];
    sedans[0] = new Sedan();
    Auto[] autos = sedans;

    autos[0] = new Roadster();
}
```

It is useful to be able to assign an array of Sedan instances to an array of Auto instances; this allows you to write methods that take an array of Auto instances as a parameter. Unfortunately, it isn't typesafe; the last statement in the method assigns a Roadster instance to the autos array. That would be fine if the autos array was actually of type Auto[], but it is in fact of type Sedan[], and the assignment fails at runtime.[7]

This behavior is a bit unfortunate. It would be nice if generics provided a better solution. Consider the following example:

```
interface IFirstItem<T>
{
    T GetFirstItem();
}
class MyFirstList<T> : List<T>, IFirstItem<T>
{
    public MyFirstList () { }

    public T GetFirstItem()
    {
        return this[0];
    }
}
```

---

[7]The reason for this behavior is a bit complex. If you want all the details, Eric Lippert has an excellent series of blog posts on covariance and contravariance in C#.

Here you define an interface named IFirstItem<T> and a list class that implements it. You then write some code to use it.

```
void TestService()
{
    MyFirstList<Sedan> sedans = new MyFirstList<Sedan>();
    sedans.Add(new Sedan());

    PerformService(sedans);
}
void PerformService(IFirstItem<Auto> autos)
{
}
```

You are passing an IFirstItem<Sedan> to a function that takes an IFirstItem<Auto>, and that's not allowed. The compiler is worried that PerformService() will lose the fact that the Auto is really a Sedan and try to do something that will generate an exception. It's the same situation you had with the array.

If you examine the IFirstItem<T> interface, you will realize that there is no issue; the only thing that it does is pull an instance of type T out, and there is no way for that to cause an issue. What you need is a way to tell the compiler that the type parameter T is used only as output.

You can do that through the following:

```
interface IFirstItem<out T>
{
    T GetFirstItem();
}
```

The code now works. This is an example of generic covariance; the compiler now knows that it is safe to convert from the type of T to a less-derived type, so it allows you to do the conversion.

You now try to extend the interface by adding an additional method.

```
interface IFirstItem<out T>
{
    T GetFirstItem();
    void NotLegal(T parameter);
}
```

This generates an error.[8] You said that you are going to use the generic parameter T only for output, but the NotLegal() method uses it for input.

Contravariance

Contravariance applies in a different case. Consider the following:

```
interface IEqual<in T>
{
    bool IsEqual(T x, T y);
}
```

---

[8]Invalid variance: The type parameter T must be contravariantly valid on IFirstItem<T>.NotLegal(T). T is covariant.

```
class Comparer : IEqual<object>
{
    public bool IsEqual(object x, object y)
    {
        return true;
    }
}
class GenericContravariance
{
    void Example()
    {
        Comparer comparer = new Comparer();
        TestEquality(comparer);
    }
    void TestEquality(IEqual<Auto> equalizer)
    {
    }
}
```

In this case, instances of type T flow only into the interface and are never visible outside of the interface. That allows you to do something that seems a bit surprising; you can pass an IEqual<object> for use as an IEqual<Auto>. That just seems wrong. However, if you look a bit closer, you will figure out that if you have an IEqual<Auto>, you will want to use it in code such as this:

```
Auto auto1 = ...;
Auto auto2 = ...;
bool equal = equalizer.IsEqual(auto1, auto2);
```

In that situation, it is perfectly safe to use an IEqual<object>, since you can safely convert the Auto arguments into object arguments. You indicate this situation by adding the in keyword to the type parameter.

Generics and Efficiency

As you learned earlier in this chapter, the runtime will replace all generic type parameters with their appropriate argument types when constructing instances of those types. Such an implementation could result in a considerable amount of memory use, with separate implementations for List<string>, List<Employee>, and all other uses of List<T>.

The .NET Runtime will take advantage of the fact that variables of type string and Employee are the same size, and therefore the generated code is identical (except for the type of the arguments) for all reference types and generate it only once.

Value types are of differing sizes, and the runtime therefore generates a different implementation for each use of a value type as a generic type argument.

Generic Naming Guidelines

Generic type names show up in two places.

- In the declaration of the generic type and therefore any time a developer is writing code using the generic type

- In the implementation of the generic type

It is helpful to choose generic type parameter names that aid in the understanding of both of these cases. I suggest the following guidelines when naming generic type parameters:

- If there is a single type parameter that can be any type, name it T.

- If a single type parameter has a nongeneric meaning, include that meaning in the name, and name it something like TEntity or TComparable. This will make it much more understandable for the user of the generic type.

- If there are multiple type parameters, give them useful names, such as in Dictionary<TKey, TValue>.[9]

Beyond that, consider whether a particular name improves readability.

---

[9]There has been considerable discussion about the best naming convention for this case. The one I have given is consistent with the .NET Framework Design Guidelines, but the T prefix does seem out of place at times.

■ ■ ■

CHAPTER 18

Indexers, Enumerators, and Iterators

It is sometimes useful to be able to treat an object as if it were an array and access it by index. This can be done by writing an *indexer* for the object. In the same way that a property looks like a field but has accessors to perform get and set operations, an indexer looks like an array but has accessors to perform array-indexing operations.

Pretty much every object with an indexer will also have an enumerator. Enumerators and iterators provide two ways of returning a sequence of values from an object.

Indexing with an Integer Index

A class that contains a database row might implement an indexer to access the columns in the row.

```
using System;
using System.Collections.Generic;
class DataValue
{
    public DataValue(string name, object data)
    {
        Name = name;
        Data = data;
    }
    public string Name { get; set; }
    public object Data { get; set; }
}
class DataRow
{
    public DataRow()
    {
        m_row = new List<DataValue>();
    }

    public void Load()
    {
        /* load code here */
        m_row.Add(new DataValue("Id", 5551212));
        m_row.Add(new DataValue("Name", "Fred"));
        m_row.Add(new DataValue("Salary", 2355.23 m));
    }
```

```
        // the indexer - implements a 1-based index.
    public DataValue this[int column]
    {
        get { return(m_row[column - 1]); }
        set { m_row[column - 1] = value; }
    }
    List<DataValue>m_row;
}
class Test
{
    public static void Main()
    {
        DataRow row = new DataRow();
        row.Load();
        Console.WriteLine("Column 0: {0}", row[1].Data);
        row[1].Data = 12;     // set the ID
    }
}
```

The DataRow class has functions to load a row of data, functions to save the data, and an indexer function to provide access to the data. In a real class, the Load() function would load data from a database.

The indexer function is written the same way that a property is written, except that it takes an indexing parameter. The indexer is declared using the name this since it has no name.[1]

Indexing with a String Index

A class can have more than one indexer. For the DataRow class, it might be useful to be able to use the name of the column for indexing.

```
using System;
using System.Collections.Generic;
class DataValue
{
    public DataValue(string name, object data)
    {
        Name = name;
        Data = data;
    }
    public string Name { get; set; }
    public object Data { get; set; }
}
class DataRow
{
    public DataRow()
    {
        m_row = new List<DataValue>();
    }
```

---

[1]The choice of using this as a keyword was a bit controversial, but it was chosen because there weren't any better choices apparent and because reusing an existing keyword doesn't take away a name that developers would like to use elsewhere.

```csharp
    public void Load()
    {
        /* load code here */
        m_row.Add(new DataValue("Id", 5551212));
        m_row.Add(new DataValue("Name", "Fred"));
        m_row.Add(new DataValue("Salary", 2355.23 m));
    }
    public DataValue this[int column]
    {
        get { return(m_row[column - 1]); }
        set { m_row[column - 1] = value; }
    }
    int FindColumn(string name)
    {
        for (int index = 0; index < m_row.Count; index++)
        {
            if (m_row[index].Name == name)
            {
                return(index + 1);
            }
        }
        return(-1);
    }
    public DataValue this[string name]
    {
        get { return(this[FindColumn(name)]); }
        set { this[FindColumn(name)] = value; }
    }
    List<DataValue> m_row;
}
class Test
{
    public static void Main()
    {
        DataRow row = new DataRow();
        row.Load();
        DataValue val = row["Id"];
        Console.WriteLine("Id: {0}", val.Data);
        Console.WriteLine("Salary: {0}", row["Salary"].Data);
        row["Name"].Data = "Barney";     // set the name
        Console.WriteLine("Name: {0}", row["Name"].Data);
    }
}
```

The string indexer uses the FindColumn() function to find the index of the name and then uses the int indexer to do the proper thing.

Indexing with Multiple Parameters

Indexers can take more than one parameter to simulate a multidimensional virtual array. The following example implements a chessboard that can be accessed using standard chess notation (a letter from *A* to *H* followed by a number from 1 to 8). The first indexer is used to access the board using string and integer indices, and the second indexer uses a single string like "C5."

```csharp
using System;

public class Player
{
    string m_name;

    public Player(string name)
    {
        m_name = name;
    }
    public override string ToString()
    {
        return(m_name);
    }
}

public class Board
{
    Player[,] board = new Player[8, 8];

    int RowToIndex(string row)
    {
        string temp = row.ToUpper();
        return((int) temp[0] - (int) 'A');
    }

    int PositionToColumn(string pos)
    {
        return(pos[1] - '0' - 1);
    }

    public Player this[string row, int column]
    {
        get
        {
            return(board[RowToIndex(row), column - 1]);
        }
        set
        {
            board[RowToIndex(row), column - 1] = value;
        }
    }

    public Player this[string position]
    {
        get
        {
            return(board[RowToIndex(position),
                        PositionToColumn(position)]);
        }
```

```
        set
        {
            board[RowToIndex(position),
                    PositionToColumn(position)] = value;
        }
    }
}
class Test
{
    public static void Main()
    {
        Board board = new Board();

        board["A", 4] = new Player("White King");
        board["H", 4] = new Player("Black King");

        Console.WriteLine("A4 = {0}", board["A", 4]);
        Console.WriteLine("H4 = {0}", board["H4"]);
    }
}
```

Design Guidelines for Indexers

Indexers should be used only in situations where the class is arraylike.[2]

Object Enumeration

A class that contains values can implement the IEnumerable < T > alias, which specifies that this class can generate an ordered sequence of values. Enumerators and iterators are two ways (one old, one new) of implementing object enumeration.

Enumerators and Foreach

To understand what is required to enable foreach, it helps to know what goes on behind the scenes.
    When the compiler sees the following foreach block:

```
foreach (string s in myCollection)
{
    Console.WriteLine("String is {0}", s);
}
```

    it transforms this code into the following:[3]

```
IEnumerator enumerator = ((IEnumerable) myCollection).GetEnumerator();
while (enumerator.MoveNext())
```

---

[2]I've seen cases where a class that was not arraylike implemented an indexer instead of a method that took an integer. It's very weird and difficult to understand.
[3]This is a bit oversimplified. If the IEnumerator implements IDisposable, the compiler will wrap the enumeration in a try-finally statement to ensure that the Dispose method is called. More on this later.

```
{
    string s = (string) enumerator.Current();
    Console.WriteLine("String is {0}", s);
}
```

The first step of the process is to cast the item to iterate to IEnumerable. If that succeeds, the class supports enumeration, and an IEnumerator interface reference to perform the enumeration is returned. The MoveNext() and Current members of the class are then called to perform the iteration.

Enabling Enumeration

To make a class enumerable, you will implement the IEnumerable interface on a class. To do that, you need a class that can walk through a list (this uses the IntList example from Chapter 17).

```
public class IntListEnumerator : IEnumerator
{
    IntList m_intList;
    int m_index;
    internal IntListEnumerator(IntList intList)
    {
        m_intList = intList;
        Reset();
    }
    public void Reset()
    {
        m_index = -1;
    }
    public bool MoveNext()
    {
        m_index++;
        return m_index < m_intList.Count;
    }
    public object Current
    {
        get { return (m_intList[m_index]); }
    }
}
```

The IntList class can then use this enumerator class.

```
public class IntList: IEnumerable
{
    int m_count = 0;
    int[] m_values;
    public IntList(int capacity)
    {
        m_values = new int[capacity];
    }
    public void Add(int value)
```

```
    {
        m_values[m_count] = value;
        m_count++;
    }
    public int this[int index]
    {
        get { return m_values[index]; }
        set { m_values[index] = value; }
    }
    public int Count { get { return m_count; } }
    public IEnumerator GetEnumerator()
    {
        return new IntListEnumerator(this);
    }
}
```

The user can now write the following:

```
IntList intList = new IntList(3);
intList.Add(1);
intList.Add(2);
intList.Add(4);

foreach (int number in intList)
{
    Console.WriteLine(number);
}
```

The IntListEnumerator class is a simple state machine that keeps track of where it is in the list, returning items in enumeration order.

ENUMERATION HISTORY

Because enumeration was added to C# in several stages, there are no less than four ways to implement enumerations in C#. They are, in order of introduction:

1. The enumeration class can implement the IEnumerator interface. This is like the previous example, but the type of the Current property is object (so it can be generic in a world without generics).

2. The approach shown in the previous example can be used, but modified so that the type of the Current property is not object. This pattern-based approach works in C# and VB but might not work in all .NET languages. In the early days of C#, many classes used this approach and implemented IEnumerator implicitly, effectively implementing both of these approaches.

3. Implement the generic IEnumerator < T > interface. Many classes implemented the approaches of #1 and #2 as well.

4. Iterators can be used.

The first two were in C# 1.0, the third one was introduced when generic types showed up in C# 2.0, and the last one is the current approach. It's more than a little confusing. Thankfully, most classes use iterators, which, as you will see, are the simplest approach.

Iterators

Before the introduction of iterators, writing enumerators was an onerous task.[4] You had to write all the boilerplate code and get it correct, and if you had a data structure such as a tree, you had to write the traversal method that would keep track of where you were in the tree for each call.

Making that sort of thing easier is exactly what compilers are good at, and C# therefore provides support to make this easier, in a feature known as an *iterator*. Iterators automate the boilerplate code and, more importantly, let you express the state machine as if it were normal procedural code.

```
public class IntListNew: IEnumerable
{
    int m_count = 0;
    int[] m_values;
    public IntListNew(int capacity)
    {
        m_values = new int[capacity];
    }
    public void Add(int value)
    {
        m_values[m_count] = value;
        m_count++;
    }
    public int this[int index]
    {
        get { return m_values[index]; }
        set { m_values[index] = value; }
    }
    public int Count { get { return m_count; } }
    public IEnumerator GetEnumerator()
    {
        for (int index=0; index < m_count; index++)
        {
            yield return m_values[index];
        }
    }
}
```

The iterator GetEnumerator() works as follows:

1. When the class is first enumerated, the code in the iterator is executed from the start.

2. When a yield return statement is encountered, that value is returned as one of the enumeration values, and the compiler remembers where it is in the code in the enumerator.

---

[4] But we did it. And we had to trudge through waist-high snowdrifts to get to our offices, and our characters only had 7 bits (the last part is true, actually).

3. When the next value is asked for, execution of code continues immediately after the previous yield return statement.

The compiler will do all the hard work of creating the state machine that makes that possible.[5] In more complex classes, such as a tree class, it is common to have several yield return statements in a single iterator.

■ **Note**   So, why is the statement yield return and not just yield? It might have been, if iterators were in the first version of C#, but using yield by itself would have required that yield be a new keyword, which would have broken any existing code that used yield as a variable name. Putting it next to return made it a contextual keyword, preserving the use of the identifier yield elsewhere.

Named Iterators

It is possible for a class to support more than one method of iterating. A named iterator can be added to your class.

```
public IEnumerable ReversedItems()
{
    for (int index = m_count - 1; index >= 0; index--)
    {
        yield return m_values[index];
    }
}
```

And it can used as follows:

```
foreach (int number in intList.ReversedItems())
{
    Console.WriteLine(number);
}
```

NAMED ITERATORS OR LINQ METHODS?

C# provides multiple ways of doing a list reversal and other such transformations; an iterator method can be defined on the class or a Linq method, as described in Chapter 28.

There are some cases where the choice is obvious. A tree class might want to support pre-order, in-order, post-order, and breadth-first searches, and the only way to do that is through a named iterator. On the other hand, if you are dealing with a class somebody else wrote, you can't add a named iterator, so you will need to rely on Linq.

In the cases where there is a choice, my recommendation is to start with a single iterator and use Linq methods. If profiling shows a performance bottleneck in that code, then go back and add the named iterator.

---

[5]There is a considerable amount of code generation magic going on here. I recommend using a decompiler to look at the generated code.

Iterators and Generic Types

Generic iterators are defined by implementing IEnumerable < T > and returning IEnumerator < T >.

```
public class MyListNew<T> : IEnumerable<T>
{
    int m_count = 0;
    T[] m_values;
    public MyListNew(int capacity)
    {
        m_values = new T[capacity];
    }
    public void Add(T value)
    {
        m_values[m_count] = value;
        m_count++;
    }
    public T this[int index]
    {
        get { return m_values[index]; }
        set { m_values[index] = value; }
    }
    public int Count { get { return m_count; } }
    IEnumerator IEnumerable.GetEnumerator()
    {
        return GetEnumerator();
    }
    public IEnumerator<T> GetEnumerator()
    {
        for (int index = 0; index < m_count; index++)
        {
            yield return m_values[index];
        }
    }
    public IEnumerable<T> ReversedItems()
    {
        for (int index = m_count - 1; index >= 0; index--)
        {
            yield return m_values[index];
        }
    }
}
```

This is very straightforward, with two small caveats:

- In addition to implementing the generic version of GetEnumerator(), you need to explicitly implement the nongeneric version as well (see the bold code). This allows languages that don't support generics to iterate over your class.

- A using System.Collections; statement is required to use the nongeneric IEnumerable type.

Iterators and Resource Management

An iterator might hold a valuable resource, such as a database connection or a file. It would be very useful for that resource to be released when the iterator has completed, and in fact, the foreach statement will ensure that resources are released by calling Dispose() if the enumerator implements IDisposable.

Iterators do their part as well. Consider the following code:

```
class ByteStreamer
{
    string m_filename;
    public ByteStreamer(string filename)
    {
        m_filename = filename;
    }
    public IEnumerator<byte> GetEnumerator()
    {
        using (FileStream stream = File.Open(m_filename, FileMode.Open))
        {
            yield return (byte) stream.ReadByte();
        }
    }
}
```

This looks just like the normal pattern with the using statement. The compiler will take any cleanup required by the stream instance and make sure it is performed when Dispose() is called at the end of the enumeration.

This does not, however, extend to exception handling; a yield return can appear only in a try block that does not have a catch block. It can never appear in a catch or finally block.

CHAPTER 19

■ ■ ■

Strings

All strings in C# are instances of the System.String type in the Common Language Runtime. Because of this, there are many built-in operations available that work with strings. For example, the String class defines an indexer function that can be used to iterate over the characters of the string.

```
using System;
class Test
{
    public static void Main()
    {
        string s = "Test String";

        for (int index = 0; index < s.Length; index++)
        {
            Console.WriteLine("Char: {0}", s[index]);
        }
    }
}
```

Operations

The string class is an example of an immutable type, which means that the characters contained in the string cannot be modified by users of the string. All operations that produce a modification of the input string that are performed by the string class return a modified version of the string rather than modifying the instance on which the method is called. Here's an example:

```
string s = "Test String";
s.Replace("Test", "Best");
Console.WriteLine(s);
```

This takes the string, replaces Test with Best, and then throws away the result. What you want to write is this:

```
s = s.Replace("Test", "Best");
```

Immutable types are used to make reference types that have value semantics (in other words, act somewhat like value types).

The String class supports the comparison and searching methods shown in Tables 19-1 and 19-2.

Table 19-1. *String Comparison and Search Methods*

Item	Description
Compare()	Compares two strings
CompareOrdinal()	Compares two string regions using an ordinal comparison
CompareTo()	Compares the current instance with another instance
EndsWith()	Determines whether a substring exists at the end of a string
StartsWith()	Determines whether a substring exists at the beginning of a string
IndexOf()	Returns the position of the first occurrence of a substring
IndexOfAny()	Returns the position of the first occurrence of any character in a string
LastIndexOf()	Returns the position of the first occurrence of a substring
LastIndexOfAny()	Returns the position of the last occurrence of any character in a string

The String class supports the modification methods in Table 19-2, which all return a new string instance.

Table 19-2. *String Modification Methods*

Item	Description
Concat()	Concatenates two or more strings or objects together. If objects are passed, the ToString() function is called on them.
CopyTo()	Copies a specified number of characters from a location in this string into an array.
Insert()	Returns a new string with a substring inserted at a specific location.
Join()	Joins an array of strings together with a separator between each array element.
Normalize()	Normalizes the string into a Unicode form.
PadLeft()	Righ- aligns a string in a field.
PadRight()	Left-aligns a string in a field.
Remove()	Deletes characters from a string.
Replace()	Replaces all instances of a character with a different character.
Split()	Creates an array of strings by splitting a string at any occurrence of one or more characters.
Substrng()	Extracts a substring from a string.
ToLower()	Returns a lowercase version of a string.
ToUpper()	Returns an uppercase version of a string.
Trim()	Removes whitespace from a string.
TrimEnd()	Removes a string of characters from the end of a string.
TrimStart()	Removes a string of characters from the beginning of a string.

String Literals

String literals are described in Chapter 32.

String Encodings and Conversions

C# strings are always Unicode strings. When dealing only in the .NET world, this greatly simplifies working with strings.

Unfortunately, it's sometimes necessary to deal with the messy details of other kinds of strings, especially when dealing with text files produced by older applications. The System.Text namespace contains classes that can be used to convert between an array of bytes and a character encoding such as ASCII, Unicode, UTF7, or UTF8. Each encoding is encapsulated in a class such as ASCIIEncoding.

To convert from a string to a block of bytes, the GetEncoder() method on the encoding class is called to obtain an Encoder, which is then used to do the encoding. Similarly, to convert from a block of bytes to a specific encoding, GetDecoder() is called to obtain a decoder.

Converting Objects to Strings

The function object.ToString() is overridden by the built-in types to provide an easy way of converting from a value to a string representation of that value. Calling ToString() produces the default representation of a value; a different representation may be obtained by calling String.Format(). See the section on formatting in Chapter 39 for more information.

An Example

The split function can be used to break a string into substrings at separators.

```
using System;
class Test
{
    public static void Main()
    {
        string s = "Oh, I hadn't thought of that";
        char[] separators = new char[] {' ', ','};
        foreach (string sub in s.Split(separators))
        {
            Console.WriteLine("Word: {0}", sub);
        }
    }
}
```

This example produces the following output:

```
Word: Oh
Word:
Word: I
Word: hadn't
Word: thought
Word: of

Word: that
```

The separators character array defines what characters the string will be broken on. The Split() function returns an array of strings, and the foreach statement iterates over the array and prints it out.

In this case, the output isn't particularly useful because the "," string gets broken twice. This can be fixed by using the regular expression classes.

StringBuilder

Though the String.Format() function can be used to create a string based on the values of other strings, it isn't necessarily the most efficient way to assemble strings. The runtime provides the StringBuilder class to make this process easier.

The StringBuilder class supports the properties and methods described in Table 19-3 and Table 19-4.

Table 19-3. *StringBuilder Properties*

Property	Description
Capacity	Retrieves or sets the number of characters the StringBuilder can hold.
[]	The StringBuilder indexer is used to get or set a character at a specific position.
Length	Retrieves or sets the length.
MaxCapacity	Retrieves the maximum capacity of the StringBuilder.

Table 19-4. *StringBuilder Methods*

Method	Description
Append()	Appends the string representation of an object
AppendFormat()	Appends a string representation of an object, using a specific format string for the object
EnsureCapacity()	Ensures the StringBuilder has enough room for a specific number of characters
Insert()	Inserts the string representation of a specified object at a specified position
Remove()	Removes the specified characters
Replace()	Replaces all instances of a character with a new character

The following example demonstrates how the StringBuilder class can be used to create a string from separate strings:

```
using System;
using System.Text;
class Test
{
    public static void Main()
    {
        string s = "I will not buy this record, it is scratched";
        char[] separators = new char[] {' ', ','};
        StringBuilder sb = new StringBuilder();
```

```
        int number = 1;
        foreach (string sub in s.Split(separators))
        {
            sb.AppendFormat("{0}: {1} ", number++, sub);
        }
        Console.WriteLine("{0}", sb);
    }
}
```

This code will create a string with numbered words and will produce the following output:

```
1: I 2: will 3: not 4: buy 5: this 6: record 7:   8: it 9: is 10: scratched
```

Because the call to split() specified both the space and the comma as separators, it considers there to be a word between the comma and the following space, which results in an empty entry.

Regular Expressions

If the searching functions found in the String class aren't powerful enough, the System.Text namespace contains a regular expression class named Regex. Regular expressions provide a very powerful method for doing search and/or replace functions.

While this section has a few examples of using regular expressions, a detailed description of them is beyond the scope of the book. There is considerable information about regular expressions in the MSDN documentation. Several regular expression books are available, and the subject is also covered in most books about Perl. *Mastering Regular Expressions, Third Edition* (O'Reilly, 2006) by Jeffrey Friedl and *Regular Expression Recipes: A Problem-Solution Approach* (Apress, 2004) by Nathan A. Good are two great references.

The regular expression class uses a rather interesting technique to get maximum performance. Rather than interpret the regular expression for each match, it writes a short program on the fly to implement the regular expression match, and that code is then run.[1]

The previous example using Split() can be revised to use a regular expression, rather than single characters, to specify how the split should occur. This will remove the blank word that was found in the preceding example.

```
// file: regex.cs
using System;
using System.Text.RegularExpressions;
class Test
{
    public static void Main()
    {
        string s = "Oh, I hadn't thought of that";
        Regex regex = new Regex(@" |, ");
        char[] separators = {' ', ','};
        foreach (string sub in regex.Split(s))
        {
            Console.WriteLine("Word: {0}", sub);
        }
    }
}
```

---

[1]The program is written using the .NET intermediate language—the same one that C# produces as output from a compilation. See Chapter 36 for information on how this works.

This example produces the following output:

```
Word: Oh
Word: I
Word: hadn't
Word: thought
Word: of
Word: that
```

In the regular expression, the string is split either on a space or on a comma followed by a space.

Regular Expression Options

When creating a regular expression, several options can be specified to control how the matches are performed (see Table 19-5). Compiled is especially useful to speed up searches that use the same regular expression multiple times.

Table 19-5. *Regular Expression Options*

Option	Description
Compiled	Compiles the regular expression into a custom implementation so that matches are faster
ExplicitCapture	Specifies that the only valid captures are named
IgnoreCase	Performs case-insensitive matching
IgnorePatternWhitespace	Removes unescaped whitespace from the pattern to allow # comments
Multiline	Changes the meaning of ^ and $ so they match at the beginning or end of any line, not the beginning or end of the whole string
RightToLeft	Performs searches from right to left rather than from left to right
Singleline	Single-line mode, where . matches any character including \n

More Complex Parsing

Using regular expressions to improve the function of Split() doesn't really demonstrate their power. The following example uses regular expressions to parse an IIS log file. That log file looks something like this:

```
#Software: Microsoft Internet Information Server 4.0
#Version: 1.0
#Date: 1999-12-31 00:01:22
#Fields: time c-ip cs-method cs-uri-stem sc-status
00:01:31 157.56.214.169 GET /Default.htm 304
00:02:55 157.56.214.169 GET /docs/project/overview.htm 200
```

The following code will parse this into a more useful form:

```
// file=logparse.cs
// compile with: csc logparse.cs
using System;
using System.Net;
using System.IO;
using System.Text.RegularExpressions;
using System.Collections;

class Test
{
    public static void Main(string[] args)
    {
        if (args.Length  == 0) // we need a file to parse
        {
            Console.WriteLine("No log file specified.");
        }
        else
        {
            ParseLogFile(args[0]);
        }
    }
    public static void ParseLogFile(string    filename)
    {
        if (!System.IO.File.Exists(filename))
        {
            Console.WriteLine ("The file specified does not exist.");
        }
        else
        {
            FileStream f = new FileStream(filename, FileMode.Open);
            StreamReader stream=new StreamReader(f);

            string line;
            line = stream.ReadLine();     // header line
            line = stream.ReadLine();     // version line
            line = stream.ReadLine();     // Date line

            Regex regexDate = new Regex(@"\:\s(?<date>[^\s]+)\s");
            Match match = regexDate.Match(line);
            string date = "";
            if (match.Length != 0)
            {
                date = match.Groups["date"].ToString();
            }

            line = stream.ReadLine();     // Fields line

            Regex regexLine =
                new Regex(          // match digit or :
                    @"(?<time>(\d|\:)+)\s" +
                        // match digit or .
```

```
                   @"(?<ip>(\d|\.)+)\s" +
                        // match any non-white
                   @"(?<method>\S+)\s" +
                        // match any non-white
                   @"(?<uri>\S+)\s" +
                        // match any non-white
                   @"(?<status>\d+)");

        // read through the lines, add an
        // IISLogRow for each line
    while ((line = stream.ReadLine()) != null)
    {
        //Console.WriteLine(line);
        match = regexLine.Match(line);
        if (match.Length != 0)
        {
            Console.WriteLine("date: {0} {1}", date,
                            match.Groups["time"]);
            Console.WriteLine("IP Address: {0}",
                            match.Groups["ip"]);
            Console.WriteLine("Method: {0}",
                            match.Groups["method"]);
            Console.WriteLine("Status: {0}",
                            match.Groups["status"]);
            Console.WriteLine("URI: {0}\n",
                            match.Groups["uri"]);
        }
    }
    f.Close();
    }
  }
}
```

The general structure of this code should be familiar. There are two regular expressions used in this example. The date string and the regular expression used to match it are as follows:

```
#Date: 1999-12-31 00:01:22
\:\s(?<date>[^\s]+)\s
```

In the code, regular expressions are usually written using the verbatim string syntax, since the regular expression syntax also uses the backslash character. Regular expressions are most easily read if they are broken down into separate elements. The following matches the colon (:):

```
\:
```

The backslash (\) is required because the colon by itself means something else. The following matches a single character of whitespace (tab or space):

```
\s
```

In the following line, the ?<date> names the value that will be matched so it can be extracted later:

```
(?<date>[^\s]+)
```

The [^\s] is called a *character group*, with the ^ character meaning "none of the following characters." This group therefore matches any nonwhitespace character. Finally, the + character means to match one or more occurrences of the previous description (nonwhitespace). The parentheses are used to delimit how to match the extracted string. In the preceding example, this part of the expression matches 1999-12-31.

To match more carefully, the \d (digit) specifier could have been used, with the whole expression written as follows:

```
\:\s(?<date>\d\d\d\d-\d\d-\d\d)\s
```

That covers the simple regular expression. A more complex regular expression is used to match each line of the log file. Because of the regularity of the line, Split() could also have been used, but that wouldn't have been as illustrative. The clauses of the regular expression are as follows:

```
(?<time>(\d|\:)+)\s        // match digit or : to extract time
(?<ip>(\d|\.)+)\s          // match digit or . to get IP address
(?<method>\S+)\s           // any non-whitespace for method
(?<uri>\S+)\s              // any non-whitespace for uri
(?<status>\d+)             // any digit for status
```

CHAPTER 20

■ ■ ■

Enumerations

Enumerations are useful when a value in the program can have only a specific set of values. An enumeration might be used where a control supports only four colors or for a network package that supports only two protocols.

A Line-Style Enumeration

In the following example, a line-drawing class uses an enumeration to declare the styles of lines it can draw:

```
using System;
public class Draw
{
    public enum LineStyle
    {
        Solid,
        Dotted,
        DotDash,        // trailing comma is optional
    }

    public void DrawLine(int x1, int y1, int x2, int y2, LineStyle lineStyle)
    {
        switch (lineStyle)
        {
            case LineStyle.Solid:
                // draw solid
                break;

            case LineStyle.Dotted:
                // draw dotted
                break;

            case LineStyle.DotDash:
                // draw dotdash
                break;
```

```
                default:
                    throw(new ArgumentException("Invalid line style"));
            }
        }
}
class Test
{
    public static void Main()
    {
        Draw draw = new Draw();
        draw.DrawLine(0, 0, 10, 10, Draw.LineStyle.Solid);
        draw.DrawLine(5, 6, 23, 3, (Draw.LineStyle) 35);
    }
}
```

The LineStyle enum defines the values that can be specified for the enum, and then that same enum is used in the function call to specify the type of line to draw.

While enums do prevent the accidental specification of values outside of the enum range, the values that can be specified for an enum are not limited to the identifiers specified in the enum declaration. The second call to DrawLine() is legal, so an enum value passed into a function must still be validated to ensure that it is in the range of valid values.[1] The Draw class throws an invalid argument exception if the argument is invalid.

Enumeration Base Types

Each enumeration has an underlying type that specifies how much storage is allocated for that enumeration. The valid base types for enumeration are byte, sbyte, short, ushort, int, uint, long, and ulong. If the base type is not specified, the base type defaults to int. The base type is specified by listing the base type after the enum name.

```
enum SmallEnum : byte
{
    A,
    B,
    C,
    D
}
```

Specifying the base type can be useful if size is a concern or if the number of entries would exceed the number of possible values for int.

Initialization

By default, the value of the first enum member is set to 0 and incremented for each subsequent member. Specific values may be specified along with the member name.

---

[1] See the description of the System.Enum class later in this chapter for another way to deal with this situation.

```
enum Values
{
    A = 1,
    B = 5,
    C = 3,
    D = 42
}
```

Computed values can also be used, as long as they depend only on values already defined in the enum.

```
enum Values
{
    A = 1,
    B = 2,
    C = A + B,
    D = A * C + 33
}
```

If an enum is declared without a 0 value, this can lead to problems.

```
enum Values
{
    A = 1,
    B = 2,
    C = A + B,
    D = A * C + 33
}
class Test
{
    public static void Member(Values value)
    {
        // do some processing here
    }
    public static void Main()
    {
        Values value = 0;
        Member(value);
    }
}
```

In this case, Member() is called with a value that is not defined, and the program may exhibit undefined behavior.[2] Many developers add:

```
None = 0,
```

to all of their enumerations to make this apparent.

_____

[2]The wrong thing might happen, the program might crash, your cat's hair might fall out—that sort of thing.

> ## ENUMERATIONS TO MAKE THIS A

The previous example exhibits a behavior that trips up a lot of people; there is no validation of enumeration values when an assignment is performed. This means that an enumeration variable can be assigned any value that is valid for the underlying type of the enum. The following is an example of valid code:

```
Values value = 1837102383
```

When writing code that uses enumerators, you must consider values outside of the defined set of values. This is often done by using the Enum.IsDefined() method.

Bit Flag Enums

Enums may also be used as bit flags by specifying a different bit value for each bit. Here's a typical definition:

```
using System;
[Flags]
enum BitValues : uint
{
    NoBits = 0,
    Bit1 = 0x00000001,
    Bit2 = 0x00000002,
    Bit3 = 0x00000004,
    Bit4 = 0x00000008,
    Bit5 = 0x00000010,
    AllBits = 0xFFFFFFFF
}
class Test
{
    public static void Member(BitValues value)
    {
        // do some processing here
    }
    public static void Main()
    {
        Member(BitValues.Bit1 | BitValues.Bit2);
    }
}
```

The [Flags] attribute before the enum definition is used so that designers and browsers can present a different interface for enums that are flag enums. In such enums, it would make sense to allow the user to OR several bits together, which wouldn't make sense for nonflag enums.

The Main() function ORs two bit values together and then passes the value to the member function.

Conversions

Enum types can be converted to their underlying type and back again using an explicit conversion.

```
enum Values
{
    A = 1,
    B = 5,
    C = 3,
    D = 42
}
class Test
{
    public static void Main()
    {
        Values v = (Values) 2;
        int ival = (int) v;
    }
}
```

The literal 0 can be converted to an enum type without a cast, using a special-case implicit conversion. This is allowed so that the following code can be written:

```
public void DoSomething(BitValues bv)
{
    if (bv == 0)
    {
    }
}
```

The if statement would have to be written as follows if implicit conversion wasn't present:

```
if (bv == (BitValues) 0)
```

That's not bad for this example, but it could be quite cumbersome in actual use if the enum is nested deeply in the hierarchy.

```
if (bv == (CornSoft.PlotLibrary.Drawing.LineStyle.BitValues) 0)
```

That's a lot of typing.

The System.Enum Type

Like the other predefined types, the Enum type has some methods that make enums in C# a fair bit more useful than enums in C++.

The first of these is that the ToString() function is overridden to return the textual name for an enum value so that the following can be done:

```
using System;

enum Color
{
    Red,
    Green,
    Yellow
}

public class Test
{
    public static void Main()
    {
        Color c = Color.Red;

        Console.WriteLine("c is {0}", c);
    }
}
```

The example produces:

```
c is Red
```

rather than merely giving the numeric equivalent of Color.red. Other operations can be done as well.

```
using System;

enum Color
{
    Red,
    Green,
    Yellow
}

public class Test
{
    public static void Main()
    {
        Color c = Color.Red;

            // enum values and names
        foreach (int i in Enum.GetValues(c.GetType()))
        {
            Console.WriteLine("Value: {0} ({1})", i, Enum.GetName(c.GetType(), i));
        }
```

```
        // or just the names
        foreach (string s in Enum.GetNames(c.GetType()))
        {
            Console.WriteLine("Name: {0}", s);
        }

        // enum value from a string, ignore case
        c = (Color) Enum.Parse(typeof(Color), "Red", true);
        Console.WriteLine("string value is: {0}", c);

        // see if a specific value is a defined enum member
        bool defined = Enum.IsDefined(typeof(Color), 5);
        Console.WriteLine("5 is a defined value for Color: {0}", defined);     }
}
```

The output from this example is as follows:

```
Value: 0 (Red)
Value: 1 (Green)
Value: 2 (Yellow)
Name: Red
Name: Green
Name: Yellow
string value is: Red
5 is a defined value for Color: False
```

In this example, the values and/or names of the enum constants can be fetched from the enum, and the string name for a value can be converted to an enum value. Finally, a value is checked to see whether it is the same as one of the defined constants.[3]

---

[3]This is sufficient to check for validity if the enum is not a flags enum. If it is a flags enum, it is more work.

■ ■ ■

CHAPTER 21

Attributes

In most programming languages, some information is expressed through declaration, and other information is expressed through code. For example, in the following class member declaration

```
public int Test;
```

the compiler and runtime will reserve space for an integer variable and set its accessibility so that it is visible everywhere. This is an example of declarative information; it's nice because of the economy of expression and because the compiler handles the details for you.

Typically, the types of declarative information that can be used are predefined by the language designer and can't be extended by users of the language. A user who wants to associate a specific database field with a field of a class, for example, must invent a way of expressing that relationship in the language, a way of storing the relationship, and a way of accessing the information at runtime. In a language like C++, a macro might be defined that stores the information in a field that is part of the object. Such schemes work, but they're error-prone and not generalized. They're also ugly.

The .NET Runtime supports attributes, which are merely annotations that are placed on elements of source code, such as classes, members, parameters, and so on. Attributes can be used to change the behavior of the runtime, provide transaction information about an object, or convey organizational information to a designer. The attribute information is stored with the metadata of the element and can be easily retrieved at runtime through a process known as *reflection*.

C# uses a conditional attribute to control when member functions are called. A usage of the conditional attribute would look like this:

```
using System.Diagnostics;
class Test
{
    [Conditional("DEBUG")]
    public void Validate()
    {
    }
}
```

While it is possible to write your own custom attributes, most programmers will use predefined attributes much more often than writing their own.

Using Attributes

Suppose it was important to keep track of the code reviews that had been performed on classes so that you could determine when code reviews were finished. The code review information could be stored in a database, which would allow easy queries about status, or it could be stored in comments, which would make it easy to look at the code and the information at the same time.

Or an attribute could be used, which would enable both kinds of access.

To do that, an attribute class is needed. An attribute class defines the name of an attribute, how it can be created, and the information that will be stored. The gritty details of defining attribute classes will be covered in the section "An Attribute of Your Own."

The attribute class will look like this:

```
using System;
[AttributeUsage(AttributeTargets.Class)]
public class CodeReviewAttribute: System.Attribute
{
    public CodeReviewAttribute(string reviewer, string date)
    {
        m_reviewer = reviewer;
        m_date = date;
    }
    public string Comment
    {
        get { return(m_comment); }
        set { m_comment = value; }
    }
    public string Date
    {
        get { return(m_date); }
    }
    public string Reviewer
    {
        get { return(m_reviewer); }
    }
    string m_reviewer;
    string m_date;
    string m_comment;
}
[CodeReview("Eric", "01-12-2000", Comment = "Bitchin' Code")]
class Complex
{
}
```

The AttributeUsage attribute before the class specifies that this attribute can be placed only on classes. When an attribute is used on a program element, the compiler checks to see whether the use of that attribute on that program element is allowed.

The naming convention for attributes is to append Attribute to the end of the class name. This makes it easier to tell which classes are attribute classes and which classes are normal classes. All attributes must derive from System.Attribute.

The class defines a single constructor that takes a reviewer and a date as parameters, and it also has the public string property Comment.

When the compiler comes to the attribute use on class Complex, it first looks for a class derived from Attribute named CodeReview. It doesn't find one, so it next looks for a class named CodeReviewAttribute, which it finds.

Next, it checks to see whether the attribute is allowed for this usage (on a class).

Then, it checks to see whether there is a constructor that matches the parameters you've specified in the attribute use. If it finds one, an instance of the object is created—the constructor is called with the specified values.

If there are named parameters, it matches the name of the parameter with a field or property in the attribute class, and then it sets the field or property to the specified value.

After this is done, the current state of the attribute class is saved to the metadata for the program element for which it was specified.

At least, that's what happens *logically*. In actuality, it only *looks* like it happens that way; see the "Attribute Pickling" sidebar for a description of how it is implemented.

ATTRIBUTE PICKLING

THERE are a few reasons why it doesn't really work the way it's described, and they're related to performance. For the compiler to actually create the attribute object, the .NET Runtime environment would have to be running, so every compilation would have to start up the environment, and every compiler would have to run as a managed executable.

Additionally, the object creation isn't really required, since you're just going to store the information away.

The compiler therefore validates that it *could* create the object, call the constructor, and set the values for any named parameters. The attribute parameters are then pickled[1] into a chunk of binary information, which is tucked away with the metadata of the object.

A Few More Details

Some attributes can be used only once on a given element. Others, known as *multiuse* attributes, can be used more than once. This might be used, for example, to apply several different security attributes to a single class. The documentation on the attribute will describe whether an attribute is single-use or multiuse.

In most cases, it's clear that the attribute applies to a specific program element. However, consider the following case:

```
using System.Runtime.InteropServices;
class Test
{
    [return: MarshalAs(UnmanagedType.LPWStr)]
    public static extern string GetMessage();
}
```

In most cases, an attribute in that position would apply to the member function, but this attribute is really related to the return type. How can the compiler tell the difference?

There are several situations in which this can happen.

- Method vs. return value

- Event vs. field or property

- Delegate vs. return value

- Property vs. accessor vs. return value of getter vs. value parameter of setter

For each of these situations, there is a case that is much more common than the other case, and it becomes the default case. To specify an attribute for the nondefault case, the element the attribute applies to must be specified.

---

[1]The process is called *pickling* to differentiate it from serialization.

```
using System.Runtime.InteropServices;
class Test
{
    [return: MarshalAs(UnmanagedType.LPWStr)]
    public static extern string GetMessage();
}
```

The return: indicates that this attribute should be applied to the return value.

The element may be specified even if there is no ambiguity. Table 21-1 describes the identifiers.

Table 21-1. *Attribute Identifiers*

Specifier	Description
assembly	The attribute is on the assembly.
module	The attribute is on the module.
type	The attribute is on a class or struct.
method	The attribute is on a method.
property	The attribute is on a property.
event	The attribute is on an event.
field	The attribute is on a field.
param	The attribute is on a parameter.
return	The attribute is on the return value.

Attributes that are applied to assemblies or modules must occur after any using clauses and before any code.

```
using System;
[assembly:CLSCompliant(true)]

class Test
{
    Test() {}
}
```

This example applies the ClsCompliant attribute to the entire assembly. All assembly-level attributes declared in any file that is in the assembly are grouped together and attached to the assembly.

To use a predefined attribute, start by finding the constructor that best matches the information to be conveyed. Next, write the attribute, passing parameters to the constructor. Finally, use the named parameter syntax to pass additional information that wasn't part of the constructor parameters.

For more examples of attribute use, look at Chapter 37.

An Attribute of Your Own

To define attribute classes and reflect on them at runtime, there are a few more issues to consider. This section will discuss some things to consider when designing an attribute.

There are two major things to determine when writing an attribute. The first is the program elements that the attribute may be applied to, and the second is the information that will be stored by the attribute.

Attribute Usage

Placing the AttributeUsage attribute on an attribute class controls where the attribute can be used. The possible values for the attribute are defined in the AttributeTargets enumeration and described in Table 21-2.

Table 21-2. *AttributeTargets Values*

Usage	Meaning
Assembly	The program assembly
Module	The current program file
Class	A class
Struct	A struct
Enum	An enumerator
Constructor	A constructor
Method	A method (member function)
Property	A property
Field	A field
Event	An event
Interface	An interface
Parameter	A method parameter
ReturnValue	The method return value
Delegate	A delegate
All	Anywhere
ClassMembers	Class, struct, enum, constructor, method, property, field, event, delegate, interface

As part of the AttributeUsage attribute, one of these can be specified or a list of them can be ORed together.

The AttributeUsage attribute is also used to specify whether an attribute is single-use or multiuse. This is done with the named parameter AllowMultiple. Such an attribute would look like this:

```
[AttributeUsage(AttributeTargets.Method | AttributeTargets.Event, AllowMultiple = true)]
```

Attribute Parameters

The information the attribute will store should be divided into two groups: the information that is required for every use and the optional items.

The information that is required for every use should be obtained via the constructor for the attribute class. This forces the user to specify all the parameters when they use the attribute.

Optional items should be implemented as named parameters, which allows the user to specify whichever optional items are appropriate.

If an attribute has several different ways in which it can be created, with different required information, separate constructors can be declared for each usage. Don't use separate constructors as an alternative to optional items.

Attribute Parameter Types

The attribute pickling format supports only a subset of all the .NET Runtime types, and therefore, only some types can be used as attribute parameters. The types allowed are the following:

- bool, byte, char, double, float, int, long, short, string

- object

- System.Type

- An enum that has public accessibility (not nested inside something nonpublic)

- A one-dimensional array of one of the previous types

Fetching Attribute Values

Once attributes are defined on some code, it's useful to be able to find the attribute values. This is done through reflection.

The following code shows an attribute class, the application of the attribute to a class, and the reflection on the class to retrieve the attribute:

```
using System;
using System.Reflection;
[AttributeUsage(AttributeTargets.Class, AllowMultiple = true)]
public class CodeReviewAttribute: System.Attribute
{
    public CodeReviewAttribute(string reviewer, string date)
    {
        m_reviewer = reviewer;
        m_date = date;
    }
    public string Comment
    {
        get { return(m_comment); }
        set { m_comment = value; }
    }
    public string Date
    {
        get { return(m_date); }
    }
    public string Reviewer
    {
        get { return(m_reviewer); }
    }
    string m_reviewer;
    string m_date;
    string m_comment;
}
```

```
[CodeReview("Eric", "01-12-2000", Comment = "Bitchin' Code")]
[CodeReview("Gurn", "01-01-2000", Comment = "Revisit this section")]
class Complex
{
}
class Test
{
    public static void Main()
    {
        Type type = typeof(Complex);
        foreach (CodeReviewAttribute att in
                    type.GetCustomAttributes(typeof(CodeReviewAttribute), false))
        {
            Console.WriteLine("Reviewer: {0}", att.Reviewer);
            Console.WriteLine("Date: {0}", att.Date);
            Console.WriteLine("Comment: {0}", att.Comment);
        }
    }
}
```

The Main() function first gets the type object associated with the type Complex. It then iterates over all the CodeReviewAttribute attributes attached to the type and writes the values out.

Alternately, the code could get all the attributes by omitting the type in the call to GetCustomAttributes().

```
        foreach (object o in type.GetCustomAttributes(false))
        {
            CodeReviewAttribute att = o as CodeReviewAttribute;
            if (att != null)
            {
                // write values here...
            }
        }
```

This example produces the following output:

```
Reviewer: Eric
Date: 01-12-2000
Comment: Bitchin' Code
Reviewer: Gurn
Date: 01-01-2000
Comment: Revisit this section
```

The false value in the call to GetCustomAttributes tells the runtime to ignore any inherited attributes. In this case, that would ignore any attributes on the base class of Complex.

In the example, the type object for the Complex type is obtained using typeof. It can also be obtained in the following manner:

```
Complex c = new Complex();
Type t = c.GetType();
Type t2 = Type.GetType("Complex");
```

■ ■ ■

CHAPTER 22

Delegates, Anonymous Methods, and Lambdas

Delegates are similar to interfaces, in that they specify a contract between a caller and an implementer. Rather than specifying a set of methods, a delegate merely specifies the form of a single function. Also, interfaces are created at compile time and are a fixed aspect of a type, whereas delegates are created at runtime and can be used to dynamically hook up callbacks between objects that were not originally designed to work together.

Delegates are used as the basis for events in C#, which are the general-purpose notification mechanisms used by the .NET Framework, and they are the subject of the next chapter.

Anonymous methods and lambdas provide two alternatives to specify the code that is hooked up to a delegate.

Using Delegates

The specification of the delegate determines the form of the function. To create an instance of the delegate, you must use a function that matches that form. Delegates are sometimes referred to as *safe function pointers*, which isn't a bad analogy, but they do a lot more than act as function pointers.

Because of their dynamic nature, delegates are useful when the user may want to change behavior. If, for example, a collection class implements sorting, it might want to support different sort orders. The sorting could be controlled based on a delegate that defines the comparison function.

```
using System;
public class Container
{
    public delegate int CompareItemsCallback(object obj1, object obj2);
    public void Sort(CompareItemsCallback compare)
    {

        // not a real sort, just shows what the
        // inner loop code might do
        int x = 0;
        int y = 1;
        object item1 = m_arr[x];
        object item2 = m_arr[y];
        int order = compare(item1, item2);
    }
```

```
        object[] m_ arr = new object[1];     // items in the collection
}
public class Employee
{
    public Employee(string name, int id)
    {
        m_name = name;
        m_id = id;
    }
    public static int CompareName(object obj1, object obj2)
    {
        Employee emp1 = (Employee) obj1;
        Employee emp2 = (Employee) obj2;
        return(String.Compare(emp1. m_name, emp2. m_name));
    }
    public static int CompareId(object obj1, object obj2)
    {
        Employee emp1 = (Employee) obj1;
        Employee emp2 = (Employee) obj2;

        if (emp1. m_id > emp2. m_id)
        {
            return(1);
        }
        else if (emp1. m_id < emp2. m_id)
        {
            return(-1);
        }
        else
        {
            return(0);
        }
    }
    string m_name;
    int m_id;
}
class Test
{
    public static void Main()
    {
        Container employees = new Container();
        // create and add some employees here

            // create delegate to sort on names, and do the sort
        Container.CompareItemsCallback sortByName =
            new Container.CompareItemsCallback(Employee.CompareName);
        employees.Sort(sortByName);
            // employees is now sorted by name
    }
}
```

The delegate defined in the Container class takes the two objects to be compared as parameters and returns an integer that specifies the ordering of the two objects. Two static functions are declared that match this delegate as part of the Employee class, with each function describing a different kind of ordering.

When the container needs to be sorted, a delegate can be passed in that describes the ordering that should be used, and the sort function will do the sorting.[1]

Delegates to Instance Members

Users who are familiar with C++ will find a lot of similarity between delegates and C++ function pointers, but there's more to a delegate than there is to a function pointer.

When dealing with Windows functions, it's fairly common to pass in a function pointer that should be called when a specific event occurs. Since C++ function pointers can refer only to static functions, and not member functions,[2] there needs to be some way to communicate some state information to the function so that it knows what object the event corresponds to. Most functions deal with this by taking a pointer, which is passed through to the callback function. The parameter (in C++ at least) is then cast to a class instance, and then the event is processed.

In C#, delegates can encapsulate both a function to call and an instance to call it on, so there is no need for an extra parameter to carry the instance information. This is also a typesafe mechanism, because the instance is specified at the same time the function to call is specified.

```
using System;
public class User
{
    string m_name;
    public User(string name)
    {
        m_name = name;
    }
    public void Process(string message)
    {
        Console.WriteLine("{0}: {1}", m_name, message);
    }
}
class Test
{
    delegate void ProcessHandler(string message);

    public static void Main()
    {
        User user = new User("George");
        ProcessHandler handler = new ProcessHandler(user.Process);

        handler("Wake Up!");
    }
}
```

In this example, a delegate is created that points to the User.Process() function, with the user instance, and the call through the delegate is identical to calling user.Process() directly.

---

[1]Well, it would if it were actually implemented.
[2]You might ask, "What about member function pointers?" Member functions do indeed do something similar, but the syntax is rather opaque. Delegates in C# are both easier to use and more functional.

Multicasting

As mentioned earlier, a delegate can refer to more than one function. Basically, a delegate encapsulates a list of functions that should be called in order. The Delegate class provides functions to take two delegates and return one that encapsulates both or to remove a delegate from another.

To combine two delegates, the Delegate.Combine() function is used. The last example can be easily modified to call more than one function.

```
using System;
public class User
{
    string m_name;
    public User(string name)
    {
        m_name = name;
    }
    public void Process(string message)
    {
        Console.WriteLine("{0}: {1}", m_name, message);
    }
}

class Test
{
    delegate void ProcessHandler(string message);

    static public void Process(string message)
    {
        Console.WriteLine("Test.Process(\"{0}\")", message);
    }
    public static void Main()
    {
        User user = new User("George");

        ProcessHandler handler = new ProcessHandler(user.Process);
        handler = (ProcessHandler) Delegate.Combine(handler, new ProcessHandler(Process));

        handler("Wake Up!");
    }
}
```

Invoking handler now calls both delegates.

There are a couple of problems with this approach, however. The first is that it's not simple to understand. More importantly, however, is that it isn't typesafe at compile time; Delegate.Combine() both takes and returns the type Delegate, so there's no way at compile time to know whether the delegates are compatible.

To address these issues, C# allows the += and -= operators to be used to call Delegate.Combine() and Delegate.Remove(), and it makes sure the types are compatible. The call in the example is modified to the following:

```
handler += new ProcessHandler(Process);
```

When invoked, the subdelegates encapsulated in a delegate are called synchronously in the order that they were added to the delegate. If an exception is thrown by one of the subdelegates, the remaining subdelegates will not be called. If this behavior is not desirable, the list of subdelegates (otherwise known as an *invocation list*) can be obtained from the delegate, and each subdelegate can be called directly. Instead of this:

```
handler("Wake Up!");
```

the following can be used:

```
foreach (ProcessHandler subHandler in handler.GetInvocationList())
{
    try
    {
        subHandler("Wake Up!");
    }
    catch (Exception e)
    {
        // log the exception here...
    }
}
```

code like this could also be used to implement "black-ball" voting, where all delegates could be called once to see whether they were able to perform a function and then called a second time if they all voted yes.

Wanting to call more than one function may seem to be a rare situation, but it's common when dealing with events, which will be covered in Chapter 23.

Delegates As Static Members

One drawback of this approach is that the user who wants to use the sorting has to create an instance of the delegate with the appropriate function. It would be nicer if they didn't have to do that, and that can be done by defining the appropriate delegates as static members of Employee.

```
using System;
public class Container
{
    public delegate int CompareItemsCallback(object obj1, object obj2);
    public void Sort(CompareItemsCallback compare)
    {
        // not a real sort, just shows what the
        // inner loop code might do
        int x = 0;
        int y = 1;
        object item1 = arr[x];
        object item2 = arr[y];
        int order = compare(item1, item2);
    }
    object[] arr = new object[1];    // items in the collection
}
```

```
class Employee
{
    Employee(string name, int id)
    {
        m_name = name;
        m_id = id;
    }
    public static readonly Container.CompareItemsCallback SortByName =
        new Container.CompareItemsCallback(CompareName);
    public static readonly Container.CompareItemsCallback SortById =
        new Container.CompareItemsCallback(CompareId);

    public static int CompareName(object obj1, object obj2)
    {
        Employee emp1 = (Employee) obj1;
        Employee emp2 = (Employee) obj2;
        return(String.Compare(emp1. m_name, emp2. m_name));
    }
    public static int CompareId(object obj1, object obj2)
    {
        Employee emp1 = (Employee) obj1;
        Employee emp2 = (Employee) obj2;

        if (emp1. m_id > emp2. m_id)
        {
            return(1);
        }
        else if (emp1. m_id < emp2. m_id)
        {
            return(-1);
        }
        else
        {
            return(0);
        }
    }
    string m_name;
    int m_id;
}
class Test
{
    public static void Main()
    {
        Container employees = new Container();
        // create and add some employees here

        employees.Sort(Employee.SortByName);
            // employees is now sorted by name
    }
}
```

This is a lot easier. The users of Employee don't have to know how to create the delegate—they can just refer to the static member.

Anonymous Methods

Delegates work very nicely for scenarios where the code to execute is known ahead of time, such as a button event handler. But they don't work very well in some other situations. For example, if I have a list of employees and I want to find the first one who is older than 40, I need to do something like the following:

```
class Employee
{
    public Employee(string name, int age, decimal salary)
    {
        Name = name;
        Age = age;
        Salary = salary;
    }

    public string Name { get; set; }
    public int Age { get; set; }
    public decimal Salary { get; set; }
}
class EmployeeFilterByAge
{
    int m_age;

    public EmployeeFilterByAge(int age)
    {
        m_age = age;
    }

    public bool OlderThan(Employee employee)
    {
        return employee.Age > m_age;
    }
}
```

The OlderThan() method can be passed to a selection method,[3] which will return true if the employee is older than the specified age. This can then be used in the following code:

```
List<Employee> employees = new List<Employee>();
employees.Add(new Employee("John", 33, 22000m));
employees.Add(new Employee("Eric", 42, 18000m));
employees.Add(new Employee("Michael", 33, 19500m));

EmployeeFilterByAge filterByAge = new EmployeeFilterByAge(40);
int index = employees.FindIndex(filterByAge.OlderThan);
```

---

[3]In this usage, the method is known as a *predicate*.

This does what I want, but I have to create the `EmployeeFilterByAge` class, which takes some extra time and effort. I would prefer a way to express the comparison that I want in fewer lines of code and in a way that makes it more obvious what I am doing. Something like this:

```
int index = employees.FindIndex(
    delegate(Employee employee)
    {
        return employee.Age > 40;
    });
```

The compiler will do the heavy lifting, converting the few lines of code here into a separate class with a delegate that can be called directly. This construct is known as an *anonymous delegate* and was a popular addition to C# 2.0. There is, however, quite a bit of extra syntax to simply express the condition.

```
employee.Age > 40
```

This was addressed in C# 3.0, with the addition of lambdas.

Lambdas

The term *lambda* comes from a mathematical construct known as the *lambda calculus*, which is used in many functional programming languages. It provides a more concise way of expressing a function. It simplifies the declaration of the function to the following:

```
(parameters) => expression
```

The following method takes an integer parameter and returns a value that is one greater:

```
int AddOne(int x)
{
    return x + 1;
}
```

Expressed as a lambda, this becomes the following:

```
(int x) => { return x + 1; }
```

The lambda syntax supports a few simplifications.[4] First, if the type of the parameter can be determined based on the context where the lambda is written, the type can be omitted.

```
(x) => { return x + 1; }
```

If there is only one parameter to the function, the parentheses can be omitted.

```
x => { return x + 1; }
```

---

[4] I'm not sure I like the simplifications. It is simpler to write the code, but the form `(int x) => { return x + 1; }` is clearer than `x => x + 1`, at least initially.

Finally, if the only thing the body of the lambda does is return a value, the curly brackets and return statement can be omitted.

```
x => x + 1
```

This gives you the simplest version of the lambda expression. You can revisit the earlier call to FindIndex() using a lambda instead of an anonymous delegate.

```
int index = employees.FindIndex(employee => employee.Age > 40);
```

■ **Note**   For many more lambda examples, see Chapter 29.

Implementation

The implementation of the previous lambda is quite simple; the compiler creates the following method:

```
private static bool MyAgeFilter(Employee employee)
{
    return employee.Age > 40;
}
```

It's not going to call it MyAgeFilter, however. It will use a generated name like ' <Example>b__0'.

Variable Capturing

Consider the following code:

```
List<Employee> employees = new List<Employee>();
employees.Add(new Employee("John", 33, 22000m));
employees.Add(new Employee("Eric", 42, 18000m));
employees.Add(new Employee("Michael", 32, 19500m));

int ageThreshold = 40;
Predicate<Employee> match = e => e.Age > ageThreshold;
ageThreshold = 30;

int index = employees.FindIndex(match);
Console.WriteLine(index);
```

Does this code locate John because his age is greater than 40, or does it locate Eric because his age is greater than 32?

The answer to that question depends on what the usage of ageThreshold means in the lambda expression. In lambda expressions, the variable is *captured*, which means that the expression uses the value of ageThreshold at the time that the expression is evaluated, not the value of it when the lambda was defined. It therefore locates Eric. This distinction is most important in cases where the lambda escapes the current scope.

To capture the variable, it creates a class.

```
class DisplayClass
{
    public int ageThreshold;
    public bool MyPredicate(Employee employee)
    {
        return employee.Age > ageThreshold;
    }
}
```

The usage is roughly[5] the following:

```
DisplayClass d = new DisplayClass ();
d.ageThreadhold = 40;
Predicate<Employee> match = d.MyPredicate;
d.ageThreshold = 30;

int index = employees.FindIndex(match);
```

Guidelines

I recommend the following guidelines for lambdas.

Parameter Naming

Lambda parameters should be named with the same care you would use for other parameters. Compare the readability of this lambda:

```
int index = employees.FindIndex(employee => employee.Age > 40);
```

with this one:

```
int index = employees.FindIndex(x => x.Age > 40);
```

The first is considerably easier to understand. This is especially important when an expression involves more than one lambda.[6]

Method, Anonymous Delegate, or Lambda?

C# provides three choices; which of these constructs should you use?

The lambda syntax is so much nicer than the anonymous delegate one that I see no reason to ever use the anonymous delegate one, which leaves two choices. Choosing between them is an aesthetic choice, and there are differing opinions. This is what I recommend:

- Use lambdas any place you are passing code as a parameter to another method.

- Use methods to hook to events.

---

[5]The names have been changed to improve clarity.
[6]You will likely see lots of code that just uses x for lambda parameters.

There are two reasons for the second guideline. The first has to do with unsubscribing from an event.

■ **Note**   It would be helpful to read Chapter 23 before you read this section.[7]

Consider the following:

```
Console.CancelKeyPress += (o, args) =>
    {
        Console.WriteLine("Boo");
        args.Cancel = true;
    };

Console.CancelKeyPress -= (o, args) =>
    {
        Console.WriteLine("Boo");
        args.Cancel = true;
    };
```

This looks like the standard event pattern; the first call subscribes to the event, and the second one unsubscribes. It *is* a bit ugly because you need to write the whole lambda over, but it has a more serious problem.

It doesn't work. While the two lambdas appear to be identical, they do not generate the same instance of a delegate, and therefore the statement to unsubscribe to the event does nothing,[8] which is bad.

The second reason is readability. Event handlers tend to have more code in them than the simple expressions in this chapter, which makes the extra syntax of a method less important. It is also nice to be able to see what the type of the parameter is when reading the code.[9] If you have a few event handlers to set up at the beginning of a method, you end up with all of your event handling code in a single method, which doesn't make it very readable. Finally, I find it much easier to read the subscription line without all the handler code getting in the way. The following:

```
Console.CancelKeyPress += HandleControlC;
```

is much easier to read than the lambda equivalent.

---

[7]I'll wait for you here.

[8]You can get the behavior you want by assigning the lambda to a variable and using that same variable to subscribe and unsubscribe, but at that point you're pretty close to using a method.

[9]Yes, you can specify a parameter name in the lambda, but almost nobody does.

■ ■ ■

CHAPTER 23

Events

Chapter 22 discussed how delegates can be used to pass a reference to a method so that it can be called in a general way. Being able to call a method in such a way is useful in graphical user interfaces, such as the one provided by the classes in System.Windows.Controls. It's fairly easy to build such a framework by using delegates, but there are significant limitations to the delegate approach. Events remove those limitations.

A Simple Example Using Delegates

The following is a simple example using delegates:

```
using System;
public class Button
{
    public delegate void ClickHandler(object sender, EventArgs e);
    public ClickHandler Click;

    protected void OnClick()
    {
        if (Click != null)
        {
            Click(this, EventArgs.Empty);
        }
    }

    public void SimulateClick()
    {
        OnClick();
    }
}

class Test
{
    static public void ButtonHandler(object sender, EventArgs e)
    {
        Console.WriteLine("Button clicked");
    }
```

```
    public static void Main()
    {
        Button button = new Button();
        button.Click = ButtonHandler;
        button.SimulateClick();
    }
}
```

The Button class is supporting a click "event"[1] by having the ClickHandler delegate tell what kind of method can be called to hook up, and a delegate instance can then be assigned to the event. The OnClick() method then calls this delegate, and everything works fine—at least in this simple case.

The situation gets more complicated in a real-world scenario. In real applications, a button such as this one would live in a form, and a button click might be of interest to more than one component of the application. Doing this isn't a problem with delegates because more than one method can be called from a single delegate instance. In the previous example, if another class also wanted to be called when the button was clicked, the += operator could be used, like this:

```
button.Click += OtherMethodToCall;
```

Unfortunately, if the other class wasn't careful, it might do the following:

```
button.Click = OtherMethodToCall;
```

This would be bad, because it would mean that the ButtonHandler would be unhooked, and only the new method would be called.

To unhook from the click, the right thing to do is use this code:[2]

```
button.Click -= OtherMethodToCall;
```

However, the following might be used instead:

```
button.Click = null;
```

This is also wrong.

What is needed is some way of protecting the delegate field so that it's accessed only using the += and -= operators.

Add and Remove Functions

One way to do this is to make the delegate field private and write a couple of methods that can be used to add or remove delegates.

```
using System;
public class Button
{
    public delegate void ClickHandler(object sender, EventArgs e);
    private ClickHandler click;
```

---

[1] This isn't an "event" in the C# sense of the word but just the abstract concept of something happening.
[2] This syntax may look weird since a new instance of the delegate is created just so it can be removed from the delegate. When Delegate.Remove() is called, it needs to find the delegate in the invocation list, so a delegate instance is required.

```csharp
    public void AddClick(ClickHandler clickHandler)
    {
        click += clickHandler;
    }

    public void RemoveClick(ClickHandler clickHandler)
    {
        click -= clickHandler;
    }

    protected void OnClick()
    {
        if (click != null)
        {
            click(this, EventArgs.Empty);
        }
    }

    public void SimulateClick()
    {
        OnClick();
    }
}

class Test
{
    static public void ButtonHandler(object sender, EventArgs e)
    {
        Console.WriteLine("Button clicked");
    }

    public static void Main()
    {
        Button button = new Button();

        button.AddClick(ButtonHandler);

        button.SimulateClick();

        button.RemoveClick(ButtonHandler);
    }
}
```

In this example, the AddClick() and RemoveClick() methods have been added, and the delegate field is now private. It's now impossible for users of the class to do the wrong thing when they hook or unhook.

This example is reminiscent of the example in Chapter 16. You had two accessor methods, and adding properties made those two methods look like a field. Let's add a feature to the compiler so there's a "property-like" delegate named Click. The compiler can write the AddClick() and RemoveClick() methods for you, and it can also change a use of + = or - = to the appropriate add or remove call. This gives you the advantage of having the Add and Remove methods without having to write them.

You need a keyword for this compiler enhancement, and event seems like a good choice.

```csharp
using System;
public class Button
{
    public delegate void ClickHandler(object sender, EventArgs e);

    public event ClickHandler Click;

    protected void OnClick()
    {
        if (Click != null)
        {
            Click(this, EventArgs.Empty);
        }
    }

    public void SimulateClick()
    {
        OnClick();
    }
}

class Test
{
    static public void ButtonHandler(object sender, EventArgs e)
    {
        Console.WriteLine("Button clicked");
    }

    public static void Main()
    {
        Button button = new Button();

        button.Click += ButtonHandler;

        button.SimulateClick();

        button.Click - = ButtonHandler;
    }
}
```

When the event keyword is added to a delegate, the compiler creates a private field to store the delegate and creates public add_Click() and remove_Click() methods. It also emits a bit of metadata that says there is an event named Click and associates the event with the add and remove methods so that object browsers can tell there's an event on this class.

In Main(), the event is accessed as if it were a delegate, but since the add and remove methods are the only ways to access the private delegate, + = and - = are the only operations that can be performed on the event.

That's the basic story for events. The arguments to the event handler, object sender and EventArgs e, are by convention and should be followed by other classes that expose events. The sender argument allows the user of the code to know which object fired the event, and the e argument contains the information associated with the event. In this case, there's no additional information to pass, so EventArgs is used. If additional information needed to be passed, a class should be derived from EventArgs with the additional information. For example, the KeyEventArgs class in the .NET Framework looks like this:

```
using System;
using System.Windows.Forms;
class KeyEventArgs: EventArgs
{
    Keys    keyData;

    KeyEventArgs(Keys keyData)
    {
        this.keyData = keyData;
    }

    public Keys KeyData
    {
        get
        {
            return(keyData);
        }
    }

    // other functions here...
}
```

The OnKey method will take a parameter of type Keys, encapsulate it into a KeyEventArgs class, and then call the delegate.

Safe Event Invocation

The previous examples use code that looks like this to call events:

```
if (Click != null)
{
    Click(this, EventArgs.Empty);
}
```

In a multithreaded environment, there is a small possibility that the thread might be interrupted after the null check but before the event was called and that the interrupting thread would unsubscribe from the event.
   This can be prevented through the following construct:

```
ClickHandler clickHandler = Click;
if (clickHandler != null)
{
    clickHandler(this, EventArgs.Empty);
}
```

The clickHandler is now guaranteed to be non-null when the code calls it.

■ **Note**   This has really only moved the race condition; there is now a case where the user may have unsubscribed to an event but could still be called after the unsubscription. There are some examples of using locking to prevent this, but it seems like a very corner case to me.

EventHandler <T>

The base class library provides the generic delegate EventHandler <T>. This delegate can be used instead of declaring an event-specific delegate. Following the first example, you would declare the Key event as follows:

```
public delegate void KeyHandler(object sender, KeyEventArgs e);

public event KeyHandler KeyDown;
```

Using EventHandler <T>, this can be simplified to the following:

```
public event EventHandler <KeyEventsArgs> KeyDown;
```

WHAT ABOUT EVENTARGS <T> ?

The EventHandler <T> delegate makes it easy to declare the event, but if you want to pass information along with the event, you still have to create a separate class derived from EventArgs. Many people have requested a generic EventArgs <T> class[3] so that if all you wanted to pass was a string, you could write something like this:

```
public event EventHandler<EventArgs <string>> StringReceived;
```

Then you would be done with it. This is also very useful if you want to pass a class that is already defined (such as an Employee class) in the event args where the class isn't derived from EventArgs.[4]

It's useful enough that you can find an implementation of EventArgs <T> if you search for EventArgs <T> in your favorite search engine. I've written a basic implementation and found it to be quite useful in some scenarios.

One downside of this approach is that it is tempting to use a predefined type, such as an int, to pass data that would be more understandable if it were stored in a specific class. It also prevents you from adding more properties to your event args class without breaking the users of your class.

Custom Add and Remove

Because the compiler creates a private delegate fields for every event that is declared, a class that declares numerous events will use one field per event. The Control class in System.Windows.Forms declares more than 25 events, but there are usually just a couple of these events hooked up for a given control. Defining 25 fields and using only a few is wasteful. What's needed is a way to avoid allocating the storage for the delegate unless it is needed.

The C# language supports this by allowing the add() and remove() methods that are provided by the compiler to be replaced with an implementation that stores the delegates in a more space-efficient manner. One typical way of doing this is to define a Dictionary to store the delegates.

---

[3]I don't happen to know the base class library team's opinion in this area, but if it were added now, it would conflict with the existing EventArgs <T> classes that people are already using, so calling it that would be a breaking change. Perhaps they could call it EventArgsEx <T>.
[4]And more often, can't be defined that way, since C# supports only single inheritance.

```
public class Button
{
    ConcurrentDictionary<object, EventHandler>m_delegateStore =
        new ConcurrentDictionary<object, EventHandler>();
    static object clickEventKey = new object();

    public event EventHandler Click
    {
        add
        {
            m_delegateStore.AddOrUpdate(
                clickEventKey,
                value,
                (key, oldValue) =>
                    (EventHandler)Delegate.Combine(oldValue, value));
        }

        remove
        {
            m_delegateStore.AddOrUpdate(
                clickEventKey,
                null,
                (key, oldValue) =>
                    (EventHandler)Delegate.Remove(oldValue, value));
        }
    }
    protected void OnClick()
    {
        EventHandler handler;

        if (m_delegateStore.TryGetValue(clickEventKey, out handler))
        {
            handler(this, EventArgs.Empty);
        }
    }
    public void SimulateClick()
    {
        OnClick();
    }
}
class Test
{
    static public void ButtonHandler(object sender, EventArgs e)
    {
        Console.WriteLine("Button clicked");
    }
```

```
    public static void Main()
    {
        Button button = new Button();

        button.Click += ButtonHandler;

        button.SimulateClick();

        button.Click - = ButtonHandler;
    }
}
```

The add() and remove() methods are written using a syntax similar to the one used for properties, and they use the m_delegateStore concurrent dictionary to store the delegate. One problem with using a hash table is coming up with a key that can be used to store and fetch the delegates. There's nothing associated with an event that can serve as a unique key, so clickEventKey is an object that's created only so that you can use it as a key for the dictionary. It's static because the same unique value can be used for all instances of the Button class.

CHAPTER 24

■ ■ ■

Dynamic Typing

The vast majority of code written with C# is strongly typed. But there are scenarios where a strongly typed system doesn't work, such as when dealing with some COM objects or working with dynamically typed languages. This chapter explores the support that C# provides for dynamically typed programming.

The dynamic Keyword

Dynamic provides a new way to declare variables. Consider the following code:

```
Employee george = new Employee("George", 15, 10M);
var jane = new Employee("Jane", 13, 9M);
dynamic astro = new Employee("Rastro", 7, 1M);
```

The first line declares that George is of type Employee. The second line uses var to declare that the type of jane will be whatever the type of the expression is, which is also Employee in this example.

The dynamic keyword is very different, in that it does not equate to a specific type. It means "I don't know what type this thing is, so just keep a reference to it. We'll figure out what it can do later." Since all of these variables are references to instances of the Employee class, you can write the following:

```
Console.WriteLine(george.Name);
Console.WriteLine(jane.Name);
Console.WriteLine(astro.Name);
```

When you write george.Name or jane.Name, it means something very simple. Since you know that the type is Employee, you know that there is property named Name, and you merely call the getter of the Name property of the instance.[1]

When you write astro.Name, it means something very different; since you declared astro to be dynamic, all you know is that it is an instance of some object, but you don't know what that object can do when you compile the code.

To evaluate astro.Name, you need to do the following:

1. Determine whether astro has a member named Name.

2. Determine whether the usage of astro.Name is valid in this context.

---

[1]If you care, it's a method named get_Name. It's still named that even if you don't care.

3. Figure out that Name is a property and has a specific get method.

4. Call the property getter.

5. Determine how the return type of the property getter should be treated and whether any conversions are required.

All of this is done through the component of the .NET runtime known as the dynamic runtime. It is a lot more work than accessing a property where you know the underlying type, which is not surprisingly a fair bit slower than making a direct call.[2]

Dynamic Failure

When dynamic is used, many compile-time failures become runtime failures. Consider the following code:

```
string value = "a,b,c,d,e";

string[] items = value.Split(',');

foreach (string item in items)
{
    Console.WriteLine(item);
}
```

When it is rewritten to use dynamic, you can easily make mistakes.

```
dynamic value = "a,b,c,d,e";

string[] items = value.SplitItUp(',');

foreach (string item in items)
{
    Console.WriteLine(item);
}
```

In this version, I have accidentally tried to call the SplitItUp() method instead of the Split() method. The compiler accepts my code and can't tell me about my error until the code is executed.

Generic Arithmetic with dynamic

One of the areas where C# lacks support is generic arithmetic. There is no IArithmetic interface implemented by the built-in numeric types (int, short, long, *et al.*). This prevents the following code from working:

```
public static T Add<T>(T first, T second)
{
    return first + second;
}
```

---

[2]A quick test of 10 million property accesses showed 12ms for direct access, 390ms for dynamic, and 2500ms using reflection.

This lack of support is frustrating for those who want to create mathematical libraries; a matrix multiplication operation must be written twice, once for float and once for double, despite the code being identical. Can dynamic provide a way to get around this?

In fact, it can; the dynamic runtime provides support for determining whether a type supports operations (see DynamicObject.TryBinaryOperation() for more information), and using that support, you can write the following:

```
public static T Add<T>(T first, T second)
{
    return (dynamic) first + (dynamic) second;
}
public static void Test()
{
    Console.WriteLine(Add(5, 10));
    Console.WriteLine(Add(5.134, 10));
    Console.WriteLine(Add(10, 33.182274));
}
```

This generates the following:

```
15
15.134
43.182274
```

This is exactly what you would expect, and it can be used to write generic algorithms. Unfortunately, it suffers from two problems.

- The add operation is not typesafe; I can write code that tries to add two non-numeric types together.

- It's slow, taking approximately 50 times longer than performing the mathematical operations directly.

The slow performance likely excludes the use of this technique in many scenarios.[3]

Usage Guidelines

The use of dynamic has performance disadvantages, but performance is not the only issue; because the compiler doesn't know what the underlying type is, Visual Studio doesn't support statement completion on types declared with dynamic.[4]

Because of these disadvantages, dynamic should be used only in the following situations:

- When it provides the capability to do something that cannot be done otherwise in C#, such as calling code in Python

- When it significantly simplifies the use of existing COM APIs

---

[3]There's a nicer approach to do generic calculations; see www.codeproject.com/Articles/8531/Using-generics-for-calculations.

[4]At least, it doesn't currently. Doing so would require it to create objects of the target type and use dynamic to find out what properties and methods they expose. That's similar to what UI controls do to show up in designers, so it seems feasible.

■ ■ ■

CHAPTER 25

User-Defined Conversions

C# allows conversions to be defined between classes or structs and other objects in the system. User-defined conversions are always static functions, which must either take as a parameter or return as a return value the object in which they are declared. This means that conversions can't be declared between two existing types, which makes the language simpler.

A Simple Example

This example implements a struct that stores Roman numerals. It could also be written as a class, but since it acts like a built-in value type, a struct makes more sense.

```
struct RomanNumeral
{
    public RomanNumeral(short value)
    {
        if (value > 5000)
        {
            throw (new ArgumentOutOfRangeException());
        }
        m_value = value;
    }
    public static explicit operator RomanNumeral(short value)
    {
        RomanNumeral retval;
        retval = new RomanNumeral(value);
        return retval;
    }

    public static implicit operator short(RomanNumeral roman)
    {
        return roman.m_value;
    }

    static string NumberString(ref int value, int magnitude, char letter)
    {
        StringBuilder numberString = new StringBuilder();

        while (value >= magnitude)
```

```
            {
                value -= magnitude;
                numberString.Append(letter);
            }
            return numberString.ToString();
        }

        public static implicit operator string(RomanNumeral roman)
        {
            int temp = roman.m_value;

            StringBuilder retval = new StringBuilder();

            retval.Append(RomanNumeral.NumberString(ref temp, 1000, 'M'));
            retval.Append(RomanNumeral.NumberString(ref temp, 500, 'D'));
            retval.Append(RomanNumeral.NumberString(ref temp, 100, 'C'));
            retval.Append(RomanNumeral.NumberString(ref temp, 50, 'L'));
            retval.Append(RomanNumeral.NumberString(ref temp, 10, 'X'));
            retval.Append(RomanNumeral.NumberString(ref temp, 5, 'V'));
            retval.Append(RomanNumeral.NumberString(ref temp, 1, 'I'));

            return retval.ToString();

        }

        private short m_value;
}
class Test
{
    public static void Main()
    {
        short s = 12;
        RomanNumeral numeral = new RomanNumeral(s);

        s = 165;
        numeral = (RomanNumeral) s;

        Console.WriteLine("Roman as int: {0}", (int)numeral);
        Console.WriteLine("Roman as string: {0}", (string)numeral);

        short s2 = numeral;
    }
}
```

This struct declares a constructor that can take a short value, and it also declares a conversion from a short to a RomanNumeral. The conversion is declared as an explicit conversion because it isn't a conversion that will always succeed; in this case, it may throw an exception if the number is bigger than the magnitude supported by the struct. There is a conversion to short that is declared implicit, because the value in a RomanNumeral will always fit in a short. And finally, there's a conversion to string that gives the romanized version of the number.[1]

---

[1]No, this struct doesn't handle niceties such as replacing "IIII" with "IV," nor does it handle converting the romanized string to a short. The remainder of the implementation is left as an exercise for the reader.

When an instance of this struct is created, the constructor can be used to set the value. An explicit conversion can be used to convert the integer value to a RomanNumeral. To get the romanized version of the RomanNumeral, you could write the following:

```
Console.WriteLine(roman);
```

If this is done, the compiler reports that there is an ambiguous conversion present. The class includes implicit conversions both to short and to string, and Console.WriteLine() has overloads that take both versions, so the compiler doesn't know which one to call.

In the example, an explicit cast is used to disambiguate, but it's a bit ugly. It would probably be best to overload ToString() and remove the string conversion.

Pre- and Post-Conversions

In the preceding example, the basic types that were converted to and from the RomanNumeral were exact matches to the types that were declared in the struct itself. A user-defined conversion can also be used in scenarios where the source or destination types are not exact matches to the types in the conversion functions.

If the source or destination types are not exact matches, then the appropriate standard (i.e., built-in) conversion must be present to convert from the source type to the source type of the user-defined conversion and/or from the destination type of the user-defined conversion, and the type of the conversion (implicit or explicit) must also be compatible.

Perhaps an example will be a bit clearer. In the preceding example, the following line

```
short s = numeral;
```

calls the implicit user-defined conversion directly. Since this is an implicit use of the user-defined conversion, there can also be another implicit conversion at the end.

```
int i = numeral;
```

Here, the implicit conversion from RomanNumeral to short is performed, followed by the implicit conversion from short to long.

In the explicit case, there was the following conversion in the example:

```
numeral = (RomanNumeral) 165;
```

Since the usage is explicit, the explicit conversion from int to RomanNumeral is used. Also, an additional explicit conversion can occur before the user-defined conversion is called.

```
long bigvalue = 166;
short smallvalue = 12;
numeral = (RomanNumeral) bigvalue;
numeral = (RomanNumeral) smallvalue;
```

In the first conversion, the long value is converted by explicit conversion to an integer, and then the user-defined conversion is called. The second conversion is similar, except that an implicit conversion is performed before the explicit user-defined conversion.

Conversions Between Structs

User-defined conversions that deal with classes or structs rather than basic types work in a similar way, except that there are a few more situations to consider. Since the user conversion can be defined in either the source or destination type, there's a bit more design work to do, and the operation is a bit more complex. For details, see the "How It Works" section later in this chapter.

Adding to the RomanNumeral example in the previous section, a struct that handles binary numbers can be added.

```
struct BinaryNumeral
{
    public BinaryNumeral(int value)
    {
        m_value = value;
    }
    public static implicit operator BinaryNumeral(int value)
    {
        return new BinaryNumeral(value);
    }
    public static implicit operator int(BinaryNumeral binary)
    {
        return binary.m_value;
    }
    public static implicit operator string(BinaryNumeral binary)
    {
        StringBuilder retval = new StringBuilder();

        return retval.ToString();
    }

    private int m_value;
}
class Test
{
    public static void Main()
    {
        RomanNumeral roman = new RomanNumeral(12);
        BinaryNumeral binary;
        binary = (BinaryNumeral)(int)roman;
    }
}
```

The classes can be used together, but since they don't really know about each other, it takes a bit of extra typing. Converting from a RomanNumeral to a BinaryNumeral requires first converting to an int.

It would be nice to write the Main() function as follows:

```
binary = roman;
roman = (RomanNumeral) binary;
```

This makes the types look like the built-in types, with the exception that RomanNumeral has a smaller range than binary and therefore will require an explicit conversion in that section.

To get this, a user-defined conversion is required on either the RomanNumeral or BinaryNumeral class. In this case, it goes on the RomanNumeral class, for reasons that should become clear in the "Design Guidelines" section of this chapter.

The classes are modified as follows, adding two conversions:

```
struct RomanNumeral
{
    public static implicit operator BinaryNumeral(RomanNumeral roman)
    {
        return new BinaryNumeral((short) roman);
    }

    public static explicit operator RomanNumeral(
    BinaryNumeral binary)
    {
        return new RomanNumeral((short) binary);
    }
}
class Test
{
    public static void Main()
    {
        RomanNumeral roman = new RomanNumeral(122);
        BinaryNumeral binary;
        binary = roman;
        roman = (RomanNumeral) binary;
    }
}
```

With these added user-defined conversions, conversions between the RomanNumeral and BinaryNumeral types can now take place.

Classes and Pre- and Post-Conversions

As with basic types, classes can also have standard conversions that occur either before or after the user-defined conversion, or even before *and* after. The only standard conversions that deal with classes, however, are conversions to a base or derived class, so those are the only ones considered.

For implicit conversions, it's pretty simple, and the conversion occurs in three steps:

1. A conversion from a derived class to the source class of the user-defined conversion is optionally performed.

2. The user-defined conversion occurs.

3. A conversion from the destination class of the user-defined conversion to a base class is optionally performed.

To illustrate this, the example will be modified to use classes rather than structs, and a new class that derives from RomanNumeral will be added.

```
class RomanNumeral
{
    public RomanNumeral(short value)
    {
        if (value > 5000)
        {
            throw(new ArgumentOutOfRangeException());
        }
        m_value = value;
    }
    public static explicit operator RomanNumeral(short value)
    {
        return new RomanNumeral(value);
    }

    public static implicit operator short(RomanNumeral roman)
    {
        return roman.m_value;
    }

    static string NumberString(
    ref int value, int magnitude, char letter)
    {
        StringBuilder numberString = new StringBuilder();

        while (value >= magnitude)
        {
            value -= magnitude;
            numberString.Append(letter);
        }
        return numberString.ToString();
    }

    public static implicit operator string(
    RomanNumeral roman)
    {
        int temp = roman.m_value;

        StringBuilder retval = new StringBuilder();

        retval.Append(RomanNumeral.NumberString(ref temp, 1000, 'M'));
        retval.Append(RomanNumeral.NumberString(ref temp, 500, 'D'));
        retval.Append(RomanNumeral.NumberString(ref temp, 100, 'C'));
        retval.Append(RomanNumeral.NumberString(ref temp, 50, 'L'));
        retval.Append(RomanNumeral.NumberString(ref temp, 10, 'X'));
        retval.Append(RomanNumeral.NumberString(ref temp, 5, 'V'));
        retval.Append(RomanNumeral.NumberString(ref temp, 1, 'I'));

        return retval.ToString();
    }
```

```csharp
    public static implicit operator BinaryNumeral(RomanNumeral roman)
    {
        return new BinaryNumeral((short) roman);
    }

    public static explicit operator RomanNumeral(
    BinaryNumeral binary)
    {
        return new RomanNumeral((short)(int) binary);
    }
    private short m_value;
}
class BinaryNumeral
{
    public BinaryNumeral(int value)
    {
        m_value = value;
    }

    public static implicit operator BinaryNumeral(int value)
    {
        return new BinaryNumeral(value);
    }

    public static implicit operator int(BinaryNumeral binary)
    {
        return binary.m_value;
    }

    public static implicit operator string(BinaryNumeral binary)
    {
        StringBuilder    retval = new StringBuilder();

        return retval.ToString();
    }

    private int m_value;
}
class RomanNumeralAlternate : RomanNumeral
{
    public RomanNumeralAlternate(short value): base(value)
    {
    }
    public static implicit operator string(RomanNumeralAlternate roman)
    {
        return "NYI";
    }
}
```

```
class Test
{
    public static void Main()
    {
            // implicit conversion section
        RomanNumeralAlternate roman;
        roman = new RomanNumeralAlternate(55);

        BinaryNumeral binary = roman;
            // explicit conversion section
        BinaryNumeral binary2 = new BinaryNumeral(1500);
        RomanNumeralAlternate roman2;

        roman2 = (RomanNumeralAlternate) binary2;
    }
}
```

The operation of the implicit conversion to BinaryNumeral is as expected; an implicit conversion of roman from RomanNumeralAlternate to RomanNumeral occurs, and then the user-defined conversion from RomanNumeral to BinaryNumeral is performed.

The explicit conversion section may have some people scratching their heads. The user-defined function from BinaryNumeral to RomanNumeral returns a RomanNumeral, and the post-conversion to RomanNumeralAlternate can never succeed.

The conversion could be rewritten as follows:

```
using System;
using System.Text;
class RomanNumeral
{
    public RomanNumeral(short value)
    {
        if (value > 5000)
        {
            throw(new ArgumentOutOfRangeException());
        }
        m_value = value;
    }
    public static implicit operator short(RomanNumeral roman)
    {
        return roman.m_value;
    }

    static string NumberString(
        ref int value, int magnitude, char letter)
    {
        StringBuilder numberString = new StringBuilder();

        while (value >= magnitude)
        {
            value -= magnitude;
            numberString.Append(letter);
        }
```

```csharp
        return numberString.ToString();
    }

    public static implicit operator string(RomanNumeral roman)
    {

        int temp = roman.m_value;

        StringBuilder retval = new StringBuilder();

        retval.Append(RomanNumeral.NumberString(ref temp, 1000, 'M'));
        retval.Append(RomanNumeral.NumberString(ref temp, 500, 'D'));
        retval.Append(RomanNumeral.NumberString(ref temp, 100, 'C'));
        retval.Append(RomanNumeral.NumberString(ref temp, 50, 'L'));
        retval.Append(RomanNumeral.NumberString(ref temp, 10, 'X'));
        retval.Append(RomanNumeral.NumberString(ref temp, 5, 'V'));
        retval.Append(RomanNumeral.NumberString(ref temp, 1, 'I'));

        return retval.ToString();

    }
    public static implicit operator BinaryNumeral(RomanNumeral roman)
    {
        return new BinaryNumeral((short) roman);
    }

    public static explicit operator RomanNumeral(BinaryNumeral binary)
    {
        int val = binary;
        if (val >= 1000)
        {
            return (RomanNumeral)
                    new RomanNumeralAlternate((short) val);
        }
        else
        {
            return new RomanNumeral((short) val);
        }
    }

    private short m_value;
}
class BinaryNumeral
{
    public BinaryNumeral(int value)
    {
        m_value = value;
    }
    public static implicit operator BinaryNumeral(int value)
    {
        return new BinaryNumeral(value);
    }
```

```
    public static implicit operator int(BinaryNumeral binary)
    {
        return binary.m_value;
    }

    public static implicit operator string(BinaryNumeral binary)
    {
        StringBuilder retval = new StringBuilder();

        return retval.ToString();
    }

    private int m_value;
}
class RomanNumeralAlternate : RomanNumeral
{
    public RomanNumeralAlternate(short value) : base(value)
    {
    }

    public static implicit operator string(
    RomanNumeralAlternate roman)
    {
        return "NYI";
    }
}
class Test
{
    public static void Main()
    {
            // implicit conversion section
        RomanNumeralAlternate roman;
        roman = new RomanNumeralAlternate(55);
        BinaryNumeral binary = roman;

        // explicit conversion section
        BinaryNumeral binary2 = new BinaryNumeral(1500);
        RomanNumeralAlternate roman2;

        roman2 = (RomanNumeralAlternate) binary2;
    }
}
```

The user-defined conversion operator now doesn't return a RomanNumeral; it returns a RomanNumeral reference to a RomanNumeralAlternate object, and it's perfectly legal for that to be a reference to a derived type. Weird, perhaps, but legal. With the revised version of the conversion function, the explicit conversion from BinaryNumeral to RomanNumeralAlternate may succeed, depending on whether the RomanNumeral reference is a reference to a RomanNumeral object or a RomanNumeralAlternate object.

Design Guidelines

When designing user-defined conversions, the following guidelines should be considered.

Implicit Conversions Are Safe Conversions

When defining conversions between types, the only conversions that should be implicit ones are those that don't lose any data and don't throw exceptions.

This is important, because implicit conversions can occur without it being obvious that a conversion has occurred.

Define the Conversion in the More Complex Type

This basically means not cluttering up a simple type with conversions to a more complex one. For conversions to and from one of the predefined types, there is no option but to define the conversion as part of the class, since the source isn't available.

Even if the source *were* available, however, it would be really strange to define the conversions from int to BinaryNumeral or RomanNumeral in the int class.

Sometimes, as in the example, the classes are peers to each other, and there is no obvious simpler class. In that case, pick a class, and put both conversions there.

One Conversion to and from a Hierarchy

In my examples, there was only a single conversion from the user-defined type to the numeric types and one conversion from numeric types to the user-defined type. In general, it is good practice to do this and then to use the built-in conversions to move between the destination types. When choosing the numeric type to convert from or to, choose the one that is the most natural size for the type.

For example, in the BinaryNumeral class, there's an implicit conversion to int. If the user wants a smaller type, such as short, a cast can easily be done.

If multiple conversions are available, the overloading rules will take effect, and the result may not always be intuitive for the user of the class. This is especially important when dealing with both signed and unsigned types.

Add Conversions Only As Needed

I've seen a collection class that defined an implicit conversion to integer, which returned the count of items in the class. Don't do the unexpected with user-defined conversions; extraneous conversions only make the user's life harder.

Conversions That Operate in Other Languages

Some of the .NET languages don't support the conversion syntax, and calling conversion functions—which have weird names—may be difficult or impossible. To make classes easily usable from these languages, alternate versions of the conversions should be supplied. If, for example, an object supports a conversion to string, it should also support calling ToString() on that function. Here's how it would be done on the RomanNumeral class:

```
using System;
using System.Text;
```

```csharp
class RomanNumeral
{
    public RomanNumeral(short value)
    {
        if (value > 5000)
        {
            throw(new ArgumentOutOfRangeException());
        }
        m_value = value;
    }
    public static explicit operator RomanNumeral(short value)
    {
        return new RomanNumeral(value);
    }

    public static implicit operator short(RomanNumeral roman)
    {
        return roman.m_value;
    }

    static string NumberString(
    ref int value, int magnitude, char letter)
    {
        StringBuilder numberString = new StringBuilder();

        while (value >= magnitude)
        {
            value -= magnitude;
            numberString.Append(letter);
        }
        return numberString.ToString();
    }

    public static implicit operator string(RomanNumeral roman)
    {
        int temp = roman.m_value;

        StringBuilder retval = new StringBuilder();

        retval.Append(RomanNumeral.NumberString(ref temp, 1000, 'M'));
        retval.Append(RomanNumeral.NumberString(ref temp, 500, 'D'));
        retval.Append(RomanNumeral.NumberString(ref temp, 100, 'C'));
        retval.Append(RomanNumeral.NumberString(ref temp, 50, 'L'));
        retval.Append(RomanNumeral.NumberString(ref temp, 10, 'X'));
        retval.Append(RomanNumeral.NumberString(ref temp, 5, 'V'));
        retval.Append(RomanNumeral.NumberString(ref temp, 1, 'I'));

        return retval.ToString();
```

```
    }
    public short ToShort()
    {
        return (short) this;
    }

    public override string ToString()
    {
        return (string) this;
    }

    private short m_value;
}
```

The ToString() function is an override because it overrides the ToString() method in object.

How It Works

To finish the section on user-defined conversions, there are a few details on how the compiler views conversions that warrant a bit of explanation. Those who are really interested in the gory details can find them in the C# Language Reference.

This section can be safely skipped.

Conversion Lookup

When looking for candidate user-defined conversions, the compiler will search the source class and all of its base classes and the destination class and all of its base classes.

This leads to an interesting case.

```
public class S
{
    public static implicit operator T(S s)
    {
        // conversion here
        return new T();
    }
}
public class TBase
{
}
public class T: TBase
{
}
public class Test
{
    public static void Main()
    {
        S myS = new S();
```

```
        TBase tb = (TBase) myS;
    }
}
```

In this example, the compiler will find the conversion from S to T, and since the use is explicit, match it for the conversion to TBase, which will succeed only if the T returned by the conversion is really only a TBase.

Revising things a bit, removing the conversion from S and adding it to T, you get this:

```
// error
class S
{
}
class TBase
{
}
class T: TBase
{
    public static implicit operator T(S s)
    {
        return new T();
    }
}
class Test
{
    public static void Main()
    {
        S myS = new S();
        TBase tb = (TBase) myS;
    }
}
```

This code doesn't compile. The conversion is from S to TBase, and the compiler can't find the definition of the conversion, because class T isn't searched.

CHAPTER 26

■ ■ ■

Operator Overloading

Operator overloading allows operators to be defined on a class or struct so that it can be used with operator syntax. This is most useful on data types where there is a good definition for what a specific operator means, thereby allowing an economy of expression for the user.

Overloading the relational operators (==, !=, >, <, >=, <=) is covered in the section of Chapter 32 that explains how to overload the Equals() function from the .NET Framework.

Overloading conversion operators is covered in Chapter 25.

Unary Operators

All unary operators are defined as static functions that take a single operator of the class or struct type and return an operator of that type. The following operators can be overloaded:

```
+ - ! ~ ++ -- true false
```

The first six unary overloaded operators are called when the corresponding operation is invoked on a type. The true and false operators are available for boolean types where the following:

```
if (a == true)
```

is not equivalent to this:

```
if (! (a == false))
```

This happens in the SQL types in the System.Data.SQL namespace, which have a null state that is neither true nor false, and it also happens in nullable types. In this scenario, the compiler will use the overloaded true and false operators to correctly evaluate such statements. These operators must return type bool.

There is no way to discriminate between the pre- and post-increment or decrement operation. Because the operators are static (and therefore have no state), this distinction is not important.

Binary Operators

All binary operators take two parameters, and at least one of which must be the class or struct type in which the operator is declared. A binary operator can return any type but would typically return the type of the class or struct in which it is defined.

The following binary operators can be overloaded:

```
+ - * / % & | ^ << >> == != >= <= > <
```

An Example

The following class implements some of the overloadable operators:

```
struct RomanNumeral
{
    public RomanNumeral(int value)
    {
        m_value = value;
    }
    public override string ToString()
    {
        return m_value.ToString();
    }
    public static RomanNumeral operator -(RomanNumeral roman)
    {
        return new RomanNumeral(-roman.m_value);
    }
    public static RomanNumeral operator +(
        RomanNumeral roman1,
        RomanNumeral roman2)
    {
        return new RomanNumeral(roman1.m_value + roman2.m_value);
    }

    public static RomanNumeral operator ++(RomanNumeral roman)
    {
        return new RomanNumeral(roman.m_value + 1);
    }
    int m_value;
}
class Test
{
    public static void Main()
    {
        RomanNumeral roman1 = new RomanNumeral(12);
        RomanNumeral roman2 = new RomanNumeral(125);

        Console.WriteLine("Increment: {0}", roman1++);
        Console.WriteLine("Addition: {0}", roman1 + roman2);
    }
}
```

This example generates the following output:

```
Increment: 12
Addition: 138
```

Restrictions

It is not possible to overload any of the following:

- Member access

- Method invocation (function calling)

- The =, &&, ||, ?:, and new operators

This is for the sake of simplicity; although you can do interesting things with such overloadings, it greatly increases the difficulty in understanding code, since programmers would have to always remember that member invocation (for example) could be doing something special.[1] The new operator can't be overloaded because the .NET Runtime is responsible for managing memory, and in the C# idiom, new just means "give me a new instance of."

It is also not possible to overload the compound assignment operators (+=, *=, and so on), since they are always expanded to the simple operation and an assignment. This avoids cases where one would be defined and the other wouldn't be or when (shudder) they would be defined but with different meanings.

Guidelines

Operator overloading is a feature that should be used only when necessary. By "necessary," I mean in ways that make things easier and simpler for the user.

Good examples of operator overloading would be defining arithmetic operations on a complex number or matrix class.

Bad examples would be defining the increment (++) operator on a string class to mean "increment each character in the string." A good guideline is that unless a typical user would understand what the operator does without any documentation, it shouldn't be defined as an operator. Don't make up new meanings for operators.

In practice, the equality (==) and inequality (!=) operators are the ones that will be defined most often, since if this is not done, there may be unexpected results.[2]

If the type behaves like a built-in data type, such as the BinaryNumeral class, it may make sense to overload more operators. At first look, it might seem that since the BinaryNumeral class is really just a fancy integer, it could just derive from the System.Int32 class and get the operators for free.

This won't work for a couple of reasons. First, value types can't be used as base classes, and Int32 is a value type. Second, even if it was possible, it wouldn't really work for BinaryNumeral, because a BinaryNumeral isn't an integer; it supports only a small part of the possible integer range. Because of this, derivation would not be a good design choice. The smaller range means that even if BinaryNumeral were derived from int, there isn't an implicit conversion from int to BinaryNumeral, and any expressions would therefore require casts.

Even if these weren't true, however, it still wouldn't make sense, since the whole point of having a data type is to have something that's lightweight, and a struct would be a better choice than a class. Structs, of course, can't derive from other objects.

A Complex Number Class

The following struct implements a complex number, with a few overloaded operators. Note that there are nonoverloaded versions for use by languages that don't support overloaded operators.

---

[1] One could, however, argue that member access can be overloaded through properties.
[2] As you saw earlier, if your type is a reference type (class), using == will compare to see whether the two things you're comparing reference the same object, rather than seeing whether they have the same contents. If your type is a value type, == will compare the contents of the value type, if operator == is defined.

```
struct Complex
{
    public float m_real;
    public float m_imaginary;

    public Complex(float real, float imaginary)
    {
        m_real = real;
        m_imaginary = imaginary;
    }
    public float Real
    {
        get { return m_real; }
        set { m_real = value; }
    }
    public float Imaginary
    {
        get { return m_imaginary; }
        set { m_imaginary = value; }
    }
    public override string ToString()
    {
        return (String.Format("({0}, {1}i)", m_real, m_imaginary));
    }
    public static bool operator ==(Complex c1, Complex c2)
    {
        return (c1.m_real == c2.m_real) &&
                (c1.m_imaginary == c2.m_imaginary);
    }
    public static bool operator !=(Complex c1, Complex c2)
    {
        return !(c1 == c2);
    }
    public override bool Equals(object o2)
    {
        return this == (Complex) o2;
    }
    public override int GetHashCode()
    {
        return m_real.GetHashCode() ^ m_imaginary.GetHashCode();
    }
    public static Complex operator +(Complex c1, Complex c2)
    {
        return new Complex(c1.m_real + c2.m_real, c1.m_imaginary + c2.m_imaginary);
    }
}
```

```csharp
    public static Complex operator -(Complex c1, Complex c2)
    {
        return new Complex(c1.m_real - c2.m_real, c1.m_imaginary - c2.m_imaginary);
    }

    // product of two complex numbers
    public static Complex operator *(Complex c1, Complex c2)
    {
        return new Complex(c1.m_real * c2.m_real - c1.m_imaginary * c2.m_imaginary,
                           c1.m_real * c2.m_imaginary + c2.m_real * c1.m_imaginary);
    }

    // quotient of two complex numbers
    public static Complex operator /(Complex c1, Complex c2)
    {
        if ((c2.m_real == 0.0f) &&
            (c2.m_imaginary == 0.0f))
        {

            throw new DivideByZeroException("Can't divide by zero Complex number");
        }

        float newReal =
            (c1.m_real * c2.m_real + c1.m_imaginary * c2.m_imaginary) /
            (c2.m_real * c2.m_real + c2.m_imaginary * c2.m_imaginary);
        float newImaginary =
            (c2.m_real * c1.m_imaginary - c1.m_real * c2.m_imaginary) /
            (c2.m_real * c2.m_real + c2.m_imaginary * c2.m_imaginary);

        return new Complex(newReal, newImaginary);
    }

    // non-operator versions for other languages...
    public static Complex Add(Complex c1, Complex c2)
    {
        return c1 + c2;
    }
    public static Complex Subtract(Complex c1, Complex c2)
    {
        return c1 - c2;
    }
    public static Complex Multiply(Complex c1, Complex c2)
    {
        return c1 * c2;
    }
    public static Complex Divide(Complex c1, Complex c2)
    {
        return c1 / c2;
    }
}
```

```
class Test
{
    public static void Main()
    {
        Complex c1 = new Complex(3, 1);
        Complex c2 = new Complex(1, 2);

        Console.WriteLine("c1 == c2: {0}", c1 == c2);
        Console.WriteLine("c1 != c2: {0}", c1 != c2);
        Console.WriteLine("c1 + c2 = {0}", c1 + c2);
        Console.WriteLine("c1 - c2 = {0}", c1 - c2);
        Console.WriteLine("c1 * c2 = {0}", c1 * c2);
        Console.WriteLine("c1 / c2 = {0}", c1 / c2);
    }
}
```

■ ■ ■

CHAPTER 27

Nullable Types

It is sometimes useful to know whether a value has been defined. This concept is present for reference types (classes) by using the `null` value. Nullable types are used to support this concept with value types (structs).

A Simple Example

Assume you are writing a customer-tracking system and have created the following class:

```
class Customer
{
    public Customer(string name, string company)
    {
        Name = name;
        Company = company;
    }

    public string Name { get; set; }
    public string Company { get; set; }
    public string City { get; set; }
    public int YearOfBirth { get; set; }
}
```

In addition to the name and company for each customer, you want to store the city where they live and the year of their birth if the customer is willing to provide that information. Storing the city information is simple; you store the name if you know it, or you store `null` to indicate that you don't know the information. You have a problem storing the `YearOfBirth`, however, since there is no way to indicate "don't know" in a value type such as `int`.[1] How can you deal with this?

You could choose a specific value (such as 0) to indicate that the user did not provide their date of birth, but then you run the risk of generating reports showing that your average customer is slightly more than 2,000 years old, which will happen if you forget to check for that specific value.

A nicer approach would be to create a type that implemented an "integer value or unknown" abstraction.[2]

---

[1]Floating-point numbers define a NaN (Not a Number) that maybe could be used for this, but arithmetic with NaN values is actually defined.
[2]This is a very common database abstraction.

```
struct Integer
{
    int m_value;
    bool m_hasValue;

    public int Value
    {
        get
        {
            if (!m_hasValue)
            {
                throw new InvalidOperationException("Integer does not have a value");
            }
            return m_value;
        }
        set
        {
            m_value = value;
            m_hasValue = true;
        }
    }
    public bool HasValue
    {
        get { return m_hasValue; }
        set { m_hasValue = value; }
    }
    public Integer(int value)
    {
        m_value = value;
        m_hasValue = true;
    }
    public static implicit operator Integer(int value)
    {
        return new Integer(value);
    }
    public static Integer Null
    {
        get { return new Integer(); }
    }
}
```

With this struct, you can write the following:

```
static void IntegerExample()
{
    Integer value = 15;
    Process(value);
    Integer nullInteger = Integer.Null;
    Process(nullInteger);
}
```

```
static void Process(Integer integer)
{
    Console.WriteLine(integer.HasValue ? integer.Value.ToString() : "null");
}
```

With the Integer struct, you can tell whether there is a value, and if you try to use a value that is not defined, you will get an exception. There are a few things that I don't like, however. I would like to be able to write the following:

```
Integer YearOfBirth = null;
```

instead of this:

```
Integer YearOfBirth = Integer.Null;
```

But there is no way to express that in my struct. I would also like to be able to modify the Integer struct into a ValueOrNull <T> struct so that I don't have to write one for every value type, but I am unable to write the implicit operator to convert from T to ValueOrNull <T>, so I'd end up having to write something like this:

```
ValueOrNull<int> value = new ValueOrNull<int>(15);
```

which doesn't make me happy. Finally, I'd prefer a shorter syntax so that I don't have to write ValueOrNull <int> all of the time. It sounds like I need some compiler help to get what I want, and that is what C# provides with nullable types: a Nullable <T> implementation in the base class library, plus some compiler support[3] to make it easier to use.

Using Nullable Types

With nullable support, it is now possible to write the following:

```
static void NullableExample()
{
    int? value = 15;
    Process(value);
    int? nullValue = null;
    Process(nullValue);
}
static void Process(int? value)
{
    Console.WriteLine(value.HasValue ? value.Value.ToString() : "null");
}
```

The use of int? is precisely equivalent to Nullable <int> but with a sweeter syntax.[4] You can write expressions using nullable types.

---

[3]What is technically known as *syntactical sugar*.
[4]Syntactical sugar gives us a sweeter syntax.

```
int? i = 10;
int? j = 20;
int? n = null;

int? k = i * j;
int? s = k+n;
```

When this code is run, k will have a value of 200, and s will be `null`.

Null Coalescing

There is one more area that could use some support. It is common to want to go from the nullable world back to the non-nullable world, which involves using the value from the nullable if it is present or a default value if it is not. This can be written simply using the ternary operator.

```
int final = value.HasValue ? value.Value : 15;
```

To make this a bit easier, `Nullable <T>` provides a method.

```
int final = value.GetValueOrDefault(15);
```

Finally, C# gives you a shortcut syntax to calling the `GetValueOrDefault()` method.

```
int final = value ?? 15;
```

The `??` operator is known as the *null coalescing* operator, because it takes the null value and joins it back into the non-nullable world.

Nullable Types and Equality

Nullable types in C# and the null values in the database world have different definitions of equality. In the database world, if two null values are compared to each other, the result is `null`, while in the C# world, if two null values are compared, the result is `true`.

C# BEHAVIOR VS. DATABASE BEHAVIOR

During the design of nullable types, there was a considerable amount of discussion around how equality should work. On one side was the database view, and supporting the database concept of nullable was one of the main motivations for adding nullable support. On the other side was the existing behavior of C#; comparing two null reference instances returned `true`, and if nullable used the database definition, it would be different between the two and surprising to developers. The existing equality operators were also all defined as taking two parameters and returning a boolean value, not a nullable boolean value.

After working through a number of proposals, it was decided to go with the behavior that was a better fit into the existing C# design and make `null == null` return true.

■ ■ ■

CHAPTER 28

Linq to Objects

Linq is a programming paradigm that melds a declarative approach with the more traditional[1] procedural approach. Because the declarative approach is different from the procedural approach used in other C# code, it requires a different mental model. Until you have become comfortable with that new model, the code is going to be a bit puzzling at times, but hang in there. There is a lot to like in Linq; you can use it to write code that is smaller, easier to write and understand, and less likely to contain bugs.

There are three main parts of the Microsoft Linq offering[2]:

- Linq to objects, which operates against collections and collection-like classes.

- Linq to XML, which is used to perform XML processing.

- Linq to SQL, which is used to execute database queries.

This chapter will cover Linq to objects, and the following chapters will cover the XML and SQL variants.

Getting Started with Linq to Objects

We've been volunteered to help a friend keep track of the grades for a class. Our first task is to compute the current average for each student, so we open up our laptop, start up Visual Studio, and begin coding:

```
class Assignment
{
    public string Name { get; set; }
    public int Score { get; set; }
}
class Student
{
    public Student()
    {
        Assignments = new List<Assignment>();
    }

    public string Name { get; set; }
    public List<Assignment> Assignments { get; set; }
```

---

[1] More traditional for those of us who grew up with procedural languages.
[2] The paradigm that Linq uses can easily be extended and applied to other areas.

```
    public double GetAverageScore()
    {
        double sum = 0;
        foreach (Assignment assignment in Assignments)
        {
            sum += assignment.Score;
        }

        return sum / Assignments.Count;
    }
}
```

That works fine. But it's a bit annoying that we have to write a method to compute the average, and we certainly don't want to have to do it multiple times. Let's see if we can generalize it a bit. Here's the starting point of a more general average method:

```
public static double AverageV1(List<Assignment> values)
{
    double sum = 0;
    foreach (Assignment assignment in values)
    {
        sum += assignment.Score;
    }

    return sum / values.Count;
}
```

This only works for the Assignment type. Is there a way to get rid of the assignment.Score reference in the foreach and make it work for any type? To do so, we will need a way of reaching into an instance and pulling out (or "selecting") the data value to perform the average on. That is a perfect place for a bit of delegate/lambda magic:

```
public static double AverageV2(List<Assignment> values, Func<Assignment, int> selector)
{
    double sum = 0;
    foreach (Assignment value in values)
    {
        sum += selector(value);
    }

    return sum / values.Count;
}
```

System.Func<T, TResult> is a delegate that defines a function that takes an argument of input type T and returns a value of the output type TResult. By making it an argument to the Average method, we allow the caller to specify how to extract the value.

To call it, we'll need to specific the function to pull the score out of the assignment:

```
double average = Helpers.AverageV2(Assignments, a => a.Score);
```

The second parameter is a lambda that takes an assignment and returns a score. We are still wedded to the Assignment type, but perhaps we can make it generic:

```
public static double AverageV3<T>(List<T> values, Func<T, int> selector)
{
    double sum = 0;
    foreach (T value in values)
    {
        sum += selector(value);
    }

    return sum / values.Count;
}
```

By replacing the hard-coded uses of the Argument type with a generic argument T, this method can now be used to get the sum of any list.[3] There are a few more improvements we can make:

```
public static double AverageV4<T>(this IEnumerable<T> values, Func<T, int> selector)
{
    double sum = 0;
    int count = 0;
    foreach (T value in values)
    {
        sum += selector(value);
        count++;
    }

    return sum / count;
}
```

Making it an extension method makes it easier to call, and having it take an IEnumerable<T> rather than List<T> makes it work on any sequence of values. It can be called as follows:

```
double average = Assignments.AverageV4(a => a.Score);
```

At this point, our work is done, we have a method that does exactly what we want. And then a friend points us to the documentation for IEnumerable<T>, and we will find that somebody else has already done this work for us, giving us a method that is used exactly like the one we just wrote:

```
double average = Assignments.Average(a => a.Score);
```

Such methods are what I call sequence methods,[4] and they are the basis for everything that Linq does.

---

[3] You may have noticed that hard-coded int as the second type parameter. What would be very nice would be to write an average method that worked across all "numeric" types, but—unlike some other languages—C# and .NET don't have a type system that makes that possible, so we're stuck with separate overloads if we want to use different numeric types. We can kind of get around this by defining our own data types that implement an interface that defines the arithmetic operations, but it's easier and cleaner to define the methods multiple times, one for each numeric type.

[4] From what I can tell, there is no generally accepted term. From the language perspective, they're just methods, and therefore they don't have separate names.

Filtering Data

Our next task is to count the number of missing assignments each student has. We write the following:

```
public int CountOfAssignmentsWithZeroScores()
{
    int count = 0;
    foreach (Assignment assignment in Assignments)
    {
        if (assignment.Score == 0)
        {
            count++;
        }
    }

    return count;
}
```

This sort of list traversal has been bread-and-butter code for years, and most programmers have written it thousands of times. It's not a hard thing to do, but it is a tedious thing to do it over and over. Linq provides an interesting alternative.

First, we need to filter the assignment to only those with non-zero scores:

```
Assignments.Where(a => a.Score == 0);
```

and then we can get the count of those assignments:

```
Assignments.Where(a => a.Score == 0).Count();
```

The Where() method functions the same way a WHERE statement does in SQL; we start with all the assignments, but only those that pass the condition make it past the Where() method to be counted.

The previous statement can be written in a different way using another overload of the Count() method:

```
Assignments.Count(a => a.Score == 0);
```

In this version, we are counting all the items in the sequence that meet the condition.[5]

Transforming Data

Our next project is to produce a simple flat list that has the student's name and average score. We'll start by defining a class that can hold the data that we want:

```
class NameAndGrade
{
    public NameAndGrade(string name, double average)
    {
        Name = name;
        Average = average;
    }
```

---

[5] This overloading of method names to do two different things is confusing. A name like CountWhere() makes more sense to me.

```
    public string Name { get; set; }
    public double Average { get; set; }
}
```

Now that we have the class, we can create an expression that will generate a collection of NameAndGrade instances:

```
students.Select(s => new NameAndGrade(s.Name, s.GetAverageScore()));
```

This uses the Select() method, which takes the current sequence and converts it into a sequence of another type.[6] In this case, a sequence of Student is transformed into a sequence of NameAndGrade.

It's more than a bit cumbersome to have to define a separate class to hold the new information when you use a Select() method. This is the sort of tedium that programmers hate and compilers are quite good at.

C# therefore provides support to generate a new class automatically that will hold the items that result from the select, so it is possible to simply write the following:

```
var nameAndAverages = students.Select(
    s => new {
        Name = s.Name,
        Average = s.GetAverageScore()
    });
```

In this case, the use of var is required, as there is no way to specify the name of the anonymous type that is created. The compiler does generate a class, but there's no way to find the name of it.[7] That means that you can't pass instances of the type to a method or return the type from a method; in those situations you must write the type yourself.[8]

It is of course possible to eliminate the call to the GetAverageScore() method and use another Linq expression in its place:

```
var nameAndAverages = students.Select(
        s => new
        {
            Name = s.Name,
            Average = s.Assignments.Average(a => a.Score)
        });
```

Stringing Sequences Together

The next task is to figure out the average score across all assignments. The obvious way to write it is as follows:

```
var a1 = students.Average(s => s.GetAverageScore());
```

---

[6]It would be clearer if the method was named Transform() rather than Select(), but the Select term came from the SQL world, so we're stuck with it, unless you can go back to the 1970s and change history.
[7]Technically, this is false. You can run ILDASM on the assembly and figure out what the name is, and then use that in your code, although it's a *really* bad idea to do so, so bad that you should forget I mentioned it. In this case the name is
<>f__AnonymousType0'@<'<Name>j__TPar','<Average>j__TPar'>.
[8]There was considerable discussion during the design of Linq about ways to name the anonymous type (so it could be used as a function parameter), but we were unable to come up with a satisfactory solution.

This is incorrect; the average of all the averages may not be the overall average, since students might not have the same number of assignments. Perhaps selecting the `Assignments` collection can help:

```
var a2 = students.Select(s => s.Assignments);
```

This, unfortunately, is not a collection of assignments, but a collection of collections of assignments. What is needed is an operator that will enumerate across multiple collections and join them together into a single sequence. That is done with the `SelectMany()` method:

```
var a3 = students.SelectMany(s => s.Assignments).Average(a => a.Score);
```

Behind the Curtain

To understand all that can be done with Linq, it's important to understand a few implementation details; how Linq does what it does. Consider the following expression:

```
var x = students.Where(s => s.Name.Length < 5).Skip(1).Average(s => s.Assignments.Average(a =>
a.Score));
```

That's ugly. It will look better if formatted as follows:

```
var x = students
            .Where(s => s.Name.Length < 5)
            .Skip(1)
            .Average(s.Assignments.Average(a => a.Score));
```

The C# rule is that expressions are evaluated from left to right, so the operations will happen in the following order:

1. `Where()` operates on all the students, creating a list of `Student` instances that meet the condition.

2. `Skip()` takes the list, removes the first item, and passes it on.

3. `Average()` takes the list, traverses all the items, and figures out the average.

In fact, that's almost backward from how it works, because the Linq expressions deal with `IEnumerable<T>`, not `List<T>`. The actual sequences is as follows:

1. `Where()` creates an enumerator,[9] which stores the lambda expression and the enumerator from `students`, implements `IEnumerable<Student>`, and returns this instance.

2. `Skip()` creates an enumerator, which stores the enumerator returned by the `Where()` method, remembers how many items to skip and implements `IEnumerable<Student>`, and returns this instance.

3. `Average()` stores the enumerator from `Skip()` and the lambda expression it gets and initializes `count` and `sum` variables. It then starts to calculate the average.

4. The `Average()` enumerator asks the `Skip()` enumerator for an item.

---

[9] More specifically, it creates an instance of a class that implements `IEnumerable<Student>` and returns that instance.

5. The Skip() enumerator asks the Where() enumerator for an item.

6. The Where() enumerator asks the students list for an item. It repeats this until it finds an item that passes the condition. When it gets one, it passes it on.

7. The Skip() enumerator decrements the skip count it saved. If that skip count is positive, it goes back to step 4. If not, the item is passed through.

8. The Average() method takes the item, calls the lambda to get the value from it, and increments the count and sum variables.

9. If there are no more items, Average() computes the average and returns it. If not, the process continues with step 4.

This chaining together of enumerators has a number of benefits:

- It avoids intermediate lists and is therefore more efficient.[10]

- It defers execution of an operation until it is enumerated.

- It allows some interesting operations to be performed.

In the previous example, it was the Average() method that started the enumeration, and the reason it did so is that it needs all the values to calculate its return value. If the Average() was omitted:

```
var x = students
            .Where(s => s.Name.Length < 5)
            .Skip(1);
```

only steps 1 and 2 are executed, and therefore no operations have been performed. The value of x after execution of this statement is an IEnumerable<Student>, which will not do any work until somebody gets around to enumerating over it. This behavior is very important in Linq to SQL.

The communication between methods may be something other than IEnumerable<T>. Consider the following:

```
students.OrderBy(s => s.Assignments.Count());
```

That seems straightforward enough—order the students based on the number of assignments each student has. What does the following do?

```
students
    .OrderBy(s => s.Assignments.Count())
    .ThenBy(s => s.Assignments.Average(a => a.Score));
```

It sorts first by the count of assignments, then uses the average score as a subsort for any items that are equal to the first. This is done through a clever private conversation between the OrderBy() and ThenBy() methods using the IOrderedEnumerable<T> interface, which allows the two orderings to be batched and applied together, with the count as the primary sort key and the average as the secondary sort key.

---

[10]Some methods, such as Reverse(), require full enumeration to generate the list of items.

The effect is as if both of the selectors were written together:

```
students
    .OrderByMany(
        s => s.Assignments.Count(),
        s => s.Assignments.Average(a => a.Score));
```

and the single function does all the sorting,[11] which is quite cool.

Query Expressions

As part of the goal to make Linq to SQL more SQL-like, the C# compiler supports an alternate syntax for Linq expressions. The following:

```
var x = students
            .Where(s => s.Name.Length < 5)
            .Select(s => new
            {
                Name = s.Name,
                Average = s.Assignments.Average(a => a.Score)
            });
```

can alternatively be expressed as follows:

```
var y = from s in students
        where s.Name.Length < 5
        select new
        {
            Name = s.Name,
            Average = s.Assignments.Average(a => a.Score)
        };
```

This is similar to SQL select syntax, but differs in the order in which the select, where, and from sections are specified.[12]

■ **Note** There is potential for confusion if both syntaxes are used in the same codebase. The standard C# approach makes more sense to me, and I find it easier to separate the Linq syntax from any SQL queries involved. However, this may not apply in Linq to SQL code, so the best approach may differ for different teams.

---

[11] If you are curious, the method is defined as follows:
`public static IEnumerable<T> OrderByMany<T>(this IEnumerable<T> values, params Func<T, double>[] selector)`
Implementation is left as an exercise for the reader.
[12] The order is rearranged so that IntelliSense can function in the select clause; in a normal SQL syntax order (select, from, where), IntelliSense cannot be provided in the select clause because the from clause has not yet been written.

A Sequence Method of Your Own

It's simple to write additional sequence methods. The following is a subset method that skips the even-numbered items in a sequence:

```
private class EveryOtherEnumerator<T> : IEnumerable<T>
{
    IEnumerable<T> m_baseEnumerable;

    public EveryOtherEnumerator(IEnumerable<T> baseEnumerable)
    {
        m_baseEnumerable = baseEnumerable;
    }

    public IEnumerator<T> GetEnumerator()
    {
        int count = 0;
        foreach (T value in m_baseEnumerable)
        {
            if (count % 2 == 0)
            {
                yield return value;
            }
            count++;
        }
    }

    IEnumerator IEnumerable.GetEnumerator()
    {
        return GetEnumerator();
    }
}
```

Sequence Method Reference

Linq provides a large set of methods to make your life easier. The following section groups them by function.

Aggregate Methods

An aggregate method takes a sequence and produces a single value, causing the sequence to be enumerated. Aggregates can operate on the following data types:

- Decimal
- Double
- Float
- Int
- Long

In addition, nullable values of any of these types are permitted. The aggregate methods are shown in Table 28-1:

Table 28-1. *Linq Aggregate Methods*

Method	Description
Average()	Returns the average of the values.
Count()	Returns the count of the values.
Min()	Returns the minimum of the values.
Max()	Returns the maximum of the values.
Sum()	Returns the sum of the values.
Aggregate()	Computes a general aggregate.

The aggregate method can be used to construct custom aggregators, but in practice it is simpler to write a custom sequence method instead.

Transformational Methods

The transformational methods take a sequence of one type and transform it into a sequence of another type.

Select()

The Select() method applies the supplied expression to every item in the sequence, generating a new sequence that contains all the return values. For example:

```
students.Select(s => s.Name);
```

SelectMany()

The SelectMany() method joins together a collection that exists on each item in the sequence into a single sequence. For example:

```
students.SelectMany(s => s.Assignments);
```

Cast()

The Cast() method casts all of the items in a sequence to a specific type. For example:

```
List<object> objects = new List<object>();
objects.Add("A");
objects.Add("B");
objects.Add("C");

var sequenceOfString = objects.Cast<string>();
```

Each of the items in the objects list will be cast to the string type.

ToArray()

The ToArray() method returns an array that contains all of the items in the sequence. ToArray() will force enumeration of the sequence.

ToDictionary()

The ToDictionary() method takes a sequence of instances and adds those instances to a dictionary, using the specified value as the key for the item in the dictionary.

```
List<Student> students = new List<Student>();
Dictionary<string, Student> studentDictionary = students.ToDictionary(s => s.Name);
```

The Dictionary type requires that the key values are all unique. If the keys are not unique, the ToLookup() method may be a better choice. ToDictionary() will force enumeration of the sequence.

ToList()

The ToList() method returns a List that contains all of the items in the sequence. ToList() will force enumeration of the sequence.

ToLookup()

The ToLookup() method takes a sequence of instances and adds those instances to a lookup, using the specified value as the key for the item in the lookup. The Lookup class is similar to the Dictionary class, but instead of storing a single value, it stores an IEnumerable of that value.

The Lookup type stores a collection of values that are stored for each key, so it is a good choice if the key values are not unique. ToLookup() will force enumeration of the sequence.

Extraction Methods

The extraction methods are used to take a sequence and extract a single element from the sequence. For example, the First() method is used to take the first element of a sequence:

```
Student firstStudent = students.First();
```

If the sequence is empty, an exception will be thrown.

Some of the extraction methods have an "OrDefault" variant; this variant will return the default value for the type (i.e., default(T)) instead of throwing an exception.

```
Student firstStudent = students.FirstOrDefault();
```

It is sometimes desirable to filter a list before performing the extraction. For example, the following will return the first student with a name more than five characters in length:

```
students.Where(s => s.Name.Length > 5).First();
```

There is an additional overload to the `First()` method that allows this to be written more concisely[13]:

```
students.First(s => s.Name.Length > 5);
```

The extraction methods are shown in Table 28-2.

Table 28-2. *Linq Extraction Methods*

Method	Description
First()	Returns the first element that matches a condition (or with no condition) or throws an exception if there is no element.
FirstOrDefault()	Returns the first element that matches a condition (or with no condition) or a default value if there is no element.
Last()	Returns the last element that matches a condition (or with no condition) or throws an exception if there is no element.
LastOrDefault()	Returns the last element that matches a condition (or with no condition) or a default value if there is no element.
Single()	Returns the element that matches a condition (or with no condition) if there is only one element in the sequence, or throws an exception if there is no element.
SingleOrDefault()	Returns the element that matches a condition (or with no condition) if there is only one element in the sequence, or a default value if there is no element.
ElementAt()	Returns the element at the specific index in the sequence or throws an exception if the element does not exist.
ElementAtOrDefault()	Returns the element at the specific index in the sequence or a default value if the element does not exist.
DefaultIfEmpty()	Returns the sequence if there are elements in the sequence, or a sequence containing one element with the default value in it.

Subset Methods

The subset methods are used to produce a sequence that is a subset of the original sequence. The most common of these is the `Where()` method. For example, the following generates all students who have names that are fewer than five characters in length:

```
var shortNameStudents = students.Where(s => s.Name.Length < 5);
```

The subset methods are shown in Table 28-3.

---

[13]The naming of this method is unfortunate; it would be clearer if this method were named `FirstWhere()`, so that it would be obviously distinct from `First()`.

Table 28-3. *Linq Subset Methods*

Method	Description
Where()	Returns the subset of the sequence that match the specified condition.
Distinct()	Returns the subset of the sequence with no equal elements, either using the default equality comparer or a specified equality comparer.
OfType()	Returns the subset of the sequence that are of the specified type.
Skip()	Skips *n* elements at the beginning of the sequence, and returns the remainder of the sequence.
SkipWhile()	Skips all elements at the beginning of the sequence that match the condition.
Take()	Returns *n* elements at the beginning of the sequence, then skips the remainder of the sequence.
TakeWhile()	Returns all elements at the beginning of the sequence that match the condition, then skips the remainder of the sequence.

Ordering Methods

Ordering methods are used to reorder the element in a sequence. The ordering methods are listed in Table 28-4.

Table 28-4. *Linq Ordering Methods*

Method	Description
OrderBy()	Orders the elements in a sequence in ascending order according to a key or according to a comparer.
OrderByDescending()	Orders the elements in a sequence in descending order according to a key or according to a comparer.
Reverse()	Returns a sequence of elements in the reverse order.
ThenBy()	Orders any elements that were equal by a previous ordering method according to a key or according to a comparer.
ThenByDescending()	Orders any elements that were equal by a previous ordering method in descending order according to a key or according to a comparer.

Whole Sequence Methods

Whole sequence methods perform operations on a whole sequence. For example, the following produces the set union of two lists of integers:

```
int[] list1 = { 1, 3, 5, 7, 9 };
int[] list2 = { 1, 2, 3, 5, 8, 13 };
var unionOfLists = list1.Union(list2);
```

The whole sequence methods are shown in Table 28-5.

Table 28-5. *Linq Whole Sequence Methods*

Method	Description
Intersect()	Returns the set intersection of two sequences.
Union()	Returns the set union of two sequences.
Except()	Returns the set difference between two sequences.
Concat()	Returns the concatenated elements of two lists.
Zip()	Traverses two sequences in parallel, returning a new sequence that depends on the corresponding elements in each sequence.

Comparisons can be performed either using the default equality comparer or by specifying a equality comparer. The order of the elements in the resulting sequence are not defined. All of these methods force enumeration of the sequence.

Conditional Methods

The conditional methods evaluate a sequence and return a boolean value. For example, the Any() method can be used to determine if any students have a name longer than 30 characters in length:

```
bool veryLongNameStudents = _students.Any(s => s.Name.Length > 30);
```

The conditional methods are shown in Table 28-6.

Table 28-6. *Linq Conditional Methods*

Method	Description
All()	Returns true if the condition is true for all of the elements in the sequence.
Any()	Returns true if the condition is true for any of the elements in the sequence.
Contains()	Returns true if the sequence contains the specified element.
SequenceEqual()	Returns true if the two sequences are equal.

Comparisons can be performed either using the default equality comparer or by specifying an equality comparer.

Generator Methods

Generator methods are used to generate sequences. The generator methods are shown in Table 28-7.

Table 28-7. *Linq Generator Methods*

Method	Description
Range()	Generates a sequence of integers.
Repeat()	Returns a sequence that contains one element repeated a specific number of times.
Empty()	Returns the empty sequence.

Join()

The Join() method takes two sequences and joins them together using a specific key; this is the "inner join" method that is done by databases. Consider the following:

```
class StudentEmail
{
    public string Name { get; set; }
    public string EmailAddress { get; set; }
}

List<Student> students = ...
List<StudentEmail> studentEmails = ...

var joined = students.Join(studentEmails,
                s => s.Name,
                e => e.Name,
                (s, e) => new
                    {
                            Name = s.Name,
                            EmailAddress = e.EmailAddress,
                            Average = s.GetAverageScore()
                    });
```

The Student and StudentEmail classes both store the student's name, and the name can therefore be used to hook them together.[14] The Join() specifies the second sequence, the two selectors that are used to determine what values to compare, and a function to create the resulting method.

Sample data for this join are listed in Tables 28-8 and 28-9.

Table 28-8. *Student Sample Data*

Name	Average
John	20
Bob	15
Sally	18

[14]In the real world, it would be advisable to use something more unique, such as a student identification number.

Table 28-9. *StudentEmail Sample Data*

Name	Email Address
John	John@school.org
Bob	Robert@school.org
Tony	Anthony@school.org

The result of the join is shown in Table 28-10.

Table 28-10. *Result of Join*

Name	Average	Email Address
John	20	John@school.org
Bob	15	Robert@school.org

The result set contains only those items where the key values match in both sequences.

Inside of the Join(), it creates a Lookup of the keys in the second sequence and then uses that to find the values that match the key from the first sequence, so it's reasonably efficient. Note that like the SQL operation, the Join() method is combinatorical; if there are two "John Smith" entries in the student sequence and three in the email sequence, the final sequence will contain six "John Smith" entries.

■ **Note** If you are experienced with SQL, you are probably asking yourself "where are the other types of joins?" Only the inner join is supported directly through a sequence operator, although the same operations can be performed in other ways. If you are not experienced with SQL, don't worry about it; this topic will be covered in much more detail in Chapter 30.

GroupBy()

The GroupBy() method is used to take an entire sequence and group it into different buckets, based on a specific key value. Consider the following data:

```
List<Demographics> data = new List<Demographics>();

data.Add(new Demographics("Fred",   55, 98008,  55000));
data.Add(new Demographics("Barney", 58, 98052, 125000));
data.Add(new Demographics("Wilma",  38, 98008, 250000));
data.Add(new Demographics("Dino",   12, 98001,  12000));
data.Add(new Demographics("George", 55, 98001,  80000));
data.Add(new Demographics("Elroy",   8, 98008,   8000));
data.Add(new Demographics("Judy",   16, 98008,  18000));
data.Add(new Demographics("Jane",   48, 98008, 251000));
```

The GroupBy() can be used to bucket the data by zip code:

```
var x = data.GroupBy(d => d.ZipCode);
```

The result looks a lot like a Lookup structure; there is a different key for each unique value of the key, and all the elements that were grouped are stored under one of the keys.

The following can be used to output the result:

```
foreach (var group in x)
{
    Console.WriteLine(group.Key);
    foreach (var item in group)
    {
        Console.Write("    ");
        Console.WriteLine(item);
    }
}
```

Output:

```
98008
    Fred, 55, 98008, 55000
    Wilma, 38, 98008, 250000
    Elroy, 8, 98008, 8000
    Judy, 16, 98008, 18000
    Jane, 48, 98008, 251000
98052
    Barney, 58, 98052, 125000
98001
    Dino, 12, 98001, 12000
    George, 55, 98001, 80000
```

Once the data are grouped, they can be summarized with one of the aggregate methods:

```
var x = data
        .GroupBy(d => d.ZipCode)
        .Select(d => new
            {
                ZipCode = d.Key,
                AverageSalary = d.Average(d2 => d2.Salary)
            });
```

This results in a sequence of elements containing the zip code and the average salary of all the zip codes in the group.

■ ■ ■

CHAPTER 29

Linq to XML

XML is a very popular format—a *very* popular format—which makes it a bit surprising that it has often been more than a bit of a pain for developers to deal with.

Rockin' It "Old School"

The first version of the .NET base classes provided two ways of parsing XML. The simple way to deal with XML was to use the XML DOM, which allows the developer to easily find elements in a document, validate them against a schema, and do that sort of thing. It is fairly simple to use,[1] but it is a fairly big stick; it takes a bit of time to load and parse XML and consumes quite a bit of memory.

The opposite end of the spectrum is represented by the XmlReader and XmlWriter classes. They are very fast at parsing XML, but they don't provide a lot of help; the developer has to write complex code that ends up being difficult to understand and hard to change. But they are fast.

Creating XML had the same choices: the big DOM, the XmlWriter class, and the always-popular WriteLine() approach.[2]

Soon after, the XPathDocument class showed up, which provided a middle ground for parsing; it was faster than the DOM and much easier than the XmlReader class to use. But there was no improved way to create XML documents.

Linq to XML

Linq to XML is a bit of a misnomer. Under this umbrella are the following:

- A new syntax to create XML

- A nicer way to parse XML

- Smooth interfacing with other Linq abstractions

---

[1] Assuming you are better at remembering how namespaces work than I am.
[2] Purist may cringe, but there is a lot of code written this way.

Creating XML

For a bit of context, here is some code that uses the DOM to create some XML:

```
static public string CreateXmlExample1DOM()
{
    XmlDocument xmlDocument = new XmlDocument();

    XmlNode xmlBooksNode = xmlDocument.CreateElement("books");
    xmlDocument.AppendChild(xmlBooksNode);

    XmlNode xmlBookNode = xmlDocument.CreateElement("book");
    xmlBooksNode.AppendChild(xmlBookNode);

    XmlNode xmlNameNode = xmlDocument.CreateElement("name");
    xmlNameNode.InnerText = "Fox in socks";
    xmlBookNode.AppendChild(xmlNameNode);

    XmlNode xmlPriceNode = xmlDocument.CreateElement("price");
    xmlPriceNode.InnerText = "35.99";
    xmlBookNode.AppendChild(xmlPriceNode);

    return xmlDocument.OuterXml;
}
```

Take a look at that code, and write down the XML that it generates.

My guess is that it took you a bit of time to do that, and a similar effort is required whenever that code is read. One of the major goals of Linq to XML is to make XML creation easier to write and understand. Here is the XML that it generated:[3]

```
<books>
  <book>
    <name>Fox in socks</name>
    <price>35.99</price>
  </book>
</books>
```

You will generate the same XML using the XElement class. You'll start with one of the inner elements.

```
XElement element=new XElement("name", "Fox in socks");
```

---

[3]All the XML examples in this chapter are formatted to be easy to read. The actual generated XML may differ in whitespace.

This allows both creating the element and setting the value to be performed in one statement, and it doesn't require a separate document reference to create the new element. This makes it easy to create methods that return XElements.

Now, you can add the other elements.

```
XElement element =
    new XElement("books",
        new XElement("book",
            new XElement("name", "Fox in socks"),
            new XElement("price", "35.99")
        )
    );
return element.ToString();
```

Nicely, the constructor for XElement allows you to pass a list of child elements, so for the book element, it's easy to pass the name and price children. This code is much shorter than the XDocument version; the arrangement and formatting of the code has the same structure as the XML that it is generating.

More typically, you need to be able to generate the list of books from some sort of data structure. This is easily done with a bit of Linq code to generate a sequence of book elements.

```
class Book
{
    public string Name { get; set; }
    public Decimal Price { get; set; }
}

var books = new List<Book>(){
    new Book(){ Name="Fox in socks", Price=35.99M },
    new Book(){ Name="Rocks in box", Price=12.99M },
    new Book(){ Name="Lox in crocks", Price=9.99M } };

XElement element =
    new XElement("books",
            books.Select(x => new XElement("book",
                                new XElement("name", x.Name),
                                new XElement("price", x.Price)
                )
            )
    );
```

This generates the following XML:

```
<books>
  <book>
    <name>Fox in socks</name>
    <price>35.99</price>
  </book>
  <book>
    <name>Rocks in box</name>
    <price>12.99</price>
  </book>
```

```
  <book>
    <name>Lox in crocks</name>
    <price>9.99</price>
  </book>
</books>
```

You could save some space by creating attributes instead of elements.

```
XElement element =
    new XElement("books",
            books.Select(x => new XElement("book",
                                    new XAttribute("name", x.Name),
                                    new XAttribute("price", x.Price)
                        )
                    )
                );
```

This code will yield the following XML:

```
<books>
  <book name="Fox in socks" price="35.99" />
  <book name="Rocks in box" price="12.99" />
  <book name="Lox in crocks" price="9.99" />
</books>
```

Namespaces

Revisiting an earlier bit of code, look at the following:

```
XElement element = new XElement("name", "Fox in socks");
```

If you look at the constructors for XElement, you will find that there isn't one that takes a string as the first parameter, but you do find a few that take an XName as the first element. A bit more exploration, and you find that XName declares the following conversion:

```
public static implicit operator XName(string localName);
```

This code is therefore the equivalent of this:

```
XElement element = new XElement((XName) "name", "Fox in socks");
```

The string "name" is automatically used to construct an XName, and in the process it sets the LocalName property of the XName class.

This construct gives you an element that has only a local name. If you need to create a name with a namespace, you can use the following:

```
XNamespace myNamespace = "http://www.example.com";
```

```
XElement element = new XElement(myNamespace + "books");
XNamespace defines both an implicit conversion and an addition operator:
public static implicit operator XNamespace(string namespaceName);
public static XName operator +(XNamespace namespaceName, string localName);
```

The conversion is used to create the namespace from a string, and the addition operator is used to create an XName from a namespace and a local name, resulting in the following XML:

```
<books xmlns = "http://www.example.com" />
```

A BRIEF DIGRESSION ABOUT DESIGN

Some of the design decisions made in this area are worth a bit of discussion.

The first is the choice to create XName instances directly from strings (through the overloaded conversion operator) instead of the conventional way of overloading the XElement constructors and methods to take either a string or an XName. It does make it easier to define the methods correctly and yields a bit of economy, but it's harder to understand how everything works. It can be a bit confusing when IntelliSense shows you a method that takes an XName and you can't figure out how to create one.[4]

The second decision was to be able to create XNamespace instances directly from strings. Namespaces are rarely created, and they aren't done inline in the XML creation code, so there is little benefit of not doing this with a simple constructor.

The final decision is to create an XName from an XNamespace and a string, using the addition operator. This allows the developer to write the following:

```
var element = new XElement(myNamespace + "books");
```

which is a little shorter than the alternative but arguably not quite as clear.

```
var element = new XElement(myNamespace.GetName("books"));
```

In sum, I think the overall design is just a little bit too clever and would prefer that it was a bit more conventional even at a slight cost to readability. In writing this section, I discovered that it is legal to write the following, which is just wrong:

```
var element = new XElement((XNamespace)"http://www.example.com" + "books");
```

Namespace Prefixes

It is common to want to use namespace prefixes on nodes instead of full namespaces.

---

[4] I have a rule for APIs I call "no surprises." If you want to create an XName, you first look for an instance constructor (nope), and then you look for a static factory class (also nope). Then you have to go and read the remarks in MSDN to understand what is going on.

```
<bk:books xmlns:bk="http://examplelibrary.com" xmlns:pr="http://pricelibrary.com">
  <bk:book>
    <bk:name>Fox in Sox</bk:name>
    <pr:price>12.95</pr:price>
    <bk:pages>55</bk:pages>
  </bk:book>
</bk:books>
```

You can do this by adding namespace attributes that define the prefixes at the appropriate point, and XElement will use the prefixes in the XML.

```
XNamespace booksNamespace = "http://examplelibrary.com";
XNamespace priceNamespace = "http://pricelibrary.com";

XElement element =
    new XElement(booksNamespace + "books",
        new XAttribute(XNamespace.Xmlns + "bk", booksNamespace.NamespaceName),
        new XAttribute(XNamespace.Xmlns + "pr", priceNamespace.NamespaceName),
        new XElement(booksNamespace + "book",
            new XElement(booksNamespace + "name", "Fox in Sox"),
            new XElement(priceNamespace + "price", "12.95"),
            new XElement(booksNamespace + "pages", "55")
        )
    );
```

Comments

You can easily add comments by adding an XComment instance. The following code adds a comment:

```
XElement element =
    new XElement("books",
        new XElement("book",
            new XComment("name is the short name"),
            new XElement("name", "Fox in socks"),
            new XElement("price", "35.99")
        )
    );
```

```
<books>
  <book>
    <!--name is the short name-->
    <name>Fox in socks</name>
    <price>35.99</price>
  </book>
</books>
```

XText

The XText instance can be used to add text at other places in the XML tree. For example, the following creates a book node that contains both child elements and text:[5]

```
XElement element =
    new XElement("books",
        new XElement("book",
            new XText("book status"),
            new XElement("name", "Fox in socks"),
            new XElement("price", "35.99")
        )
    );
```

This generates the following:

```
<books>
  <book>book status
    <name>Fox in socks</name>
    <price>35.99</price>
  </book>
</books>
```

XDocument

The XElement class can be used for most operations, but in some cases the extra functionality of the XDocument class can be useful. It provides the following:

- A Declaration property, which allows setting the values that will be emitted for the `<?xml ...>` instruction at the top of the generated XML file[6]

- A place to put processing instructions that pass information to applications[7]

- A way to specify the document type

The following is an example of using XDocument:

```
XDocument document = new XDocument(
    new XProcessingInstruction(
        "xml-stylesheet",
        @"type=""text/xsl"" href=""style.xsl"""),
    new XElement("books"));

document.Declaration = new XDeclaration("1.0", "utf-8", "yes");
document.Save(@"%temp%\test.xml");
```

---

[5]Try to avoid this unless you need to have it; it makes parsing much harder.
[6]Because this is part of the stored XML and not strictly part of the XML document, it is generated only if you save the XDocument. It is not present in the return value of the ToString() method.
[7]Processing instructions can also be added to XElements.

This will generate the following file:

```
<?xml version="1.0" encoding="utf-8" standalone="yes"?>
<?xml-stylesheet type="text/xsl" href="style.xsl"?>
  <books />
```

Parsing XML

The previous section wasn't very "Linq-ish," which isn't surprising since the *q* in Linq stands for "query" and creating XML is not at all about querying. This parsing section will lean on Linq much more.

Loading the XML

As with creating XML, XML can be loaded using the XDocument class or XElement class. If you want the extras of XDocument, use that class; otherwise, use XElement.

For both classes, there are two ways to load the XML.

- The XML can be loaded from a file, stream, XmlReader, or TextReader using the Load() method.

- A string of XML text can be parsed using the Parse() method.

The following is an example of the two different ways:

```
XElement element1 = XElement.Load(@"c:\test.xml");
XElement element2 = XElement.Parse("<books><book><name>Fox in Sox</name></book></books>");

Console.WriteLine(element1);
Console.WriteLine(element2);
```

The code to use XDocument would be identical, except access to the XML would be through the Root property of the XDocument.

The XElement Representation

It is important to understand the model and terminology that XElement uses for the XML tree. Consider the following XML:

```
<books>
  <book>
    <name>Fox in Sox</name>
    <price>12.95</price>
     <editions>
      <edition>
        <number>1</number>
        <year>1956</year>
        <price>1.49</price>
      </edition>
      <edition>
        <number>2</number>
        <year>1973</year>
```

```
      <price> 5.59</price>
      </edition>
     </editions>
     <pages> 55</pages>
    </book>
    <book>
     <name> Fox in Crocs</name>
    </book>
</books>
```

This XML is shown in tree form in Figure 29-1.

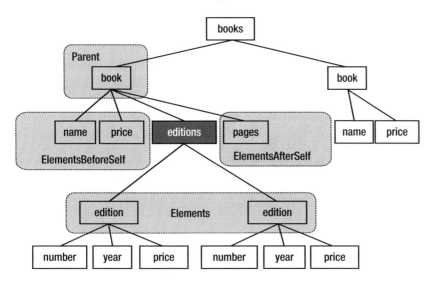

Figure 29-1. *Direct relations of the editions node*

If you declare the following variable:

```
XElement editions;
```

and assign it to the editions element (marked in black) in the middle of the diagram, the related elements will be those in Table 29-1.

Table 29-1. *Elements Related to the editions XElement via Direct Relationships*

Expression	Description
editions.Parent	The parent of the editions node (book)
editions.Elements()	The children of the editions node (edition, edition)
editions.ElementsBeforeSelf()	The siblings of the editions node that occur before the editions node (name, price)
editions.ElementsAfterSelf()	The siblings of the editions node that occur after the editions node (pages)

The Parent and Elements() expressions reference only one level above and one level below the editions element. It is possible to go further, as illustrated in Figure 29-2.

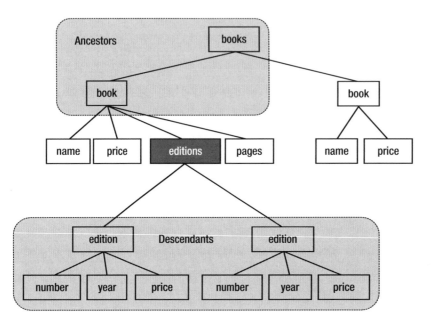

Figure 29-2. *Upper and lower relationships to the editions node*

The upper and lower relationships are described in Table 29-2.

Table 29-2. *Elements Related to the editions XElement via Upper and Lower Relationships*

Expression	Description
editions.Ancestors()	The ancestors of the editions node, in order from closest to farthest to the editions node (book, books)
editions.Descendants()	All descendants of the editions node, in document order (edition, number, year, price, edition, number, year, price)

For all of these methods, there are overloads that accept an XName parameter that returns only elements that match that XName. There are also variants of Ancestors() and Descendants() named AncestorsAndSelf() and DescendantsAndSelf() that encompass the current element.

Node Expressions

All of the previous expressions consider only the XElement instances in the tree. As you saw earlier in the chapter, there can be other nodes in the tree, such as XComment, XText, or XProcessingInstruction. To obtain the XElement instances and the other nodes, use the expressions described in Table 29-3.

Table 29-3. *XElement and All Node Expressions*

XElement Only	XElement and Other Nodes
editions.Elements()	Editions.Nodes()
editions.ElementsBeforeSelf()	Editions.NodesAfterSelf()
editions.ElementsAfterSelf()	Editions.NodesBeforeSelf()
editions.Ancestors()	No node version[8]
editions.AncestorsAndSelf()	No node version
editions.Descendants()	editions.DescendantNodes()
editions.DescendantsAndSelf()	editions.DescendantNodesAndSelf()

XELEMENT METHOD NAMING

The goal of the naming used in XElement was to make the distinction between XElement and other node types clear and to use a common naming pattern between those two operations.

Unfortunately, this resulted in one of the most used operations—accessing the children of a node—using the name Elements rather than the far more obvious name Children. The two names Elements and ElementsBeforeSelf/ElementsAfterSelf both use the term Element, despite the first referring to child elements and the second referring to sibling elements.

My preference would have been to use the natural names for the more often used element expressions (Children, SiblingsBeforeSelf, and SiblingsAfterSelf) and then accept less-natural names for the node expressions.

Finding Nodes in the Tree

Using the books example from the previous section, you want to find the names of all the books. The first version of code you write is the following:

```
var books = booksElement.Elements("book");

foreach (var book in books)
{
    Console.WriteLine(book.Element("name").Value);
}
```

That generates the desired result, but it's a bit clumsy; at the books level, you have to find all the book children, and then from the book level, you have to find all of the name children and then write them out. Perhaps Linq can help out.

---

[8]The tree is expressed only with XElement nodes, so the nodes higher in the tree must be of type XElement.

```
var bookNames = booksElement.Elements("book")
                    .SelectMany(book => book.Elements("name"))
                    .Select(name => name.Value);
```

Hmm. That looks more complicated. What about the following?

```
var bookNames = booksElement
                    .Descendants("name")
                    .Select(name => name.Value);
```

This looks promising; rather than having to walk through the tree level by level, you can reach deep into the tree and extract the values in a single operation. And, in fact, this returns the two book names that you expect. Can you do something similar with price? How about this?

```
var bookPrices = booksElement
                    .Descendants("price")
                    .Select(name => name.Value);
```

This generates four price values, not the two you expect. Not only did it find the two price elements that are children of the book elements, it also found the two price elements that are children of the edition elements.

The problem with this approach is not cases such as this one, since it's pretty obvious that you are not getting the values you expect. The problem is that future changes to the XML may use the same node names in a different context and can cause hard-to-find bugs.

■ **Tip**   Code that uses Descendants() to find nodes by name will break if the node name is reused elsewhere in the document. Use an alternate construct, such as the XPath approach in the next section.

XPathy Goodness

What is needed is a way to uniquely specify the path into the tree, which is commonly done using an XPath expression. At first glance, there is no support for XPath expressions in the XElement world, but it turns out that the support is defined using extension methods in System.Xml.XPath, and a simple using of that namespace will enable that support.[9]

In your first attempt at parsing, you wrote separate statements that walked down the tree to find the node you wanted. XPath allows you to specify the route through the tree through a single string statement.

```
var bookPrices = booksElement
                    .XPathSelectElements("book/price")
                    .Select(name => name.Value);
```

XElement also exposes an XPathEvaluate() method that can evaluate any general XPath expression, but since the expression can return several different types (bool, double, string, or IEnumerable<T>), the method return type is object, which makes it less than convenient to deal with. Consider the following XML that uses attributes to store values:

---

[9]One of the reasons code is written using Descendants() instead of XPath is that the XPath support doesn't show up without adding this using statement. Not that your author would ever do anything like that....

```
<book>
  <price full="15.99" wholesale="7.99" />
</book>
```

Extracting the wholesale price requires the following:

```
var wholesale = ((IEnumerable<object>) book
      .XPathEvaluate("price/@wholesale"))
      .Cast<XAttribute>()
      .Select(att => att.Value)
      .First();
```

That's a lot of code, and given how common attributes are, it's a bit surprising that there is no built-in helper to get them. You can add one, however.

```
public static class XPathHelper
{
    public static IEnumerable<string> XPathSelectAttributes(
        this XElement element,
        string xpathExpression)
    {
        return ((IEnumerable<object>) element.XPathEvaluate(xpathExpression))
            .Cast<XAttribute>()
            .Select(att => att.Value);
    }

    public static string XPathSelectAttribute(
        this XElement element,
        string xpathExpression)
    {
        return XPathSelectAttributes(element, xpathExpression).First();
    }
}
```

With that defined, it is now very simple to pull out the value of an attribute.

```
string wholesale = book.XPathSelectAttribute("price/@wholesale");
```

Namespaces and Parsing

It is fairly common to want to process XML documents that contain namespaces. Consider the following XML:

```
<books xmlns="http://examplelibrary.com">
  <book>
    <name>Fox in Sox</name>
    <price xmlns="http://pricelibrary.com">12.95</price>
    <pages>55</pages>
  </book>
  <book>
```

```
    <name> Fox in Crocs</name>
    <price xmlns = "http://pricelibrary.com">9.95</price>
  </book>
</books>
```

It is tempting to walk up to the books element and ask for all the book children.

```
XElement booksElement = GetExampleXmlWithNamespaces();
foreach (var book in booksElement.Elements("book"))
{
    Console.WriteLine("N: {0}", book);
}
```

That doesn't work, because there are no elements named book in the default namespace. You will need to look in the proper namespaces.

```
XNamespace booksNamespace = "http://examplelibrary.com";
XNamespace priceNamespace = "http://pricelibrary.com";
foreach (var book in booksElement.Elements(booksNamespace + "book"))
{
    Console.WriteLine(book.Element(booksNamespace + "name").Value);
    Console.WriteLine(book.Element(priceNamespace + "price").Value);
}
```

Accessing Element Values

In the previous example, you extracted the string value of the price node from the book node. It would be useful to be able to deal with that as a numeric value instead of a string. You could do it simply with the following code:

```
string temp = book.Element(priceNamespace + "price").Value;
Decimal price = Decimal.Parse(temp);
```

The temporary variable is a bit annoying, however. The XElement class defines explicit conversions to many different data types, so the previous code can be simplified to the following:

```
price = (Decimal) book.Element(priceNamespace + "price");
```

CHAPTER 30

■ ■ ■

Linq to SQL

An object-oriented language such as C# and a SQL relational database have different views of the world. This is sometimes known as an *impedance mismatch*. The concepts of an object in C# and a row in a database seem very analogous, and there have been many attempts to unify them, with Linq to SQL being one of the more successful ones.

Linq to SQL is a very big topic, and covering it thoroughly requires a full book.[1] This chapter is an introduction to using Linq to SQL.

Connecting by Hand

Before there was support to make things easier, a considerable amount of code was written to access databases by hand, something like the following:

```
class Person
{
    public string LastName { get; set; }
    public string PersonType { get; set; }

    public Person (IDataReader reader)
    {
        int i = 0;
        LastName = (string)reader[i++];
        PersonType = (string)reader[i++];
    }
}
class PersonFetcher
{
    List<Person> GetPersons(string query)
    {
        List<Person> results = new List<Person>();

        SqlDataReader reader = Database.ExecuteReader(query);
```

---

[1] Such as *Pro Linq* (Apress, 2010).

```
        while (reader.Read())
        {
            Person person = new Person(reader);
            results.Add(person);
        }

        return results;
    }
}
```

The Person constructor takes the database row and maps it across to properties on the class. This is typical of the kind of boilerplate code that was written to access databases. One big drawback is that it works only if the query returns a specific set of columns (in this case, name, age, and date of birth). If you need to have the address information, you either have to modify the class (and all the queries that use it) to now return address information, create a new class (PersonIncludingAddress), or modify the Person class so that it holds the address information if it was returned by the query or null otherwise.[2]

Another obvious drawback is that you have to write the code to perform all the operations, which isn't the most exciting part of the project. It is, however, easy to figure out what the code is doing and easy to debug, and you can take advantage of the power of the database to do efficient queries.

Query and Class Generation

It seems like you can give the user some help. Here you will give the user a way to specify a query and some other information through a few wizard dialogs, and you will create a class that will hold the query result and some way of filling that class. Then the user can write code like this:

```
PersonDataSetTableAdapters.PersonTableAdapter personTableAdapter =
    new PersonDataSetTableAdapters.PersonTableAdapter();

PersonDataSet.PersonDataTable personDataTable = personTableAdapter.GetData();

foreach (PersonDataSet.PersonRow personRow in personDataTable.Rows)
{
    Console.WriteLine(personRow.PersonType);
}
```

It is nice that you don't have to create a Person class or write the method to fetch the data and create employees, but it is not without disadvantages. It's not clear from this code what query the GetData() method is using, and if you change the definition of the underlying Person table to include a new column, you will have to update each query that references the table. This may take longer than adding a column took when you did it all by hand.

There's also another problem. One day you get a request to return a list of all the Person records where the person is an employee. That's a simple filter to write the following:

```
PersonDataSetTableAdapters.PersonTableAdapter personTableAdapter =
    new PersonDataSetTableAdapters.PersonTableAdapter();
```

---

[2] This can quite confusing; you might have a property that is null sometimes because there is no data in it and null other times because the query didn't fetch any data for it. Good luck figuring that out.

```
PersonDataSet.PersonDataTable personDataTable = personTableAdapter.GetData();

List<PersonDataSet.PersonRow> employees = new List<PersonDataSet.PersonRow>();
foreach (PersonDataSet.PersonRow personRow in personDataTable.Rows)
{
    if (personRow.PersonType == "EM")
    {
        employees.Add(personRow);
    }
}
foreach (PersonDataSet.PersonRow personRow in employees)
{
    Console.WriteLine(personRow.LastName);
}
```

When you look at the employee list, you find that it has all the names you expected. Congratulations, you have just fetched nearly 20,000 person rows from your database and then thrown away all except 273 of them. And you fetched all of the data for each person, even though you were interested only in the last name. Your query takes much longer than it needs to, takes up more network bandwidth, and puts more load on your server.

The "right way" is to go back to your dataset designer, create a new dataset type, create a query that returns only the last names of the employees, and then use that. However, if you do that, you'll soon end up with a large number of datasets and adapters, and it will be hard to figure out which one you want.

■ **Note**   Some of you are undoubtedly saying, "No, you should be using stored procedures." Hold on to that thought; I'll get back to it later in this chapter.

What is needed is a way to execute queries that is simple, is easy to understand, and doesn't create a lot of extraneous classes. Maybe you can apply some Linq techniques to the scenario.

Linq to SQL

If you have all the rows from the Person table in a List <Person>, then you can use a simple Linq query to find the employees.

```
PersonDataSetTableAdapters.PersonTableAdapter personTableAdapter =
    new PersonDataSetTableAdapters.PersonTableAdapter();

PersonDataSet.PersonDataTable personDataTable = personTableAdapter.GetData();

List<PersonDataSet.PersonRow> persons = new List<PersonDataSet.PersonRow>();
foreach (PersonDataSet.PersonRow personRow in personDataTable.Rows)
{
    persons.Add(personRow);
}

var employees = persons.Where(person => person.PersonType == "EM");
```

The query part is much nicer; you can now understand exactly what the query is doing. The setup code is complicated, and you're still fetching all the rows. Since you are always returning all of the rows, you don't need the complicated process of setting up a query. You can just go directly to the table. So, you can simplify the setup code quite a bit.

```
AdventureWorksDataContext context = new AdventureWorksDataContext();

var employeeLastNames = context.Persons
                    .Where(person => person.PersonType == "EM")
                    .Select(person => person.LastName);

foreach (var lastName in employeeLastNames)
{
    Console.WriteLine(lastName);
}
```

That is much simpler, and it's very obvious what you are doing. And you have also solved the problem of fetching all the rows, through a very clever bit of code.

In Chapter 28, I discussed that Linq execution doesn't work quite the way it looks when you first see it; the definition of a Linq expression creates only the expression, but the evaluation is deferred. You also saw how the implementations of the `OrderBy()` and `TheyBy()` operations cooperated to perform their operations together.

The same techniques are used here, except in this case the `Where()` and `Select()` operations cooperate with the `Persons` table to create a query definition from what you wrote and send that definition to your database server. In this case, they send the following SQL query to the database server:

```
select LastName
from person
where PersonType = 'EM'
```

That is the coolness of Linq to SQL; you can write what looks like client-side C# code and have it execute efficiently on the database. If you prefer a SQL-style syntax, you can write it using the same expression as follows:

```
var employeeLastNames =
    from person in context.Persons
    where person.PersonType == "EM"
    select person.LastName;
```

■ **Note**   All of the following examples assume you have already created a connection to the AdventureWorks sample SQL database and that you have used the Visual Studio database designer to drag and drop the tables and other database entities onto the design surface.

Joining Tables

It is simple to join tables, as the following example demonstrates:

```
var salesByPerson =
    context.Persons.Join(context.SalesPersons,
                         person => person.BusinessEntityID,
                         salesPerson => salesPerson.BusinessEntityID,
                         (person, salesPerson) => new
                         {
                             FirstName = person.FirstName,
                             SalesLastYear = salesPerson.SalesLastYear
                         } );
```

Or, you can do it using the SQL syntax:

```
var salesByPerson =
    from person in context.Persons
    join salesPerson in context.SalesPersons
    on person.BusinessEntityID equals salesPerson.BusinessEntityID
    select new
    {
        FirstName = person.FirstName,
        SalesLastYear = salesPerson.SalesLastYear
    };
```

As is expected, the expression is converted into a SQL join statement and shipped off to the server for execution.

WHY "EQUALS"?

You may have noticed the strange use of `equals` in the SQL syntax version. Both versions are going to hook into the `Join()` method, which takes four parameters: the table to join, two lambdas to extract the key on which the tables will be joined, and then the value to return from the join. The method requires two lambdas because each one pulls from a different source (in this example, one from `person` and one from `salesPerson`). In the Linq to Objects case, going from the following expression:

```
person.BusinessEntityID == salesPerson.BusinessEntityID
```

to the two lambas would have required a significant amount of overhead, so it was decided to use "equals" instead.

How It Works

In Chapter 28, which covered Linq to Objects, you saw that Linq defers the generation of values until they are asked for. You also saw that the `OrderBy()` and `ThenBy()` operations cooperate to perform a single operation.

Linq to SQL uses a similar technique but pushes it further; not only does it enable deferred execution, it also enables execution of the entire expression somewhere else. Here's the earlier example:

```
var employeeLastNames = context.Persons
                    .Where(person => person.PersonType == "EM")
                    .Select(person => person.LastName);
```

Starting at the root, the Persons property is of type Table <Person>, and it implements the IQueryable <Person> interface. Just as IEnumerable <T> is the main interface used by Linq to Objects, IQueryable <T> is the main interface used by Linq to SQL. IQueryable <T> defines three members.

- An ExpressionTree, which defines the operations to perform

- An ElementType, which defines the type of the elements returned by the expression

- A Provider, which defines the query provider, the part of the system that will handle the creation and execution of the query

Walking through the simple query, the operations are as follows:

1. Context.Persons exposes IQueryable <Person>.

2. The Queryable.Where() extension method accepts the queryable from step 1 and an Expression and also exposes IQueryable <Person>.

3. The Queryable.Select() extension method accepts the queryable from the Where() method and an Expression and exposes IQueryable <string>.

4. The IQueryable <string> instance is assigned to the employeeLastNames variable.

This is a bit different from the Linq to Objects approach; in this case, the Where() and Select() methods are taking this new Expression type. The Where part of the statement, as follows:

```
.Where(person => person.PersonType == "EM")
```

is roughly translated into the following:[3]

```
ParameterExpression parameterExpression1 =
        Expression.Parameter(typeof(Person), "person");
var binaryExpression = Expression.Equal(
    Expression.Property(parameterExpression1, Person.get_PersonType),
    Expression.Constant("EM", typeof(string)))
```

The resulting binaryExpression encodes the person.PersonType == "EM" expression, and that expression is then passed to somebody who can translate it into the proper form.

---

[3] I've simplified some of it to make it easier to understand.

LINQ TO OBJECTS VS. LINQ TO SQL

When the C# compiler encounters an expression such as the following:

```
person.PersonType == "EM"
```

it processes it in two steps. In the first (parsing) step, it takes the expression and converts it into an expression tree. Once it has verified that the program is correct, it converts the expression tree into the .NET IL codes that will actually implement the expression (in this case, a comparison).

In the Linq to SQL scenario, only the first half of the process is performed so that the result is the syntax tree. This syntax tree can then be passed to something else that can implement the expression; in the Linq to SQL case, it will be converted to a SQL query instead of .NET IL.

Because the expression tree is a generalized representation, it can be used in other scenarios outside of SQL; there are Linq providers to Excel, to SharePoint, or even to a REST interface such as Amazon's book search.

Modifying Data

Linq supports all of the usual CRUD (Create/Read/Update/Delete) database operations. Here's an example of performing an insert operation:

```
public static void Insert()
{
    AdventureWorksDataContext context = new AdventureWorksDataContext();

    Currency currency = new Currency();
    currency.CurrencyCode = "PNT";
    currency.Name = "Peanuts";
    currency.ModifiedDate = DateTime.Now;

    context.Currencies.InsertOnSubmit(currency);

    context.SubmitChanges();
}
```

All the operations that modify data on a single context are deferred; the changes you make are held locally in the context, until you commit them all at once by calling SubmitChanges(). Not surprisingly, if you forget to set a required value, an exception will be thrown when SubmitChanges() is called.

■ **Note** An obvious question here is "Are all the changes performed by SubmitChanges() wrapped in a transaction? The answer is "Yes, yes they are." If you want to expand the scope of a transaction to encompass more operations, you can put all the operations inside a TransactionScope, and the Submit operation will use that transaction scope instead.

Updating an object is even easier than inserting one.

```csharp
public static void Update()
{
    AdventureWorksDataContext context = new AdventureWorksDataContext();

    var peanuts = context.Currencies
                    .Where(currency => currency.CurrencyCode == "PNT")
                    .Single();

    peanuts.Name = "Roasted Peanuts";

    context.SubmitChanges();
}
```

In this case, all you have to do is modify the value of the Name property; the property setter is smart enough to remember that the change was made and then execute it when SubmitChanges() is called.

Finally, you come to the delete operation.

```csharp
public static void Delete()
{
    AdventureWorksDataContext context = new AdventureWorksDataContext();

    var peanuts = context.Currencies
                    .Where(currency => currency.CurrencyCode == "PNT")
                    .Single();

    context.Currencies.DeleteOnSubmit(peanuts);

    context.SubmitChanges();
}
```

Stored Procedures

There are two broad approaches to performing database operations. The first is to treat the database as a black box that can execute SQL statements and keep all of the details about the operations in the client program. The second is to implement the low-level database operations in the database using stored procedures and present an abstracted view to the client program.[4]

The arguments for and against each approach would fill a decent-sized book.[5] Very generally, stored procedures tend to be used for bigger, "enterprise-scale" systems, and direct SQL access tends to be used for smaller approaches, but this is not universally true. And some systems use direct access initially and then migrate to stored procedures once they figure out what operations are required.

One of the advantages of Linq to SQL is that you can just write the queries in C# code, and it's up to the system to figure out how to execute them and get the data back to you. If you need to modify them, you just change the code, recompile, and you are golden.

That same flexibility isn't present if you are using stored procedures on the database side, but you can still use Linq to SQL to talk to them.

---

[4]OK, so there's a third, where the client talks to another abstraction, a server layer that exposes specific operations. The server layer might be implemented talking directly to the database or through stored procedures.
[5]Followed by a daylong symposium, an escalating series of blog articles, and countless angry forum posts. Seriously.

```
public static void OutputManagerEmployees(int managerId)
{
    AdventureWorksDataContext context = new AdventureWorksDataContext();

    var employees = context.uspGetManagerEmployees(managerId);
    foreach (var employee in employees)
    {
        Console.WriteLine(employee.FirstName);
    }
}
```

The uspGetManagerEmployees stored procedure was added to the database designer in the same way the tables were added (in other words, via drag and drop), and the designer nicely wrapped the stored procedure so that it can be directly called from the context. That certainly is convenient, and I can even do a little work on the results.

```
public static void OutputManagerEmployeesAndFilter(int managerId)
{
    AdventureWorksDataContext context = new AdventureWorksDataContext();

    var mark = context.uspGetManagerEmployees(managerId)
                .Where(emp => emp.FirstName == "Mark")
                .First();
    Console.WriteLine(mark.LastName);
}
```

This method writes out the last name of the first employee of the manager named Mark. How does it work, and is it good code?

Well, the return type of uspGetManagerEmployees() is not an IQueryable but an ISingleResult, which implements IEnumerable. It is *not* a Linq to SQL expression but a simple method that returns a sequence of results, which you then filter with a Linq to Objects Where() expression.

That makes this bad code; you are grabbing a bunch of employees out of the database, shipping them across to the program, and then choosing a single one.

■ **Note**   This is one of the drawbacks of using stored procedures; it's easy to add a Linq to Objects expression to the result of the stored procedure, and it's not obvious what is really happening.

Linq to Entities

If you need to perform more complex database operations, such as joining tables together, consider using Linq to Entities instead of Linq to SQL. Detailed documentation about Linq to Entities can be found on MSDN.

CHAPTER 31

■ ■ ■

Other Language Details

This chapter deals with some miscellaneous details about the language, including how to use the Main()
function, how the preprocessor works, and how to write literal values.

The Main Function

The simplest version of the Main() function should already be familiar from earlier in the book.

```
using System;
class Test
{
    public static void Main()
    {
        Console.WriteLine("Hello, Universe!");
    }
}
```

Returning an Int Status

It may sometimes be useful to return a status from the Main() function, particularly if the program is called
programmatically, because the return status can be used to determine whether the application executed
successfully. This is done by declaring the return type of Main() as an integer.

```
using System;
class Test
{
    public static int Main()
    {
        Console.WriteLine("Hello, Universe!");
        return(0);
    }
}
```

Command-Line Parameters

The command-line parameters to an application can be accessed by declaring the Main() function with a string array as a parameter. The parameters can then be processed by indexing the array.[1]

```
using System;
class Test
{
    public static void Main(string[] args)
    {
        foreach (string arg in args)
        {
            Console.WriteLine("Arg: {0}", arg);
        }
    }
}
```

Multiple Mains

It is sometimes useful for testing purposes to include a static function in a class that tests the class to make sure it does the right thing. In C#, this static test function can be written as a Main() function, which makes automating such tests easy.

If there is a single main() function encountered during a compilation, the C# compiler will use it. If there is more than one main()function, the class that contains the desired Main() can be specified on the command line with the /main:<classname> option.

```
// error
using System;
class Complex
{
    static int Main()
    {
        // test code here
        Console.WriteLine("Console: Passed");
        return(0);
    }
}
class Test
{
    public static void Main(string[] args)
    {
        foreach (string arg in args)
        {
            Console.WriteLine(arg);
        }
    }
}
```

---

[1] There is no command-line parser in .NET, but there are many free libraries available.

Compiling this file with /main:Complex will use the test version of Main(), whereas compiling with /main:Test will use the real version of Main(). Compiling it without either will result in an error.

The Main() declared in the Complex type isn't declared public. In fact, there is no requirement that Main() should be public, and keeping it private is useful in cases such as these, where the test function shouldn't be visible to users of the class.

Preprocessing

The most important thing to remember about the C# preprocessor is that it doesn't exist. The features in the C/C++ processor are either totally absent or present in a limited form. In the "absent" category are include files and the ability to do text replacement with #define. The #ifdef and associated directives are present in a slightly modified form and can be used to control the compilation of code.

Getting rid of the macro version (something like #define MYINT int) of #define allows the programmer to understand more clearly what the program is saying. A name that isn't familiar must come from one of the namespaces, and there's no need to hunt through include files to find it. The C# code means what it says it means.[2]

Getting rid of macro preprocessing and #include also enables a simplified compilation structure and faster compilation, and there is no need to create a separate header file and keep it in sync with the implementation file.

When C# source files are compiled, the order of the compilation of the individual files is unimportant, and it is equivalent to them all being in one big file. There is no need for forward declarations or worrying about the order of #includes.

Preprocessing Directives

The preprocessing directives that are supported include those shown in Table 31-1.

Table 31-1. *C# Preprocessing Directives*

Directive	Description
#define identifier	Defines an identifier. Note that a value can't be set for it; it can merely be defined. Identifiers can also be defined via the command line.
#undef identifier	Undefines an identifier.
#if expression	Code in this section is compiled if the expression is true.
#elif expression	Else-if construct. If the previous directive wasn't taken and the expression is true, code in this section is compiled.
#else	If the previous directive wasn't taken, code in this section is compiled.
#endif	Marks the end of a section.

---

[2]In C++, you can define true to 0 and false to 1 if you want.

Here's an example of how they might be used:

```
#define DEBUGLOG
using System;
class Test
{
    public static void Main()
    {
        #if DEBUGLOG
        Console.WriteLine("In Main - Debug Enabled");
        #else
        Console.WriteLine("In Main - No Debug");
        #endif
    }
}
```

#define and #undef must precede any "real code" in a file, or an error occurs. The previous example can't be written as follows:

```
// error
using System;
class Test
{
    #define DEBUGLOG
    public static void Main()
    {
        #if DEBUGLOG
        Console.WriteLine("In Main - Debug Enabled");
        #else
        Console.WriteLine("In Main - No Debug");
        #endif
    }
}
```

C# also supports the Conditional attribute for controlling function calls based upon preprocessor identifiers; see Chapter 39 for more information.

Preprocessor Expressions

The operators shown in Table 31-2 can be used in preprocessor expressions.

Table 31-2. *C# Preprocessor Expressions*

Operator	Description
! ex	Expression is true if ex is false
ex == value	Expression is true if ex is equal to value
ex != value	Expression is true if ex is not equal to value
ex1 && ex2	Expression is true if both ex1 and ex2 are true
ex1 || ex2	Expression is true if either ex1 or ex2 are true

Parentheses can be used to group expressions.

```
#if !(DEBUGLOG && (TESTLOG || USERLOG))
```

If TESTLOG or USERLOG is defined and DEBUGLOG is defined, then the expression within the parentheses is true, which is then negated by the !.

Inline Warning Control

The C# compiler provides the ability to suppress compiler warnings using the /nowarn switch. Warnings that are suppressed on the command line are disabled for all files, but it may be desirable in some situations to disable a single instance of a warning. For example, if a program uses a method that has been marked as obsolete:

```
class Program
{
    static void Main(string[] args)
    {
        ObsoleteMethod();
    }
    [Obsolete]
    static void ObsoleteMethod()
    {
    }
}
```

the program will generate a warning message:

```
'Program.ObsoleteMethod()' is obsolete
```

In this case, it may be useful to disable that warning message, since the presence of an expected warning can hide other warnings.[3] This can be done by adding a #pragma warning disable directive to the program.

```
class Program
{
    static void Main(string[] args)
    {
#pragma warning disable 612
        ObsoleteMethod();
#pragma warning restore 612
    }
    [Obsolete]
    static void ObsoleteMethod()
    {
    }
}
```

The disable directive turns off the warning, and then the restore directive turns it back on. It is possible to disable multiple warnings by separating the warning numbers by commas.

---

[3]It's a pretty good idea to use the /warnaserror compiler option, which doesn't allow you to ignore any warnings. In that case, you may need to disable some warnings.

■ **Note**   If you are using Visual Studio, the warning number does not appear in the error window, so it's not obvious what the number of a warning is. If you choose View ➤ Output, the output window will be shown, and that will include the full text of the warning including the warning number.

Other Preprocessor Functions

In addition to the #if and #define functions, there are a few other preprocessor functions that can be used.

#warning and #error

#warning and #error allow warnings or errors to be reported during the compilation process. All text following #warning or #error will be output when the compiler reaches that line.

For a section of code, you could do the following:

```
#warning Check algorithm with John
```

This would result in the string "Check algorithm with John" being output when the line was compiled.

#line

The #line directive provides two different capabilities.

First, it can be used to specify the line number and/or source filename to report when the compiler encounters warnings or errors. This can be useful in cases where user-written code is folded in with user-generated code; by specifying the line number and the filename of the user-written code, the user will see the error in their code, not the combined file. Either the line number or both the line number and the filename can be specified.

```
#line 255
#line 300 "UserCode.cs"
```

The line number and filename can be reset to the default behavior using this:

```
#line 255 default
```

Second, #line can also be used to hide data from debugger stepping.

```
#line hidden
```

The debugger will then skip all subsequent lines until another #line directive is encountered.[4] This is also very useful if the code is machine-generated.

#region

The #region and #endregion directives are used to group code into named sections, which can then be collapsed or expanded inside an editor. For example, if a class implements the IXmlSerializable interface, it can be useful to group the implementation methods in a region.

---

[4]There is no #line show to directly turn off hidden, so you are stuck using #line default or setting the specific line number or filename.

```
class Employee: IXmlSerializable
{
    public string Name { get; set; }
    public Decimal Age { get; set; }

    public Employee(String name, Decimal age)
    {
        Name = name;
        Age = age;
    }

    #region IXmlSerializable

    // IXmlSerializable methods go here...
    #endregion
}
```

This region can then be collapsed so it is out of the way when looking at the other members of the type.

REGION-ITIS

Regions have been used in many different ways in C# code. In earlier versions of C# (before the introduction of partial classes), they were used to hide machine-generated code, which was a good thing. Grouping a set of interface methods together is also a good thing.

In other cases, regions are used to organize properties into one section, methods into another section, and constructors into a third. I find that such use makes it harder to read the class, since it's common to want to see items in these separate regions at once. If you find yourself wanting to use regions in this way, it usually indicates that your class is getting too big and should be broken into smaller classes.

Lexical Details

The lexical details of the language deal with things that are important at the single-character level: how to write numerical constants, identifiers, and other low-level entities of the language.

Identifiers

An identifier is a name that is used for some program element, such as a variable or a function.

Identifiers must have a letter or an underscore as the first character, and the remainder of the identifier can also include numeric characters.[5] Unicode characters can be specified using \udddd, where dddd specifies the hex value of the Unicode character.

---

[5]It's actually a fair bit more complicated than this, since C# has Unicode support. Briefly, letters can be any Unicode letter character, and characters other than the underscore (_) can also be used for combinations. See the online C# Language Reference for a full description.

When using code that has been written in other languages, some names might be C# keywords. To write such a name, an "at" character (@) can be placed before the name, which merely indicates to C# that the name is not a keyword but an identifier.

Similarly, use @ to use keywords as identifiers.

```
class Test
{
    public void @checked()
    {
    }
}
```

This class declares a member function named checked. Using this feature so that identifiers can be the same as built-in identifiers is not recommended because of the confusion it can create.

Keywords

Keywords are reserved words that cannot be used as identifiers. The keywords in C# are shown in Table 31-3.

Table 31-3. *C# Keywords*

abstract	as	base	bool	break
byte	case	catch	char	checked
class	const	continue	decimal	default
delegate	do	double	else	enum
event	explicit	extern	false	finally
fixed	float	for	foreach	goto
If	implicit	in	int	interface
internal	is	lock	long	namespace
new	null	object	operator	out
override	params	private	protected	public
readonly	ref	return	sbyte	sealed
short	sizeof	stackalloc	static	string
struct	switch	this	throw	true
try	typeof	uint	ulong	unchecked
unsafe	ushort	using	virtual	void
volatile	while			

C# also defines contextual keywords. A contextual keyword can be used as a variable, class, or property name, but when it is used in a specific context, it becomes a keyword. The partial contextual keyword is used in the specification of a partial class, where is used to define generic contraints, yield is used to implement an iterator, and value is used in a set property block to access the incoming value. Table 31-4 lists the contextual keywords.

Table 31-4. *C# Contextual Keywords*

add	dynamic	get	global	partial
remove	set	value	var	where
yield				

Literals

Literals are the way in which values are written for variables.

Boolean

There are two boolean literals: true and false.

Integer

Integer literals are written simply by writing the numeric value. Integer literals that are small enough to fit into the int data type[6] are treated as ints; if they are too big to fit into an int, they will be created as the smallest type of uint, long, or ulong in which the literal will fit.

Here are some integer literal examples:

```
123
-15
```

Integer literals can also be written in hexadecimal format, by placing 0x in front of the constant.

```
0xFFFF
0x12AB
```

Real

Real literals are used for the types float, double, and decimal. Float literals have f or F after them; double literals have d or D after them and are the default when nothing is specified, and decimal literals have m or M after them.

Exponential notation can be used by appending e followed by the exponent to the real literal.

Here are some examples:

```
1.345              // double constant
-8.99e12F          // float constant
15.66m             // decimal constant
```

Character

A character literal is a single character enclosed in single quotes, such as x. Table 31-5 shows the supported escape sequences.

---

[6]See the "Basic Data Types" section in Chapter 3.

Table 31-5. *Character Escape Sequences*

Escape Sequence	Description
\'	Single quote.
\"	Double quote. Double quotes do not need to be escaped if they are part of a character literal.
\\	Backslash.
\0	Null.
\a	Alert.
\b	Backspace.
\f	Form feed.
\n	Newline.
\r	Carriage return.
\t	Tab.
\v	Vertical tab.
\xdddd	Character dddd, where d is a hexadecimal digit.
\udddd	Unicode character dddd, where d is a hexadecimal digit.
\Udddddddd	Unicode character dddddddd, where d is a hexadecimal digit.

String

String literals are written as a sequence of characters enclosed in double quotes, such as "Hello". All of the character escape sequences are supported within strings.

Strings cannot span multiple lines, but the same effect can be achieved by concatenating them.

```
string s = "What is your favorite color?" +
           "Blue. No, Red. ";
```

When this code is compiled, a single string constant will be created, consisting of the two strings concatenated.

Verbatim Strings

Verbatim strings allow some strings to be specified more simply.

If a string contains the backslash character, such as a filename, a verbatim string can be used to turn off the support for escape sequences. Instead of writing something like this:

```
string s = "c:\\Program Files\\Microsoft Office\\Office";
```

the following can be written:

```
string s = @"c:\Program Files\Microsoft Office\Office";
```

The verbatim string syntax is also useful if the code is generated by a program and there is no way to constrain the contents of the string. All characters can be represented within such a string, though any occurrence of the double-quote character must be doubled.

```
string s = @"She said, ""Hello""";
```

In addition, strings that are written with the verbatim string syntax can span multiple lines, and any whitespace (spaces, tabs, and newlines) is preserved.

```
using System;
class Test
{
    public static void Main()
    {
        string s = @"
        C: Hello, Miss?
        O: What do you mean, 'Miss'?
        C: I'm Sorry, I have a cold. I wish to make a complaint.";
        Console.WriteLine(s);
    }
}
```

Comments

Comments in C# are denoted by a double slash for a single-line comment, and /* and */ denote the beginning and ending of a multiline comment.

```
// This is a single-line comment
/*
 * Multiline comment here
 */
```

C# also supports a special type of comment that is used to associate documentation with code; those comments are described in Chapter 38.

Expanding Internal Accessibility

The C# accessibility options (public, protected, internal, and private) generally provide sufficient flexibility in allowing other classes access to a class's members. There are two scenarios where the provided accessibilities are insufficient.

- A group of classes that are all conceptually in one namespace may be split across two assemblies if one class is large and rarely used.

- Tests are being written against a class, and the developer would prefer to keep the class methods internal.

C# provides a way to modify the specified accessibility. The InternalsVisibleTo attribute can be used to specify that the classes in another assembly be treated as if they were in the same assembly when establishing accessibility. The attribute is declared as follows:

```
[assembly: InternalsVisibleTo("ParserUnitTest")]
internal class Parser
{
    internal void Parse(string input);
}
```

A class in the ParserUnitTest assembly is now allowed to call Parser.Parse(). If one of the assemblies is signed, they both must be signed, and the public key of the assembly must be listed in the attribute.

```
[assembly: InternalsVisibleTo(
    "ParserUnitTest, PublicKey=<public-key-of-ParserUnitTest>")]
```

■ ■ ■

CHAPTER 32

Making Friends with the
.NET Framework

The information in the preceding chapters is sufficient for writing objects that will function in the .NET Runtime, but those objects may not work as expected when used in collections or when debugged. This chapter details a few ways to improve this situation.

ToString()

Overriding the ToString() function defined in the object class gives a nice representation of the values in an object. If this isn't done, object.ToString() will merely return the name of the class, which will make debugging more difficult.

Here's an example of the default behavior:

```
using System;
public class Employee
{
    public Employee(int id, string name)
    {
        m_id = id;
        m_name = name;
    }
    int m_id;
    string m_name;
}
class Test
{
    public static void Main()
    {
        Employee herb = new Employee(555, "Herb");
        Console.WriteLine("Employee: {0}", herb);
    }
}
```

The preceding code will result in the following:

```
Employee: Employee
```

By overriding ToString(), the representation can be much more useful.

```csharp
using System;
public class Employee
{
    public Employee(int id, string name)
    {
        m_id = id;
        m_name = name;
    }
    public override string ToString()
    {
        return(String.Format("{0}({1})", m_name, m_id));
    }
    int m_id;
    string m_name;
}
class Test
{
    public static void Main()
    {
        Employee herb = new Employee(555, "Herb");
        Console.WriteLine("Employee: {0}", herb);
    }
}
```

This gives a far better result:

```
Employee: Herb(555)
```

When Console.WriteLine() needs to convert an object to a string representation, it will call the ToString() virtual function, which will forward to an object's specific implementation. If more control over formatting is desired, such as implementing a floating-point class with different formats, the IFormattable interface can be overridden. IFormattable is covered in the "Custom Object Formatting" section of Chapter 38.

Object Equality

Some classes have a strong concept of equality; for example, an Employee class might have a unique identifier associated with it. Such classes should expose that concept so that other classes can use it to check for equality. There are several different ways in which object equality can be defined in C#.

- By overriding Equals(object obj)

- By overloading the == and != operators

- By implementing IEquatable<T>.Equals(T other)

The first two ways were present in all versions of C#. The first one unfortunately has a parameter of type object; this means that calling Equals() with a value type results in an unnecessary boxing and unboxing operation. It also permits you to write interesting code such as the following:

```csharp
bool result = 13.Equals("aardvark");
```

The overloaded operators (== and !=) are strongly typed and therefore do not suffer from the same issues. With the introduction of generics, the strongly typed IEquatable<T> interface was introduced, and the original version of Equals() is used only if called with a parameter of type object.

It is important that all of these implementations match. Here's an example that extends Employee:

```
public class Employee: IEquatable<Employee>
{
    public Employee(int id, string name)
    {
        m_id = id;
        m_name = name;
    }
    public bool Equals(Employee other)
    {
        return this == other;
    }
    public override bool Equals(object obj)
    {
        return Equals((Employee)obj);
    }
    public static bool operator ==(Employee emp1, Employee emp2)
    {
        if (emp1.m_id != emp2.m_id)
        {
            return false;
        }
        else if (emp1.m_name != emp2.m_name)
        {
            return false;
        }
        return true;
    }
    public static bool operator !=(Employee emp1, Employee emp2)
    {
        return !(emp1 == emp2);
    }
    int m_id;
    string m_name;
}
class Test
{
    public static void Main()
    {
        Employee herb = new Employee(555, "Herb");
        Employee herbClone = new Employee(555, "Herb");
        Employee andy = new Employee(123, "Andy");
        Console.WriteLine("Equal: {0}", herb.Equals(herbClone));
        Console.WriteLine("Equal: {0}", herb == herbClone);
        Console.WriteLine("Equal: {0}", herb == andy);
    }
}
```

This will produce the following output:

```
Equal: True
Equal: True
Equal: False
```

In this case, `operator==()` and `operator!=()` have also been overloaded, which allows the operator syntax to be used in the last line of `Main()`. These operators must be overloaded in pairs; they cannot be overloaded separately.[1]

Hashes and GetHashCode()

The .NET Framework includes two related classes, the pregeneric `HashTable` class and the `Dictionary<T>` class, which are very useful for doing fast lookup of objects by a key. They work by using a hash function, which produces an integer "key" for a specific instance of a class. This key is a condensed version of the contents of the instance. While different instances can have the same hash code, it's a rare occurrence.

A hash table uses this key as a way of drastically limiting the number of objects that must be searched to find a specific object in a collection of objects. It does this by first getting the hash value of the object, which will eliminate all objects with a different hash code, leaving only those with the same hash code to be searched. Since the number of instances with that hash code is small, searches can be much quicker.

That's the basic idea. For a more detailed explanation, please refer to a good data structures and algorithms book.[2] Hashes are a tremendously useful construct.

The `GetHashCode()` function should be overridden in user-written classes because the values returned by `GetHashCode()` are required to be related to the value returned by `Equals()`. Two objects that are the same by `Equals()` must always return the same hash code.

The default implementation of `GetHashCode()` doesn't work this way, and therefore it must be overridden to work correctly. If not overridden, the hash code will be identical only for the same instance of an object, and a search for an object that is equal but not the same instance will fail. It is therefore very important to override `GetHashCode()` for all objects that override equality.

Here I extend the example to support `GetHashCode()`:

```csharp
public class Employee: IEquatable<Employee>
{
    public Employee(int id, string name)
    {
        m_id = id;
        m_name = name;
    }
    public bool Equals(Employee other)
    {
        return this == other;
    }
    public override bool Equals(object obj)
    {
        return Equals((Employee)obj);
    }
}
```

---

[1] This is required for two reasons. The first is that if a user uses ==, they can expect != to work as well. The other is to support nullable types, for which a == b does *not* imply !(a != b).

[2] I've always liked Robert Sedgewick's *Algorithms*.

```csharp
    public override int GetHashCode()
    {
        return m_id.GetHashCode();
    }
    public static bool operator ==(Employee emp1, Employee emp2)
    {
        if (emp1.m_id != emp2.m_id)
        {
            return false;
        }
        else if (emp1.m_name != emp2.m_name)
        {
            return false;
        }
        return true;
    }
    public static bool operator !=(Employee emp1, Employee emp2)
    {
        return !(emp1 == emp2);
    }
    int m_id;
    string m_name;
}
class Test
{
    public static void Main()
    {
        Employee herb = new Employee(555, "Herb");
        Employee george = new Employee(123, "George");
        Employee frank = new Employee(111, "Frank");
        Dictionary<Employee, string> employees =
                    new Dictionary<Employee, string>();
        employees.Add(herb, "414 Evergreen Terrace");
        employees.Add(george, "2335 Elm Street");
        employees.Add(frank, "18 Pine Bluff Road");
        Employee herbClone = new Employee(555, "Herb");
        string address = employees[herbClone];
        Console.WriteLine("{0} lives at {1}", herbClone, address);
    }
}
```

The code outputs the following:

```
Herb(555) lives at 414 Evergreen Terrace
```

In the Employee class, the id member is unique, so it is used for the hash code. In the Main() function, several employees are created, and they are then used as the key values to store the addresses of the employees.

If there isn't a single unique field, the hash code should be created out of the values contained in a function. If the employee class didn't have a unique identifier but did have fields for name and address, the hash function could use those. The following shows a hash function that could be used:[3]

```
public class Employee
{
    public Employee(string name, string address)
    {
        m_name = name;
        m_address = address;
    }
    public override int GetHashCode()
    {
        return m_name.GetHashCode() ^ m_address.GetHashCode();
    }
    string m_name;
    string m_address;
}
```

This implementation of GetHashCode() simply XORs the hash codes of the elements together and returns them.

Design Guidelines

Any class that overrides Equals() should also override GetHashCode(). In fact, the C# compiler will issue an error if you forget. The reason for this error is that it prevents strange and difficult-to-debug behavior when the class is used in a Dictionary or Hashtable.

These classes depend on the fact that all instances that are equal have the same hash value. The default implementation of GetHashCode(), however, returns a value that is unique on a per-instance basis. If this implementation was not overridden, it's very easy to put objects in a hash table but not be able to retrieve them.

Value Type Guidelines

The System.ValueType class contains a version of Equals() that works for all value types, but this version of Equals() works through reflection and is therefore slow. It's therefore recommended that an Equals() be overridden for all value types.[4]

Reference Type Guidelines

For most reference types, users will expect that == will mean reference comparison, and in this case == should not be overloaded, even if the object implements Equals().

If the type has value semantics (something like a String or a BigNum), operator==() and Equals() should be overridden. If a class overloads + or -, that's a pretty good indication that it should also override == and Equals().

---

[3]This is by no means the only hash function that could be used, or even a particularly good one. Any good algorithms book will have more information on constructing good hash functions.

[4]This makes conceptual sense, since types that have a concept of value generally have a concept of equality.

CHAPTER 33

■ ■ ■

System.Array and the Collection Classes

Many useful operations can be performed with arrays and the .NET Framework collection. This chapter details how the operations are performed and which interfaces and functions are required to enable specific functionality.

Sorting and Searching

The .NET Framework collection classes provide some useful support for sorting and searching, with built-in functions to do sorting and binary searching. The Array class provides the same functionality but as static functions rather than member functions.

Sorting an array of integers is as easy as this:

```
using System;
class Test
{
    public static void Main()
    {
        int[] arr = {5, 1, 10, 33, 100, 4};
        Array.Sort(arr);
        foreach (int v in arr)
        {
            Console.WriteLine("Element: {0}", v);
        }
    }
}
```

The preceding code gives the following output:

```
4
5
10
33
100
```

This is very convenient for the built-in types, but it doesn't work for classes or structs because the sort routine doesn't know how to order them.

Specifying a Sort Order

It is useful to be able to sort a list of instances. Doing this requires that the type define the IComparable<T> interface. In this case, I am using the generic List<T> collection class:

```
public class Employee : IComparable<Employee>
{
    public Employee(string name, int id)
    {
        m_name = name;
        m_id = id;
    }
    int IComparable<Employee>.CompareTo(Employee emp2)
    {
        if (m_id > emp2.m_id)
        {
            return 1;
        }
        else if (m_id < emp2.m_id)
        {
            return -1;
        }
        else
        {
            return 0;
        }
    }
    public override string ToString()
    {
        return String.Format("{0}:{1}", m_name, m_id);
    }
    string m_name;
    int m_id;

}
class Test
{
    public static void Main()
    {
        List<Employee> employees = new List<Employee>();
        employees.Add(new Employee("George", 1));
        employees.Add(new Employee("Fred", 2));
        employees.Add(new Employee("Tom", 4));
        employees.Add(new Employee("Bob", 3));

        employees.Sort();
        foreach (Employee employee in employees)
        {
            Console.WriteLine("Employee: {0}", employee);
        }
        // Find employee id 2 in the list;
        Employee employeeToFind = new Employee(null, 2);
```

```
            int index = employees.BinarySearch(employeeToFind);
            if (index != -1)
            {
                Console.WriteLine("Found: {0}", employees[index]);
            }
        }
    }
}
```

This program gives the following output:

```
Employee: George:1
Employee: Fred:2
Employee: Bob:3
Employee: Tom:4
Found: Fred:2
```

This example used the BinarySearch() method to find an employee in the list. For this to work, the array must be sorted, or the results will not be correct.

You can define only one ordering using IComparable<T>; you could choose the employee ID or name, but there's no way to allow the user to choose which sort order they prefer.

Multiple Sort Orders

It is also possible to define multiple sort orders for a single class. Each sort order is expressed through the IComparer interface, and the appropriate interface is passed to the sort or search function.

The IComparer interface can't be implemented on Employee, however, because each class can implement an interface only once, which would allow only a single sort order.[1] A separate class is needed for each sort order, with the class implementing IComparer. The class will be very simple, since all it will do is implement the Compare() function.

```
class SortEmployeeByName : IComparer<Employee>
{
    public int Compare(Employee emp1, Employee emp2)
    {
        return String.Compare(emp1.Name, emp2.Name);
    }
}
```

The Compare() member takes two objects as parameters, and the Compare() function built into string is used for the comparison.

The sort is then performed with the following code:

```
employees.Sort(new SortEmployeeByName());
```

---

[1] IComparable *could* implement one sort order and IComparer another, but that would be very confusing to the user.

Ad Hoc Sorting Orders

Creating a class that defines the sort order is useful if there are likely to be multiple uses of that sort order. If the sort order isn't going to be shared, it can more easily be expressed by creating a lambda expression that matches the Comparison<T> delegate.

```
employees.Sort((a, b) => String.Compare(a.Name, b.Name));
```

This is certainly easier than creating a separate class for the comparison method.

Overloading Relational Operators

If a class has an ordering that is expressed by implementing IComparable<T>, it usually also makes sense to overload the other relational operators. As with == and !=, other operators must be declared as pairs, with < and > being one pair and >= and <= being the other pair.[2]

```
using System;
public class Employee: IComparable<Employee>
{
    public Employee(string name, int id)
    {
        m_name = name;
        m_id = id;
    }
    int IComparable<Employee>.CompareTo(Employee emp2)
    {
        if (m_id > emp2.m_id)
        {
            return 1;
        }
        else if (m_id < emp2.m_id)
        {
            return -1;
        }
        else
        {
            return 0;
        }
    }
    public static bool operator <(
        Employee emp1,
        Employee emp2)
    {
        var icomp = (IComparable<Employee>)emp1;
        return icomp.CompareTo (emp2) < 0;
    }
```

---

[2]For many types, the >= and <= operators can be derived from the other ones, but in some cases it is desirable to define them separately.

```csharp
    public static bool operator >(
        Employee emp1,
        Employee emp2)
    {
        var icomp = (IComparable<Employee>)emp1;
        return icomp.CompareTo (emp2) > 0;
    }
    public static bool operator <=(
        Employee emp1,
        Employee emp2)
    {
        var icomp = (IComparable<Employee>)emp1;
        return icomp.CompareTo (emp2) <= 0;
    }
    public static bool operator >=(
        Employee emp1,
        Employee emp2)
    {

        var icomp = (IComparable<Employee>)emp1;
        return icomp.CompareTo (emp2) >= 0;
    }

    public override string ToString()
    {
        return m_name + ":" + m_id;
    }

    string m_name;
    int m_id;
}
class Test
{
    public static void Main()
    {
        Employee george = new Employee("George", 1);
        Employee fred = new Employee("Fred", 2);
        Employee tom = new Employee("Tom", 4);
        Employee bob = new Employee("Bob", 3);

        Console.WriteLine("George < Fred: {0}", george < fred);
        Console.WriteLine("Tom >= Bob: {0}", tom >= bob);
    }
}
```

This example produces the following output:

```
George < Fred: trueTom >= Bob: true
```

Advanced Use of Hash Codes

In some situations, it may be desirable to define more than one hash code for a specific object. This could be used, for example, to allow an Employee to be searched for based on the employee ID or on the employee name. This is done by implementing the IHashCodeProvider interface to provide an alternate hash function, and it also requires a matching implementation of IComparer. These new implementations are passed to the constructor of the Dictionary.

```
class CompareEmployeeByName : IEqualityComparer<Employee>
{
    public bool Equals(Employee emp1, Employee emp2)
    {
        return String.Compare(emp1.Name, emp2.Name) == 0;
    }

    public int GetHashCode(Employee emp1)
    {
        return emp1.Name.GetHashCode();
    }
}
class Test
{
    public static void Main()
    {
        Employee herb = new Employee("Herb", 555);
        Employee george = new Employee("George", 123);
        Employee frank = new Employee("Frank", 111);
        Dictionary<Employee, string> employeeAddresses =
            new Dictionary<Employee, string>(new CompareEmployeeByName());

        employeeAddresses.Add(herb, "414 Evergreen Terrace");
        employeeAddresses.Add(george, "2335 Elm Street");
        employeeAddresses.Add(frank, "18 Pine Bluff Road");
        Employee herbClone = new Employee("Herb", 000);
        string address = employeeAddresses[herbClone];
        Console.WriteLine("{0} lives at {1}", herbClone, address);
    }
}
```

This generates the following:

```
Herb:0 lives at 414 Evergreen Terrace
```

This technique should be used sparingly. It's often simpler to expose a value, such as the employee name as a property, and allow that to be used as a hash key instead.

Synchronized Collections

When a collection class—such as Dictionary—is created, it is not threadsafe, because adding synchronization to such a class imposes some overhead. If a threadsafe version is needed, you can use the ConcurrentDictionary class from the System.Collections.Concurrent namespace.

For more information on threading and synchronization, see Chapter 34.

Case-Insensitive Collections

To deal with strings in a case-insensitive manner, a collection can be created using a case-insensitive comparer.

```
new Dictionary<string, string>(StringComparer.CurrentCultureIgnoreCase);
```

Collection Classes

Tables 33-1, 33-2 and 33-3 describe the collection classes provided by the .NET base class library.

Table 33-1. System.Collections.Generic *Collections*

Class	Description
Dictionary<TKey, TValue>	A collection of keys and values
HashSet<T>	A set of values
KeyedByTypeCollection<T>	A collection whose items are types that serve as keys
LinkedList<T>	A doubly linked list
Queue<T>	A first-in, first-out collection of items
SortedDictionary<TKey, TValue>	A collection of keys and values sorted by the key
SortedList<T>	A sorted list of key-value pairs
SortedSet<T>	A collection of items maintained in sorted order
Stack<T>	A last-in, first-out collection of items
SynchronizedCollection<T>	A threadsafe collection of values
SynchronizedKeyedCollection<K, T>	A threadsafe collection of values grouped by keys
SynchronizedReadOnlyCollection<T>	A threadsafe, read-only collection of values

Table 33-2. System.Collections.ObjectModel *Collections*

Class	Description
Collection<T>	A base class for collections
KeyedCollection<TKey, TItem>	Abstract base class for collections with keys in their values
ObservableCollection<T>	A collection that provides notifications when it is changed
ReadOnlyCollection<T>	Base class for a read-only wrapper around a collection
ReadOnlyObservableCollection<T>	A read-only wrapper around an observable collection

Table 33-3. System.Collections.Concurrent Collections

Class	Description
BlockingCollection<T>	Helper for building threadsafe collections
ConcurrentBag<T>	A threadsafe, unordered collection of objects
ConcurrentDictionary<TKey, TValue>	A threadsafe dictionary
ConcurrentQueue<T>	A threadsafe queue class
ConcurrentStack<T>	A threadsafe stack class
ReadOnlyObservableCollection<T>	A read-only observable collection

Design Guidelines

The intended use of an object should be considered when deciding which virtual functions and interfaces to implement. Table 33-4 provides guidelines for this.

Table 33-4. Interface and Virtual Method Uses

Object Use	Function or Interface
General	ToString()
Arrays or collections	Equals(), operator==(), operator!=(), GetHashCode()
Sorting or binary search	IComparable<T>
Multiple sort orders	IComparer<T>
Multiple hash lookups	IEqualityComparer<T>

■ ■ ■

CHAPTER 34

Threading

Modern computer operating systems allow a program to have multiple threads of execution at one time. At least, they allow the appearance of having multiple things going on at the same time.[1]

It's often useful to take advantage of this feature by allowing several operations to take place in parallel. This can be used to prevent a program's user interface from becoming unresponsive while a time-consuming task is being performed, or it can be used to execute some other task while waiting for a blocking operation (an I/O, for example) to complete.

The Common Language Runtime provides two different ways to perform such operations: through threading and through asynchronous call mechanisms.

This is a complex topic, and the material in this chapter and the next is a starting point for real-world applications. Large-scale multithreading is a complex and demanding topic and is covered in greater depth in books like *Pro .NET Performance* by Sasha Goldshtein (Apress, 2012) and *Pro .NET 4 Parallel Programming in C#* by Adam Freeman (Apress, 2010).

Data Protection and Synchronization

Performing more than one operation at once provides a valuable facility to a program, but it also provides opportunities for error.

A Slightly Broken Example

Consider the following code:

```
using System;
class Val
{
    int number = 1;

    public void Bump()
    {
        int temp = number;
        number = temp + 2;
        Console.WriteLine("number = {0}", number);
    }
```

---

[1]Many desktop computers now have more than one CPU core, so they actually can do more than one thing at a time, which makes this chapter more important than in the past.

```
        public override string ToString()
        {
            return(number.ToString());
        }

        public void DoBump()
        {
            for (int i = 0; i < 5; i++)
            {
                Bump();
            }
        }
    }

class Test
{
    public static void Main()
    {
        Val v = new Val();

        v.DoBump();
    }
}
```

In this example, the Val class holds a number and has a way to add 2 to it. When this program is run, it generates the following output:

```
number = 3
number = 5
number = 7
number = 9
number = 11
```

While that program is being executed, the operating system may be performing other tasks simultaneously. The code can be interrupted at any spot in the code,[2] but after the interruption, everything will be in the same state as before, and there's no way to know that the interruption took place.

Let's modify the program to perform operations in parallel using threads.

```
using System;
using System.Threading;
class Val
{
    int number = 1;

    public void Bump()
    {
        int temp = number;
        number = temp + 2;
        Console.WriteLine("number = {0}", number);
    }
```

_____

[2]Not quite *any* spot; the situations where it won't be interrupted are covered later.

```
    public override string ToString()
    {
        return(number.ToString());
    }
    public void DoBump()
    {
        for (int i = 0; i < 5; i++)
        {
            Bump();
        }
    }
}
class Test
{
    public static void Main()
    {
        Val v = new Val();

        for (int threadNum = 0; threadNum < 5; threadNum++)

        {

            Thread thread = new Thread(new ThreadStart(v.DoBump));

            thread.Start();

        }

    }
}
```

In this code, a ThreadStart delegate is created that refers to the function the thread should execute. When this program is run, it generates the following output:

```
number = 3
number = 5
number = 7
number = 9
number = 19
number = 21
number = 23
number = 25
number = 11
number = 27
number = 29
number = 31
number = 33
number = 13
number = 35
number = 37
number = 39
number = 15
number = 41
```

```
number = 43
number = 45
number = 17
number = 47
number = 49
number = 51
```

Is this output correct? Well, DoBump() is called 25 times, and each time it adds 2 to the result, so the expected result is 51. It does get a bit confused about when it is printing out the values, but the final result is correct.

This is a very common problem when writing multithreaded programs. The example has a latent error that might show up in some situations, but it doesn't show up when the example is run under normal conditions. Bugs like this are some of the worst to find, because they usually show up only under stressful conditions.[3]

Let's change the code to simulate an interruption by the operating system.

```
public void Bump()
{
    int temp = number;
    Thread.Sleep(1);
    number = temp + 2;
    Console.WriteLine("number = {0}", number);
}
```

This small change leads to the following output:

```
number = 3
number = 3
number = 3
number = 3
number = 3
number = 5
number = 5
number = 5
number = 5
number = 5
number = 7
number = 7
number = 7
number = 7
number = 7
number = 9
number = 9
number = 9
number = 9
number = 9
number = 11
number = 11
number = 11
number = 11
number = 11
```

---

[3]Such as at a customer's site.

That's not exactly the desired result.

The call to `Thread.Sleep(1)` will cause the current thread to sleep for one millisecond, before it has saved away the bumped value. When this happens, another thread will come in and also fetch the current value.

The code has no protection against this situation happening, but unfortunately, it's rare enough that it's hard to find. Creating multithreaded applications is one area where good design techniques are very important.

Protection Techniques

You can use several different techniques prevent problems. Code that is written to keep this in mind is known as *threadsafe* code. In general, most code isn't threadsafe because there is usually a performance penalty in writing threadsafe code.

Don't Share Data

One of the best techniques to prevent such problems is to not share data in the first place. It is often possible to architect an application so that each thread has its own data to deal with. For example, an application that fetches data from several web sites simultaneously can create a separate object for each thread.[4]

If it is possible to not share data, this is the best option, because it imposes no performance penalty and doesn't clutter the code. It requires some care, since a developer may accidentally add shared data at a later date.

Immutable Objects

In the example, you saw that problems can arise when multiple threads can modify the same piece of data. If you can change the design so that the object's data cannot be modified after creation, by creating an immutable object, you can avoid this issue.

The `string` type is a great example of achieving thread safety through immutability. There are no operations that modify a string; all the ones that look like they would modify the value of the string, such as `ToUpper()`, instead return a new `string` instance. If one thread is completing an enumeration of the characters of a string at the same time as another thread calls `ToUpper()`, the thread conducting the enumeration is unaffected because the new uppercase string is an entirely separate object that is not physically related to the original string.

Immutability does place a higher design and implementation burden on a type. The methods of the type must be designed so it is apparent to the users of the type that a modifying operation returns a new instance rather than modifying the instance it was called,[5] and it is generally wise to provide a mutable equivalent of the immutable type to support high-performance modification operations. For `string`, `StringBuilder` is the equivalent mutable type.

Exclusion Primitives

If you need to share data and it isn't practical to use immutable types, you can ask the runtime to help you. This is done through exclusion primitives, which are ways of ensuring that there is only one user of code at a time.

The `System.Threading` namespace contains a number of useful classes for ensuring that there is only one access at a time, preventing the problems in the earlier example. The most commonly used one is the `Monitor` class. The slightly broken example can be modified by surrounding the problem region of code with exclusion primitives.

---

[4]This is probably not the best choice for this scenario. See Chapter 35 for a thorough discussion of this topic.
[5]The `string` type is not a great example of this; it's very easy to write `myString.Replace("x", "y")` and then be surprised that it doesn't do anything.

```csharp
public void Bump()
{
    Monitor.Enter(this);
    int temp = number;
    Thread.Sleep(1);
    number = temp + 2;
    Console.WriteLine("number = {0}", number);
    Monitor.Exit(this);
}
```

The call to Monitor.Enter() passes in the this reference for this object. The monitor's job is to make sure that if a thread has called Monitor.Enter() with a specific value, any other call to Monitor.Enter() with the same value will block until the first thread has called Monitor.Exit(). When the first thread calls Thread.Sleep(), the second thread will call Monitor.Enter() and pass the same object as the first thread did, and therefore the second thread will block.

■ **Note** Those of you who've done Win32 programming may be familiar with using EnterCriticalSection() and LeaveCriticalSection() to block access. The Monitor methods are similar, but unlike the Win32 functions, the Monitor functions lock on a specific object. This provides finer lock granularity and better performance.

There's a slight problem with the implementation of Bump(). If an exception was thrown in the block that is protected, Monitor.Exit() will never be called, and no other thread will ever be able to enter the block. That is bad. To make sure Monitor.Exit() is always called, the calls need to be wrapped in a try-finally. This is important enough that C# provides a special statement to do just that.

The lock Statement

This scenario is common enough that C# provides a statement to make it easier to do the right thing. The lock statement is simply a thin wrapper around calls to Monitor.Enter() and Monitor.Exit(). This code:

```csharp
object m_lockObject = new object();
void MyMethod
{
    lock(m_lockObject)
    {
        // statements
    }
}
```

is translated by the compiler to the following:

```csharp
object m_lockObj = new object();
void MyMethod
{
    System.Threading.Monitor.Enter(m_lockObj);
    try
```

```
    {
        // statements
    }
    finally
    {
        System.Threading.Monitor.Exit(m_lockObj);
    }
}
```

The object that is used in the lock statement reflects the granularity at which the lock should be obtained. If the data to be protected is instance data, it's typical to create a private member variable and use it to prevent concurrent access.

If the data to be protected is a static data item, it should be locked using a unique static reference object. This is done simply by adding a static field of type object to the class.

```
static readonly object staticLock = new object();
```

This object is then used in the lock statement.

■ **Caution**   It's important to not use lock with an object that is accessible outside of the class. If other classes can see it, they could also lock on it. Avoid using string or Type instances in lock statements, because what appears to be separate instances may point to the same instance internally and could result in the same situation.

Interlocked Operations

Many processors support some instructions that cannot be interrupted. These are useful when dealing with threads, because no locking is required to use them. In the Common Language Runtime, these operations are encapsulated in the Interlocked class in the System.Threading namespace. This class exposes Add(), Increment(), Decrement(), Exchange(), and CompareExchange() methods, which can be used on int and long data types.

The problem example could be rewritten using these instructions:

```
public void Bump()
{
    Interlocked.Add(ref number, 2);
}
```

It is guaranteed by the runtime that the increment operations will not be interrupted. If interlocked works for an application, it can provide a nice performance boost because it avoids the overhead of locking.

Mutexes

The lock statement works well for a single process,[6] but there are some cases where it's useful to have a lock that works across all the processes on a machine. A common case is when there should never be more than one instance of an application running on a system. In this case, the application can create a mutex to ensure this.

---

[6]Technically, they work only across a single application domain.

```csharp
public class MyProgram
{
    const string MyMutexName = "MyProgramMutex";
    static void Main()
    {
        try
        {
            Mutex.OpenExisting(MyMutexName);
            Console.WriteLine("Mutex exists, exiting...");
            return;
        }
        catch (WaitHandleCannotBeOpenedException)
        {
        }
        using (Mutex mutex = new Mutex(true, MyMutexName))
        {
            Console.WriteLine("I have the Mutex");
            Thread.Sleep(10 * 1000);
        }
    }
}
```

Mutexes are considerably more expensive than using the lock statement and should be used only for cross-process scenarios.

Access Reordering and Volatile

To avoid the overhead of synchronization, some programmers will build their own optimization primitives. In C#, however, there are some surprising subtleties in what the language and runtime guarantee with respect to instruction ordering, especially to those who are familiar with the x86 architecture, which doesn't typically perform instruction reordering.

This topic is complex, but it isn't necessary to fully understand it if you stick to the synchronization methods discussed earlier in this chapter.

To illustrate this, consider the following example:

```csharp
class Problem
{
    int m_x;
    int m_y;
    int m_curx;
    int m_cury;

    public Problem()
    {
        m_x = 0;
        m_y = 0;
    }
    public void Process1()
    {
        m_x = 1;
        m_cury = m_y;
    }
```

```
    public void Process2()
    {
        m_y = 1;
        m_curx = m_x;
    }
    public void TestCurrent()
    {
        Console.WriteLine("curx, cury: {0} {1}", m_curx, m_cury);
    }
}
class ReorderingTest
{
    public static void Main()
    {
        Problem p = new Problem();

        Thread t1 = new Thread(new ThreadStart(p.Process1));
        Thread t2 = new Thread(new ThreadStart(p.Process2));
        t1.Start();
        t2.Start();

        t1.Join();
        t2.Join();

        p.TestCurrent();
    }
}
```

In this example, two threads are started: one that calls p.Process1() and another that calls p.Process2(). Figure 34-1 shows this process.

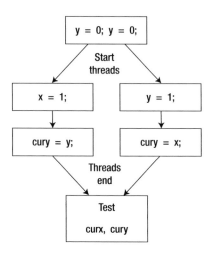

Figure 34-1. *Reordering example*

What possible values can be printed for curx and cury? It's not surprising that two possible values are as follows:

```
curx, cury: 1 0
curx, cury: 0 1
```

This makes sense from the serial nature of the code in Process1() and Process2(); either function can complete before the other one starts.

A bit less obvious[7] is the following output:

```
curx, cury: 1 1
```

This is a possibility because one of threads could be interrupted after the first instruction and the other thread could run.

The point of the example, however, is that there's a fourth possible output.

```
curx, cury: 0 0
```

This happens because of one of those things that's assumed to be true but isn't really always true. The common assumption when looking at the code in Process1() is that the lines always execute in the order in which they are written. Surprisingly, that isn't true; there are a few cases where the instructions might execute out of order.

1. First, the compiler could choose to reorder the statements, because there's no way for the compiler to know this isn't safe.

2. Second, the JIT could decide to load the values for both x and y into registers before executing either line of code.

3. Third, the processor could reorder the execution of the instructions to be faster.[8]

4. Fourth, on a multiprocessor system, the values might not be synchronized in global memory.

What is needed to address this is a way to annotate a field so that such optimizations are inhibited. C# does this with the volatile keyword.

When a field is marked as volatile, reordering of instructions is inhibited, so that

- a write cannot be moved forward across a volatile write, and

- a read cannot be move backward across a volatile read.

In the example, if curx and cury are marked volatile, the code in Process1() and Process2() cannot be reordered.

```
public void Process1()
{
    x = 1;
    cury = y;
}
```

---

[7]Though I hope it's still somewhat obvious, given the earlier content of the chapter.
[8]x86 processors don't do this, but there are other processors—including Intel's IA64 architecture—where reordering is common.

Since cury is now volatile, the write to x cannot be moved after the write to cury.

In addition to precluding such reordering, volatile also means that the JIT can't keep the variable in the register and that the variable must be stored in global memory on a multiprocessor system.

So, what is volatile good for, when you already have ways of doing synchronization?

Singletons

It is sometimes useful to restrict a class to a single shared instance, known as a *singleton*. This is easily done by taking advantage of a static constructor.

```
class SingletonIndustrious
{
    private static readonly SingletonIndustrious s_instance = new SingletonIndustrious();

    private SingletonIndustrious() { }  // nobody can call this

    public static SingletonIndustrious Instance
    {
        get { return s_instance; }
    }
}
```

The initialization of s_instance is handled for you by the runtime. This is fine if the singleton is cheap to construct. If, however, it is expensive and isn't always used, there is an issue; the runtime may choose to construct the singleton even if it is never referenced. What is needed is a lazy implementation. The traditional lazy implementation uses lock.

```
using System;
class Singleton
{
    static object s_sync = new object();
    static volatile Singleton s_singleton = null;

    private Singleton()
    {
    }
    public static Singleton Instance
    {
        get
        {
            if (s_singleton == null)
            {
                lock (s_sync)
                {
                    if (s_singleton == null)
                    {
                        s_singleton = new Singleton();
                    }
                }
            }
```

```
            return (s_singleton);
        }
    }
}
```

This works, but it requires the ugly double-check locking and is easy to get wrong. This is exactly the sort of thing that a framework should make easier.

With the Lazy<T> generic class, a nicer version can be written.

```
class Singleton
{
    private static readonly Lazy<Singleton> s_singleton =
        new Lazy<Singleton>(() => new Singleton() );

    private Singleton()
    {
    }
    public static Singleton Instance
    {
        get { return s_singleton.Value; }
    }
}
```

The implementation of Lazy will now guarantee that there is only one instance created.

Threads

The previous examples have shown a bit about threads, but there are a few more details to cover. When a Thread instance is created, a delegate to the function the thread should run is created and passed to the constructor. Since a delegate can refer to a member function[9] and a specific instance, there's no need to pass anything else to the thread.

The thread instance can be used to control the priority of the thread, set the name of the thread, or perform other thread operations, so it's necessary to save that thread instance if such operations will be performed later. A thread can get its own thread instance through the Thread.CurrentThread property.

■ **Note** Before you start writing threading code, take a look at the asynchronous support described in Chapter 35. In most cases, you will end up with a better implementation that is easier to create.

Joining

After a thread has been created to perform a task, such as doing a computation-intensive calculation, it's sometimes necessary to wait for that thread to complete. The following example illustrates this:

```
using System;
using System.Threading;
```

---

[9]You could also use a lambda, but I think you shouldn't; it will be much clearer if the code is in a separate method.

```
class ThreadSleeper
{
    int m_seconds;

    private ThreadSleeper(int seconds)
    {
        m_seconds = seconds;
    }
    public void Nap()
    {
        Console.WriteLine("Napping {0} seconds", m_seconds);
        Thread.Sleep(m_seconds * 1000);
    }
    public static Thread DoSleep(int seconds)
    {
        ThreadSleeper threadSleeper = new ThreadSleeper(seconds);
        Thread thread = new Thread(new ThreadStart(threadSleeper.Nap));
        thread.Start();
        return(thread);
    }
}

class Test
{
    public static void Main()
    {
        Thread thread = ThreadSleeper.DoSleep(5);

        Console.WriteLine("Waiting for thread to join");
        thread.Join();
        Console.WriteLine("Thread Joined");
    }
}
```

The ThreadSleeper.Nap() function simulates an operation that takes a while to perform.
ThreadSleeper.DoSleep() creates an instance of a ThreadSleeper, executes the Nap() function, and then
returns the thread instance to the main program. The main program then calls Join() on that thread to wait for
it to complete.

Using Join() works well when waiting for a single thread, but if there is more than one active thread, a call to
Join() must be made for each, which is a bit unwieldy.

A nicer solution is to use one of the utility classes.

Waiting with WaitHandle

The WaitHandle abstract class provides a simple way to wait for an event to occur.[10] In addition to waiting for a
single event to occur, it can be used to wait for more than one event and return when one or all of them occur.
The AutoResetEvent and ManualResetEvent classes derive from WaitHandle. The AutoResetEvent will release

---

[10]Note that this is an event in the general sense, not in the "C# event" sense.

a single thread only when the Set() function is called and will then reset. The ManualResetEvent may release many threads from a single call to Set() and must be cleared by calling Reset().

The previous example can be modified to use an AutoResetEvent to signal when an event is complete and to wait for more than one thread to complete.

```csharp
using System;
using System.Threading;

class ThreadSleeper
{
    int m_seconds;
    AutoResetEvent m_napDone = new AutoResetEvent(false);

    private ThreadSleeper(int seconds)
    {
        m_seconds = seconds;
    }

    public void Nap()
    {
        Console.WriteLine("Napping {0} seconds", m_seconds);
        Thread.Sleep(m_seconds * 1000);
        Console.WriteLine("{0} second nap finished", m_seconds);
        m_napDone.Set();
    }

    public static WaitHandle DoSleep(int seconds)
    {
        ThreadSleeper threadSleeper = new ThreadSleeper(seconds);
        Thread thread = new Thread(new ThreadStart(threadSleeper.Nap));
        thread.Start();
        return(threadSleeper.m_napDone);
    }
}

class Test
{
    public static void Main()
    {
        WaitHandle[] waits = new WaitHandle[2];
        waits[0] = ThreadSleeper.DoSleep(8);
        waits[1] = ThreadSleeper.DoSleep(4);
        Console.WriteLine("Waiting for threads to finish");
        WaitHandle.WaitAll(waits);
        Console.WriteLine("Threads finished");
    }
}
```

The output is as follows:

```
Waiting for threads to finish
Napping 8 seconds
Napping 4 seconds
4 second nap finished
8 second nap finished
Threads finished
```

Instead of returning a Thread, the DoSleep() function now returns a WaitHandle that will be set when the thread has completed. An array of WaitHandle is created and then is passed to WaitHandle.WaitAll() to wait for all the events to be set.

CHAPTER 35

■ ■ ■

Asynchronous and Parallel Programming

In modern programs, it's common to need to run code in small chunks to keep user interfaces responsive and to run operations in parallel to reduce latency and take advantage of multicore CPUs. C# and the .NET Framework provide the following support for asynchronous and parallel programming:

- The Task Parallel Library
- C# language support for asynchronous execution (async and await keywords)
- Parallel Linq (PLINQ)

This chapter explores how to use these facilities.

History

In earlier version of the .NET Framework, there were two ways of doing an asynchronous operation. The first one was used for I/O operations. If you were writing code to fetch data from a web site, the simplest code was synchronous.

```
public void GetWebResponse(string url)
{
    WebRequest request = WebRequest.CreateHttp(url);

    WebResponse response = request.GetResponse();

    // read the data and process it...
}
```

This is simple code to write, and you could even use the WebClient.DownloadString() method to do it in a single line of code. When you call that method, the following things happen:

1. A request is created in the proper format.
2. The request is sent over the network to the specified URL.
3. The request arrives at a server.
4. The server thinks about the request, composes an appropriate response, and sends it back.

5. The data is received back on your system.

6. The data is transferred back to your code.

This process can take a fair amount of time, during which time your program isn't doing anything else, and your program's UI is frozen. That is bad.

Windows implements a feature known as *I/O completion ports*, in which an I/O operation can be started, and then your program can go off and do something else until the operation completes, at which time the operating system will interrupt your program and present the data. This approach is supported in the .NET Framework, where a single operation is broken into two; the first one, named BeginXXX(), takes a callback function and returns an IAsyncResult, and the second one, named EndXXX(), takes an IAsyncResult and returns the result of calling the method.

You can modify the previous example as follows:

```
public void GetWebResponseStart(string url)
{
    WebRequest request = WebRequest.CreateHttp(url);

    request.BeginGetResponse(new AsyncCallback(GetWebResponseCallback), request);
}

public void GetWebResponseCallback(IAsyncResult result)
{
    WebRequest request = (WebRequest)result.AsyncState;

    WebResponse response = request.EndGetResponse(result);

    // read the data, and process it...
}
```

To start the process, you call the BeginGetResponse() method, passing in the delegate you want to be called when the operation is completed and a state object (in this case, the request) that will be passed through to your callback. After that call, your program goes on its merry way, until the operation completes. At that time, the runtime will call the callback routine you specified in the BeginGetResponse() call. In that routine, you pull the request object out of the result, extract the request, and then call EndGetResponse() to get the result of the call. Instead of the "call/wait/return" behavior that you had in the first example, you now get "call/return/do something else/pick up the data when it's ready" behavior.

This is a very good thing; not only can the program keep the UI up-to-date and responsive, but you can make multiple I/O requests at once, which gives you the chance to overlap operations. It is not, however, without its disadvantages.

- It's complicated to write. In this example, the LoadImageResponse() method starts an asynchronous read on data that is coming back on the stream, which requires yet another method and callback. It takes about 50 lines of code in my "simple" example, instead of the one line in the synchronous example.

- It has complicated exception behavior. Exceptions can be thrown from the GetWebResponseStart() method or any of the callback methods. If an exception occurs in the callback, it needs to somehow be communicated back to the calling method.

- It works only for components that have I/O completion ports underneath.

A more-general construct is needed.

Thread Pools

Chapter 34 covered the creation and use of threads, and in fact, threads are a useful general-purpose construct that can help. Assume you have an operation that takes a long time to complete.

```
class SlowOperation
{
    public static int Process()
    {
            // expensive calculation here
        return sum;
    }
}
```

If you called `Process()`, your program would just appear to hang. To prevent that, you can use a thread to perform the calculation.

```
Thread thread = new Thread(PerformSlowOperation, 0);
thread.Start();
```

You will need to figure out a way to get the value back when the thread is done, but assuming you can do that, there is another unfortunate issue; creating a thread is an expensive operation, and threads consume system resources. It may make sense to use a thread to perform a single expensive operation, but it doesn't make sense to use a thread to perform a simpler operation, and you certainly wouldn't want to use it to call `WebClient.DownloadString()`.

To reduce the number of thread creations and the number of threads taking up resources, the frameworks provide you with a thread pool, which is just a set of threads that are managed for the general use of the process. You can use the thread pool to perform the slow operation.

```
ThreadPool.QueueUserWorkItem(PerformSlowOperationThreadPool);
```

This is a more efficient use of resources, but if there are other users of the thread pool in the program, it's possible that my routine may have to wait a while before it executes. The `ThreadPool` class does provide some control over the number of threads it creates.

Introducing Tasks

The Task Parallel Library sits on top of the thread pool and provides a more abstract API. You can use the following to run the slow operation:

```
var task = new Task(() => Console.WriteLine(SlowOperation.Process()));
task.Start();
```

Or, if you want to start the task immediately, you can do it in a single line.

```
Task.Factory.StartNew(() => Console.WriteLine(SlowOperation.Process()));
```

Both of these queue a work item to the thread pool to execute the operation so that it ends up executing on a background thread.

Tasks with Return Values

If you are calling a method with a return value, you will need to have a way to wait for the task to complete.

```
var task = Task<int>.Factory.StartNew(() => SlowOperation.Process());
int i = task.Result;
Console.WriteLine(i);
```

This would seem to be a step backward; you are starting the slow operation on a thread pool thread, but you are waiting for it on the main thread. What you need is a way to run the line that starts the slow process, go away and do something else, and then come back when the operation is done to pick up the result.

The async and await Keywords

The situation you are in is very similar to the situation you had when you were writing an iterator; you want to be able to write the code that looks like it executes sequentially, but in actuality, you need it to return in the middle of the "sequential" section. Here's a simple example:

```
static async void AsyncTaskWithResult()
{
    int result = await Task<int>.Factory.StartNew(() => SlowOperation.Process());
    Console.WriteLine(result);
}
```

This functions very much like the `BeginGetResponse()`/`EndGetResponse()` example, except this time the compiler does the heavy lifting of creating a state machine that tracks the states of each request and performs the appropriate operations; it splits the code in the method into two sections (one to start the task and one to process the result) and then arranges it so that when the first section of code completes, the second section will be invoked, and then it returns, so the rest of the program can continue executing. The method could be expressed in the following pseudocode[1]:

1. If you don't have any async result information, start operation and return the task associated with it.

2. If you do have result information, get the result out of it, and write it out to the console.

If the method has more than one `await` statement in it, the state management gets more complicated, because the method will have to know which one has completed when it is called.

This method is a `void` method, but if you want, you can make an `async` method that returns a value. Perhaps you want to perform two operations and return the sum of those two operations.

```
static async Task<int> AsyncTaskWithReturnValue()
{
    int result1 = await Task<int>.Factory.StartNew(() => SlowOperation.Process1());
    int result2 = await Task<int>.Factory.StartNew(() => SlowOperation.Process2());

    return result1 + result2;
}
```

---

[1]This is a simplification; if you want more details, run `ildasm` against the generated code.

This will return the sum of the two results without blocking on the slow operations. It will be called three times.

- To start the task to call `Process1()`

- To get the result of the first task and to start the task to call `Process2()`

- To get the result of the second task, add it to the first task, and then return it

---

■ **Note**   The use of `await` as the keyword has generated a lot of discussion, since (at least in one sense) the program does not wait for the result but goes off and does other things. As is common in language design, several other options were considered, and `await` was the best one.

Tasks and Completion Ports

Tasks can also be used to unify the completion port approach and the task approach,[2] and some of the .NET Framework classes have already been modified to take advantage of this. I will return to my old friend `WebClient.DownloadString()`, which has a new method to help.

```
async void WebMethodDownload(string url)
{
    string contents = await new WebClient().DownloadStringTaskAsync(url);
    c_label.Content = contents;
}
```

This fetches the contents of a specified URL and puts it into a label control. The second line may raise some eyebrows; in typical asynchronous code, you would expect to see a call to `Dispatcher.Invoke()` to get from the background thread to the UI thread, but the C# async support ensures that the whole routine will execute using the same thread context that the routine was originally called with, which is quite slick.

■ **Note**   This means the UI thread if it was originally called on the UI thread or a thread pool thread (not necessarily the same thread) if it was called on the thread pool.

ASYNC, AWAIT, AND PARALLEL OPERATIONS

Note that so far you haven't performed any operations in parallel. The `async` support in C# is not about performing operations in parallel; it's about preventing an operation from blocking the current thread. This has confused a fair number of people, who expect `async` to always mean "parallel."

---

[2]The unification is not automatic; you need to modify your classes so that the methods return task instances, but there are helpers to make this straightforward. See the MSDN topic "TPL and Traditional .NET Asynchronous Programming" for more information.

Tasks and Parallel Operations

All of the task examples have performed only one operation at once. It is now time to explore performing operations in parallel. The following code will be your starting point. It uses async and await.

```
async void LoadImagesAsync()
{
    List<string> urls = m_smugMugFeed.Fetch();

    int i = 0;
    foreach (string url in urls)
    {
        ImageItem imageItem = new ImageItem();
        await imageItem.LoadImageAsync(url);
        AddImageToUI(imageItem);
    }
}
```

This code talks to the popular SmugMug photography site and asks for lists of popular photos.[3] You get a list of URLs of the popular photos and then loop through them using await so that you don't block the UI.

The code works nicely; it doesn't block the UI, but it downloads one photo at a time, which takes a long time.[4] What you need is code that launches multiple operations at once.

```
void LoadImage(string url)
{
    ImageItem imageItem = new ImageItem();
    imageItem.LoadImage (url);
    Dispatcher.BeginInvoke(new Action<ImageItem>(AddImageToUI), imageItem);
}

void LoadImagesAsyncNewInParallel()
{
    List<string> urls = m_smugMugFeed.Fetch();

    foreach (string url in urls)
    {
        Task.Run(() => LoadImage(url));
    }
}
```

You have pulled the inner-loop code out of the main method and put it into the LoadImage() method. This method synchronously loads the image and then adds it to the UI. Because you are running in the thread pool, you need to invoke back to the UI thread. This version takes about 50 seconds to run, considerably slower than the last version. This isn't surprising; when LoadImage() is called on a thread, it blocks until the entire operation completes. My first thought is to throw more threads at it by modifying the behavior of the thread pool.

```
ThreadPool.SetMinThreads(25, 25);
```

---

[3]For the full code that illustrates both the old and new ways of performing async operations, see the downloadable content for this book.
[4]Remember, await and async are about writing the code in one method, not about making it run fast. This approach takes about 18 seconds to fetch 100 photos.

That takes about 30 seconds, which is better but still not exciting, and the use of more threads is not free. If only there were a way to for the LoadImage() method to not block on the thread pool while it is waiting for a response so that other threads could run.

```
async void LoadImage(string url)
{
    ImageItem imageItem = new ImageItem();
    await imageItem.LoadImageAsync(url);
    await Dispatcher.BeginInvoke(new Action<ImageItem>(AddImageToUI), imageItem);
}
```

That is exactly the point of async and await: so that you don't block in time-consuming operations. Blocking on a thread pool thread may not be as obvious as blocking on a UI thread, but it's still a bad idea.

This version is fast enough that it's a bit hard to time exactly, so I'll say, "something under four seconds." The task library and the C# async support have provided a nice way to speed up the code, and the code is very similar to the synchronous code you would have written.

■ **Note**   It seems like await and async have gotten all the love in the press, but the Task class and what you can do with it are at least as important in my opinion.

Data Parallelism

The previous examples illustrated how to improve the speed of operations by not waiting when there was other work to do and by performing operations in parallel across multiple threads. The majority of the time savings came not because you could perform more than one operation at a time but because you weren't waiting for slow external operations to finish.

But what if your operations are all local to the machine? It would certainly be nice to be able to make those run faster as well. Consider the following methods:

```
static List<int> m_numbersToSum;

static long SumNumbersLessThan(int limit)
{
    long sum = 0;
    for (int i = 0; i < limit; i++)
    {
        sum += 1;
    }

    return sum;
}
static void SumOfSums()
{
    foreach (int number in m_numbersToSum)
    {
        SumNumbersLessThan(number);
    }
}
```

You have a list of the integers from 0 to 50,000 in m_numbersToSum, and you call SumNumbersLessThan() with each of those numbers. That takes about 1.37 seconds on my computer. But my system has four CPU cores on it, and it would sure be nice if I could make use of them. Enter the Parallel class.

```
static void SumOfSumsParallel()
{
    Parallel.ForEach(m_numbersToSum, number =>
        {
            SumNumbersLessThan(number);
        });
}
```

You pass in the set of numbers to sum and a lambda that contains the code you want to run. The Parallel class (part of the Parallel Task Library) farms out the calls to different tasks running on different cores, and on my machine, the method finishes in 0.43 seconds, a three-times speedup.[5] That's a nice improvement for a very small change—well, except that the code doesn't actually return the result that was calculated. That is quite simple to do in the nonparallel version, but the parallel version will take a bit more work.

```
static long m_sumOfSums;

static long SumOfSumsParallelWithResult()
{
    m_sumOfSums = 0;

    Parallel.ForEach(m_numbersToSum, number =>
    {
        long sum = SumNumbersLessThan(number);
        Interlocked.Add(ref m_sumOfSums, sum);
    });

    return m_sumOfSums;
}
```

In this case, since I am only adding up numbers, I could use the Interlocked.Add() method[6] to add each sum to a global sum. More typically, I would need to accumulate the results somewhere else and then process them at the end.

```
static ConcurrentBag<long> m_results = new ConcurrentBag<long>();

static long SumOfSumsParallelWithConcurrentBag()
{
    Parallel.ForEach(m_numbersToSum, number =>
    {
        long sum = SumNumbersLessThan(number);
        m_results.Add(sum);
    });

    return m_results.Sum();
}
```

---

[5]Your mileage may vary. Actually mileage is likely to be lower.
[6]See Chapter 34 for more information about the interlocked methods.

This uses the ConcurrentBag class, which stores an unordered collection of items. Since you don't care about this ordering of the results, this works well.[7]

HOW MANY THREADS?

As you saw earlier, the number of threads that are used in the thread pool can have a significant impact on performance. For the Parallel library, the number of threads is autotuned based upon the configuration of the machine, how the threads are being used, and the other load that is on the machine. It is possible to control this behavior (a bit) in the parallel library, but my advice is to stick with the defaults unless you are willing to invest a lot of effort into profiling.

PLinq

There is another option for this example, a parallel version of Linq known as PLinq. The previous example is very easily expressed in PLinq.

```
static long SumOfSumsPLinq()
{
    return
        m_numbersToSum
            .AsParallel()
            .Select(number => SumNumbersLessThan(number))
            .Sum();
}
```

The AsParallel() method puts you into the parallel world, and then PLinq is free to parallelize as it sees fit. This approach doesn't yield the same improvement as the previous one (only about a two-times speedup), because PLinq has to pull the sequence apart, parallelize the calls to SumNumbersLessThan(), and then put the results back together so that they can be summed up. Those operations consume some of the savings.

Design Guidelines

The task approach is much easier to use than the previous schemes, and the fact that it unifies the thread pool and completion port approaches is another point in its favor. async and await are very useful for what they are designed for. I suggest using them rather than the previous approaches.

Parallel.ForEach() and PLinq present some interesting trade-offs; the first is certainly faster when the results don't relate to one another, while PLinq may be faster if they do relate to one another, and it will likely be much better if you care about the ordering of the sequence. For more information about when to choose one over the other, see the excellent paper "When Should I Use Parallel.ForEach? When Should I Use PLINQ?" available online from Microsoft.

---

[7]There is no ConcurrentList<T>, which seems a bit strange, though it would not be terribly useful with the Parallel class, because there is no guarantee that the operations complete in the order in which you started them, and maintaining order therefore takes some extra work.

CHAPTER 36

███

Execution-Time Code Generation

If you come from a C++ background, it's likely you have a very "compile-time" view of the world. Because a C++ compiler does all code generation when the code is compiled, C++ programs are static systems that are fully known at compile time.

The Common Language Runtime provides a different way of doing things. The compile-time world still exists, but it's also possible to build dynamic systems where new code is added by loading assemblies or even by writing custom code on the fly.

Loading Assemblies

In the .NET Common Language Runtime, it's possible to load an assembly from disk and to create instances of classes from that assembly. To demonstrate this, I'll show how to build a simple logging facility that can be extended by the customer at runtime to send informational messages elsewhere.

The first step is to define the standard part of the facility.

```csharp
public interface ILogger
{
    void Log(string message);
}
public class LogDriver
{
    List<ILogger> m_loggers = new List<ILogger>();
    public LogDriver()
    {
    }
    public void AddLogger(ILogger logger)
    {
        m_loggers.Add(logger);
    }
    public void Log(string message)
    {
        foreach (ILogger logger in m_loggers)
        {
            logger.Log(message);
        }
    }
}
```

```csharp
public class LogConsole : ILogger
{
    public void Log(string message)
    {
        Console.WriteLine(message);
    }
}
```

You first define the ILogger interface that your loggers will implement and the LogDriver class that calls all the registered loggers whenever the Log() function is called. There's also a LogConsole implementation that logs messages to the console. This file is compiled to an assembly named LogDriver.dll.

In addition to this file, there's a small class to exercise the loggers.

```csharp
class Test
{
    public static void Main()
    {
        LogDriver logDriver = new LogDriver();
        logDriver.AddLogger(new LogConsole());
        logDriver.Log("Log start: " + DateTime.Now.ToString());

        for (int i = 0; i < 5; i++)
        {
            logDriver.Log("Operation: " + i.ToString());
        }

        logDriver.Log("Log end: " + DateTime.Now.ToString());
    }
}
```

This code merely creates a LogDriver, adds a LogConsole to the list of loggers, and does some logging.

Making It Dynamic

It's now time to add some dynamic ability to your system. A mechanism is needed so the LogDriver class can discover loggers in assemblies it does not know about at compile time. To keep the sample simple, the code will look for assemblies named LogAddIn*.dll.

The first step is to come up with another implementation of ILogger. The LogAddInToFile class logs messages to logger.log and lives in LogAddInToFile.dll.

```csharp
// file=LogAddInToFile.cs
// compile with: csc /r:..\logdriver.dll /target:library logaddintofile.cs
using System;
using System.Collections;
using System.IO;

public class LogAddInToFile: ILogger
{
    StreamWriter streamWriter;
```

```
    public LogAddInToFile()
    {
        streamWriter = File.CreateText(@"logger.log");
        streamWriter.AutoFlush = true;
    }

    public void Log(string message)
    {
        streamWriter.WriteLine(message);
    }
}
```

This class doesn't require much explanation. Next, the code to load the assembly needs to be added to the LogDriver class.

```
    public void ScanDirectoryForLoggers()
    {
        DirectoryInfo dir = new DirectoryInfo(@".");
        foreach (FileInfo f in dir.GetFiles(@"LogAddIn*.dll"))
        {
            ScanAssemblyForLoggers(f.FullName);
        }
    }
    void ScanAssemblyForLoggers(string filename)
    {
        Assembly a = Assembly.LoadFrom(filename);

        foreach (Type t in a.GetTypes())
        {
            if (t.GetInterface("ILogger") != null)
            {
                ILogger iLogger = (ILogger) Activator.CreateInstance(t);
                m_loggers.Add(iLogger);
            }
        }
    }
}
```

The ScanDirectoryForLoggers() function looks in the current directory for any files that match the expected file format. When one of the files is found, ScanAssemblyForLoggers() is called. This function loads the assembly and then iterates through each of the types contained in the assembly. If the type implements the ILogger interface, then an instance of the type is created using Activator.CreateInstance(), the instance is cast to the interface, and the interface is added to the list of loggers.

If an even more dynamic implementation is desirable, a FileChangeWatcher object could be used to watch a specific directory, and any assemblies copied to that directory could be then be loaded.

There are a few caveats when loading assemblies from a disk. First, the runtime locks assemblies when they are loaded. Second, it's not possible to unload a single assembly, so if unloading an assembly is required (to update a class, for example), it will need to be loaded in a separate application domain since application domains can be unloaded. For more information on application domains, consult the .NET Common Language Runtime documentation.

Code Generation at Runtime

If your code contains a complex algorithm and the performance depends on the speed of that algorithm, it may at times be more efficient to create a custom version of the algorithm and use that instead of the general-purpose one.

■ **Note**   The XML serializer and the regular expression engine are two places that use this technique to improve execution speed.

This technique involves three steps: expressing the custom version of the algorithm in code, translating that version into executable code and loading it, and calling the custom version of the code.

Expressing the Algorithm in Code

The algorithm can be expressed at two different levels: either at the C# source code level or at the .NET Intermediate Language (IL) level.

The code can be written in C# by simply creating a file with the C# source or by using the classes in the System.CodeDom namespace. Using the CodeDom namespace requires you to think like the compiler and parse the code to create the CodeDom constructs. It is usually easier to create the C# source directly.

To express the code directly in .NET IL, you can either use the classes in the Reflection.Emit namespace or, if the amount of code is small, use the DynamicMethod class.

It is significantly more work to express an algorithm in .NET IL, since you must do the work of the compiler. If you choose to take this approach, my recommendation is to first write your code in C# and compile it, use the ILDasm utility to view the resulting IL, and then base your IL on that code. Be sure to compile in release mode, because the debug mode IL contains extraneous information.

Translating and Loading the Code

If you have created the .NET IL directly, this step is pretty much done for you; you have a chunk of IL in hand, and it's fairly straightforward to get a delegate from it that you can use.

If you created C# code, you will need to use the CodeDomProvider.CompileAssemblyFromFile() method; this performs the compilation and loads the resulting assembly. You can then use reflection to create an instance of the class.

Calling the Code

Methods can be invoked in three ways.

- Using reflection and method.Invoke()
- Getting a delegate to a method and calling through that
- Getting an interface to a class and calling through an interface method

The first approach is fairly slow; the second and third approaches are at least ten times faster.

Design Guidelines

It's much easier to work at the C# code level, but if you do this, you have to pay the cost of compiling the C# code into IL, which is on the order of half a second. If you use the code often and/or the speedup is significant, this may not matter, but for small chunks of code, the cost may be prohibitive.

When calling code, make sure to use a strongly typed interface or delegate; using reflection (or dynamic typing) will be much slower.

The C# Compiler As a Service

None of the described ways of generating code is particularly straightforward or elegant. What you would really like is a way to hook into the C# compiler and have it do the hard work for you. Unfortunately, the C# compiler (including C# 5.0) is written in C++, and there is no way to hook into it from C#.

There is, however, a project (code name Roslyn) to rewrite the C# compiler in C#[1] and ship that version as C# 6.0. Preview versions of that compiler are available, which are interesting to explore.[2]

Roslyn provides many new capabilities; you can reach into the compiler at any of the compilation phases—parsing, binding, and IL generation—and get the current state and even modify it. I will limit this exploration to using Roslyn to generate code on the fly.

■ **Note**   This example uses prerelease code. It is likely that some of the details will change before this version of C# is shipped.

You will be writing code to cube (raise to the third power) numbers. Consider the following code:

```
class CuberGenerator
{
    static string CubedExpression(double x)
    {
        return x.ToString() + " * " + x.ToString() + " * " + x.ToString();
    }

    public static Func<double> GetCuber(double x)
    {
        string program =
            @"class Cuber {public static double Cubed() { return " +
            CubedExpression(x) +
            "; } }";

        Console.WriteLine(program);

        SyntaxTree tree = SyntaxTree.ParseCompilationUnit(program);
```

---

[1]And to rewrite the VB .NET compiler in VB .NET.
[2]The previews can run on both Visual Studio 2010 and Visual Studio 2012. Search for *download Roslyn CTP*.

```
        Compilation compilation = Compilation.Create(
                    "CuberGenerator.dll",
                    new CompilationOptions(OutputKind.DynamicallyLinkedLibrary),
                    new[] { tree },
                    new[] { new AssemblyFileReference(typeof(object).Assembly.Location) });

        Assembly compiledAssembly;
        using (var stream = new MemoryStream())
        {
            EmitResult compileResult = compilation.Emit(stream);
            compiledAssembly = Assembly.Load(stream.GetBuffer());
        }

        Type cuber = compiledAssembly.GetType("Cuber");
        MethodInfo getValue = cuber.GetMethod("Cubed");

        Func<double> cubedValue =
                (Func<double>)Delegate.CreateDelegate(typeof(Func<double>), getValue);
        return cubedValue;
    }
}
```

You start by creating the class that will perform the operation as a string. The string is then passed to `SyntaxTree.ParseCompilationUnit()`, which is equivalent to running the first part of the C# compiler over the class you've created. That generates a `SyntaxTree`, which contains a parsed version of the program. The syntax tree is then passed to `Compilation.Create()`, which implements the second part of compilation, converting the syntax tree to .NET IL that can be executed by the runtime. The assembly is then loaded into an `Assembly` instance, and reflection is used to locate the method to be called. This can then be called using the following code:

```
Func<double> cuber = CuberGenerator.GetCuber(7);
Console.WriteLine(cuber());
```

This example is, of course, contrived; it makes no sense to generate custom code just to cube a number. It is more reasonable if a general implementation of an algorithm is much slower than a specific one.

The `SyntaxTree` that was generated can also be used for source analysis; if you want to determine how many times a specific type is used as a method parameter, you can do that by traversing the syntax tree.

CHAPTER 37

■ ■ ■

Interop

One of the important capabilities of C# is being able to interoperate with existing code, whether it is COM-based or in a native DLL. This chapter provides a brief overview of how interop works.

For more information on interop, check out *COM and .NET Interoperability* by Andrew Troelsen (Apress, 2002).

COM Objects

Interop with COM objects is a very complex subject; COM and .NET have different—and sometimes incompatible—object models and execution environments.

If you want to use an existing COM object and you can stay within the simple COM interfaces, it is generally fairly straightforward to perform most functions. To call COM, you need to have an interop or proxy library that is generated from the COM object using the TLBIMP library (or provided directly, in the case of the Microsoft Office interop assemblies).[1] Once you have this library, you can use the types the way you would use other C# types. The .NET runtime handles translating between the .NET world and the COM world.

■ **Note** Sometimes TLBIMP doesn't quite give you the interface you want. If this is the case, you can take the assembly you got from TLBIMP and run it through a decompiler (such as JetBrain's dotPeek), which will give you C# code. You can then modify it to work the way you need it to work.

The runtime also lets .NET objects be used in place of COM objects. The TLBEXP utility is used to create a typelib that describes the COM objects so that other COM-based programs can determine the object's interface, and the REGASM utility is used to register an assembly so that it can be accessed through COM. When COM accesses a .NET class, the runtime creates the .NET object, fabricating whatever COM interfaces are required and marshaling the data between the .NET world and the COM world.

■ **Tip** You can include the interop classes directly into your assembly by setting the Embed Interop Types property to true on the reference to the interop assembly in your project.

---

[1]These are sometimes known as *primary interop assemblies* (PIAs).

Calling Native DLL Functions

C# can call C functions written in native code through a runtime feature known as *platform invoke*, or simply p/invoke. The file that the function is located in is specified by the DllImport attribute, which can also be used to specify the default character marshaling. In many cases, that attribute is all that is needed, but if a value is passed by reference, ref or out may be specified to tell the marshaler how to pass the value. Here's an example:

```
class CallMessageBox
{
    [DllImport("user32.dll")]
    static extern int MessageBox(IntPtr h, string m, string c, int type);

    public static void ShowMessageBox(string message)
    {
        int retval = MessageBox(IntPtr.Zero, message, "Caption", 0);
    }
    static void Main()
    {
        CallMessageBox.ShowMessageBox("Test");
    }
}
```

When this code runs, a message box will appear. Note that the code uses MessageBox() rather than the ASCII- or Unicode-specific versions; the runtime will automatically use the appropriate function (MessageBoxA() or MessageBoxW()) based on the platform, though you can specify in the attribute which variant to pick if you want to override the runtime's choice.

IntPtr.Zero is used to pass a pointer that is defined to match the pointer size of the underlying platform, making conversion to 64-bit (or wider) platforms much easier.

■ **Note**   The DllImport attribute works only for calling C functions; it cannot be used to hook up to C++ classes. Interop to C++ classes can be done either through COM interop or by using C++/CLI.

Pointers and Declarative Pinning

It's common for C-style functions to take pointers as their parameters. This is problematic in C#, because the actual location where an instance lives can move around when the runtime garbage collector runs. What is needed is a way to keep an instance from moving for a short period of time so that you can call a function safely. This is done using a technique known as *declarative pinning*, using the fixed keyword.

The following example calls ReadFile() from kernel32.dll:

```
using System.Runtime.InteropServices;
class FileRead
{
    const uint GENERIC_READ = 0x80000000;
    const uint OPEN_EXISTING = 3;
    SafeFileHandle handle;

    public FileRead(string filename)
    {
        // opens the existing file...
```

```
        handle = CreateFile(filename,
                GENERIC_READ,
                0,
                0,
                OPEN_EXISTING,
                0,
                0);
    }

    [DllImport("kernel32", SetLastError = true)]
    static extern SafeFileHandle CreateFile(
        string filename,
        uint desiredAccess,
        uint shareMode,
        uint attributes,          // really SecurityAttributes pointer
        uint creationDisposition,
        uint flagsAndAttributes,
        uint templateFile);

    // SetLastError = true is used to tell the interop layer to keep track of
    //underlying Windows errors
    [DllImport("kernel32", SetLastError = true)]
    static extern unsafe bool ReadFile(
        SafeFileHandle hFile,
        void* lpBuffer,
        int nBytesToRead,
        int* nBytesRead,
        int overlapped);

    public unsafe int Read(byte[] buffer, int count)
    {
        int n = 0;
        fixed (byte* p = buffer)
        {
            ReadFile(handle, p, count, &n, 0);
        }
        return n;
    }
}
class ReadFileUnsafeTest
{
    public static void Main()
    {
        FileRead fr = new FileRead(@"..\..\readfileunsafe.cs");

        byte[] buffer = new byte[128];
        ASCIIEncoding e = new ASCIIEncoding();

        // loop through, read until done...
        Console.WriteLine("Contents");
        int bytesRead = 0;
        while ((bytesRead = fr.Read(buffer, buffer.Length - 1)) != 0)
```

```
    {
        Console.Write("{0}", e.GetString(buffer, 0, bytesRead));
    }
  }
}
```

In this example, the FileRead class encapsulates the code to read from the file. It declares the functions to import and the unsafe read function.

In the Read() method, the byte[] array buffer is a managed variable, which means the garbage collector can move it at any time. The fixed statement makes it safe to pass the pointer to the buffer to ReadFile(). After the call, the flag is cleared, and execution continues.

This approach is nice in that it has very low overhead—unless garbage collection occurs while the code is inside the fixed block, which is unlikely.

This sample works fine, but the class is subject to the usual constraints on unsafe code. See the section on input and output in Chapter 38. This sample also uses SafeFileHandle to encapsulate the file handle that came back from the call to CreateFile(); this will ensure that the handle is closed.

▥ **Tip**   If you are trying to call a function in Windows, do yourself a favor and head over to www.pinvoke.net, where somebody else has likely already written what you need.

A Safe Version

Since pointer support isn't required for .NET languages, other languages need to be able to call functions such as ReadFile() without using pointers. The runtime provides a considerable amount of support to make the marshaling from managed to unmanaged types (including pointer types) transparent.

The previous example can be rewritten without using unsafe. All that is required is to change the extern declaration for the ReadFile() and Read() functions.

```
[DllImport("kernel32", SetLastError=true)]
static extern bool ReadFile(
    SafeFileHandle hFile,
    byte[] buffer,
    int nBytesToRead,
    ref int nBytesRead,
    int overlapped);

public int Read(byte[] buffer, int count)
{
    int n = 0;
    ReadFile(handle, buffer, count, ref n, 0);
    return n;
}
```

The pointer parameter for the buffer has been changed to a byte[], and the number of characters read is defined as a ref int instead of an int*.

In this version, the runtime will do the pinning of the buffer automatically for you, and because unsafe isn't required, this version isn't subject to the same restrictions as the previous example.

Structure Layout

The runtime allows a structure to specify the layout of its data members, using the StructLayout attribute. By default, the layout of a structure is automatic, which means the runtime is free to rearrange the fields. When using interop to call into native or COM code, better control is required.

When specifying the StructLayout attribute, three kinds of layout can be specified using the LayoutKind enum.

- Auto, where the runtime chooses the appropriate way to lay out the members.

- Sequential, where all fields are in declaration order. For sequential layout, the Pack property can be used to specify the type of packing.

- Explicit, where every field has a specified offset. In explicit layout, the StructOffset attribute must be used on every member to specify the offset in bytes of the element.[2]

Additionally, the CharSet property can be specified to set the default marshaling for string data members. By default, the C# compiler sets sequential layout for all structs.

Calling a Function with a Structure Parameter

To call a function with a structure parameter, the structure is defined with the appropriate parameters. This example shows how to call the GetWindowPlacement() method:

```csharp
struct WindowPlacement
{
    public uint length;
    public uint flags;
    public uint showCmd;
    public Point minPosition;
    public Point maxPosition;
    public Rectangle normalPosition;

    public override string ToString()
    {
        return String.Format("min, max, normal:\n{0}\n{1}\n{2}",
            minPosition, maxPosition, normalPosition);
    }
}
class Window
{
    [DllImport("user32")]
    static extern IntPtr GetForegroundWindow();

    [DllImport("user32")]
    static extern bool GetWindowPlacement(IntPtr handle, ref WindowPlacement wp);

    public static void Main()
    {
        IntPtr window = GetForegroundWindow();
```

---

[2]This can also be used to create C-style unions.

```
        WindowPlacement wp = new WindowPlacement();
        wp.length = (uint)Marshal.SizeOf(wp);

        bool result = GetWindowPlacement(window, ref wp);

        if (result)
        {
            Console.WriteLine(wp);
        }
    }
}
}
```

This example uses `Marshal.SizeOf()`, which will return the size of the instance on the native side after it has been marshaled. This is useful when calling many Windows functions.

Fixed-Size Buffers

It is common practice for a C-language application to use fixed-sized buffers to store data, both in memory and on disk. A fixed-size buffer of a primitive type such as `int` or `char` is very easy and quick to populate; the data that is needed to populate the entire buffer can be copied over the entire buffer using the C runtime `memcpy` function (or equivalent). The simplicity and speed of accessing fixed-size buffers come at a considerable cost in terms of code correctness and security, and fixed-size buffers are notorious as the source of many serious security breaches,[3] which is why .NET uses a different model.

In the .NET model, all access to elements in a buffer is checked, and because arrays are reference types, an array declared as part of a structure does not physically live inside the structure. Instead, a reference to the array is placed inside the structure, which points to the location of the array on the heap. This means that a `memcpy` or equivalent would not work (even if it were legal), because the memory inside the buffer is not laid out in memory correctly.

The Windows API function `GetVersionEx` is a good example of an API where fixed-size buffers are used. The single parameter that is passed to the function is a pointer to an `OSVERSIONINFO` structure, defined in C as follows:

```
typedef struct _OSVERSIONINFO {
    DWORD dwOSVersionInfoSize;
    DWORD dwMajorVersion;
    DWORD dwMinorVersion;
    DWORD dwBuildNumber;
    DWORD dwPlatformId;
    TCHAR szCSDVersion[128];
} OSVERSIONINFO;
```

This can be expressed in C# as follows:

```
unsafe struct OsVersionInfo
{
    public uint OsVersionInfoSize;
    public uint MajorVersion;
    public uint MinorVersion;
```

---

[3]If you can get code to write beyond the end of a fixed-size buffer, you can often change the code that it executes.

```
    public uint BuildNumber;
    public uint PlatformId;
    public fixed byte ServicePackVersion[128];
}
class OsVersionInfoTest
{
    [DllImport("Kernel32.dll", EntryPoint="GetVersionEx")]
    static extern bool GetVersion(ref OsVersionInfo lpVersionInfo);

    unsafe public static void Main()
    {
        OsVersionInfo versionInfo = new OsVersionInfo();
        versionInfo.OsVersionInfoSize = (uint) Marshal.SizeOf(versionInfo);
        bool res = GetVersion(ref versionInfo);
        Console.WriteLine(Marshal.PtrToStringAnsi(new IntPtr(versionInfo.ServicePackVersion)));
    }
}
```

As with all unsafe code, there is a risk involved, and if the size of memory blocks do not line up correctly, there is the potential for application crashes and security vulnerabilities.

For arrays of characters, the runtime can handle creating the inline array automatically. This definition for OsVersionInfo is cleaner and simpler to use.

```
unsafe struct OsVersionInfo
{
    public uint OsVersionInfoSize;
    public uint MajorVersion;
    public uint MinorVersion;
    public uint BuildNumber;
    public uint PlatformId;
    [MarshalAs(UnmanagedType.ByValTStr, SizeConst = 128)]
    public string ServicePackVersion;
}
```

Hooking Up to a Windows Callback

The Win32 API sometimes uses callback functions to pass information back to the caller asynchronously. The closest analogy to a callback function in C# (and in the Common Language Runtime) is a delegate, so the runtime interop layer can map a delegate to a callback. Here's an example that does so for the SetConsoleHandler() API (the one used to catch Ctrl+C):

```
using System;
using System.Threading;
using System.Runtime.InteropServices;

class ConsoleCtrl
{
    public enum ConsoleEvent
    {
        CTRL_C = 0,          // From wincom.h
        CTRL_BREAK = 1,
```

357

```
            CTRL_CLOSE = 2,
            CTRL_LOGOFF = 5,
            CTRL_SHUTDOWN = 6
    }

    public delegate void ControlEventHandler(ConsoleEvent consoleEvent);

    public event ControlEventHandler ControlEvent;

        // save delegate so the GC doesn't collect it.
    ControlEventHandler eventHandler;

    public ConsoleCtrl()
    {
            // save this to a private var so the GC doesn't collect it...
        eventHandler = new ControlEventHandler(Handler);
        SetConsoleCtrlHandler(eventHandler, true);
    }

    private void Handler(ConsoleEvent consoleEvent)
    {
        if (ControlEvent != null)
            ControlEvent(consoleEvent);
    }

    [DllImport("kernel32.dll")]
    static extern bool SetConsoleCtrlHandler(ControlEventHandler e, bool add);
}

class Test
{
    public static void MyHandler(ConsoleCtrl.ConsoleEvent consoleEvent)
    {
        Console.WriteLine("Event: {0}", consoleEvent);
    }

    public static void Main()
    {
        ConsoleCtrl cc = new ConsoleCtrl();
        cc.ControlEvent += new ConsoleCtrl.ControlEventHandler(MyHandler);

        Console.WriteLine("Enter 'E' to exit");

        Thread.Sleep(15000);  // sleep 15 seconds
    }
}
```

The ConsoleCtrl class encapsulates the API function. It defines a delegate that matches the signature of the Win32 callback function and then uses that as the type passed to the Win32 function. It exposes an event that other classes can hook up to.

The one subtlety of this example has to do with the following line:

```
ControlEventHandler eventHandler;
```

The runtime will automatically prevent any parameters that are passed to a `DllImport` function from being collected while the function is executing, but there's no way for the runtime to know that the pointer needs to be kept around. If the delegate weren't stored in a place the garbage collector could find, it would be collected the next time the garbage collector runs. If you forget to do this, your code will likely crash at some future time.

The Marshal Class

The `Marshal` class provides a set of methods that can be used to allocate different types of unmanaged memory, copy data to and from unmanaged memory, and work directly with COM.

Design Guidelines

The following are guidelines that can be used to decide what method of interop to use and how to use it.

C# or C++?

The two options for doing interop with existing C libraries are calling functions directly from C# using platform invoke (ie `DllImport`) and using a Visual C++/CLI class to encapsulate the C functions in a nice managed class.

Which is the better choice depends upon the interface being called. It's easy to tell by how much effort it takes to get it working. If it's straightforward, then doing it in C# is easy. If you find yourself asking "How do I do that in C#?" several times or you start using a lot of unsafe code, then it's likely that doing it using Managed Extensions is a better choice. This is especially true for complex interfaces, where a structure contains pointers to other structures or the sizes of a structure aren't fixed.

In such cases, you'll need to do a translation from the C-style way of doing things to the .NET-managed way of doing things. This might involve grabbing a value out of a union or walking through a structure of variable size and then putting the values into the appropriate variable on the collection class. Doing such an operation is a lot easier in C++ than it is in C#, and you likely already have working C++ code on which you can base your C# code.

Marshaling Best Practices

When importing functions into C#, consider the following best practices:

- In general, the data marshaling layer does the right thing. Choose the type that's closest to the type you want.

- For opaque types (like pointers) where all you really care about is the size of the variable, use the appropriate `SafeHandle`-derived class (or `IntPtr.Zero` if you just need to pass a null handle.

- To control data marshaling, use the `MarshalAs` attribute. This is most often used to control string marshaling.

- Rather than using a pointer type for a parameter, define it using `ref` or `out`.

- Read the "Data Marshalling Specification" section in the .NET Framework developer specifications.

- If things get ugly, switch to using C++/CLI. Switching to C++/CLI can range from writing a small wrapper that is then called from C# to using C++/CLI for large portions of an application. The optimum technique depends on the skill set of the developers available.

■ ■ ■

CHAPTER 38

.NET Base Class Library Overview

The .NET Base Class Library (BCL) contains many functions normally found in language-specific runtime libraries. It is therefore important to understand what classes are available in the BCL.

Numeric Formatting

Numeric types are formatted through the Format() member function of that data type. This can be called directly, through String.Format(), which calls the Format() function of each data type, or through Console.WriteLine(), which calls String.Format().

Adding formatting to a user-defined object is discussed in the "Custom Object Formatting" section later in this chapter. This section discusses how formatting is done with the built-in types.

There are two methods of specifying numeric formatting. A standard format string can be used to convert a numeric type to a specific string representation. If further control over the output is desired, a custom format string can be used.

Standard Format Strings

A standard format string consists of a character specifying the format, followed by a sequence of digits specifying the precision. The formats in Table 38-1 are supported.

Table 38-1. *Standard Format Strings*

Format Character	Description
C, c	Currency
D, d	Decimal
E, e	Scientific (exponential)
F, f	Fixed-point
G, g	General
N, n	Number
R, r	Round-trip
X, x	Hexadecimal

Currency

The currency format string converts the numerical value to a string containing a locale-specific currency amount. By default, the format information is determined by the current locale, but this may be changed by passing a NumberFormatInfo object. This example:

```
Console.WriteLine("{0:C}", 33345.8977);
Console.WriteLine("{0:C}", -33345.8977);
```

gives the following output:

```
$33,345.90
($33,345.90)
```

An integer following the C specifies the number of decimal places to use; two places are used if the integer is omitted.

Decimal

The decimal format string converts the numerical value to an integer. The minimum number of digits is determined by the precision specifier. The result is left-padded with zeroes to obtain the required number of digits. This example:

```
Console.WriteLine("{0:D}", 33345);
Console.WriteLine("{0:D7}", 33345);
```

gives the following output:

```
33345
0033345
```

Scientific (Exponential)

The scientific (exponential) format string converts the value to a string in the following form:

m.dddE+xxx

One digit always precedes the decimal point, and the number of decimal places is specified by the precision specifier, with six places used as the default. The format specifier controls whether E or e appears in the output. This example:

```
Console.WriteLine("{0:E}", 33345.8977);
Console.WriteLine("{0:E10}", 33345.8977);
Console.WriteLine("{0:e4}", 33345.8977);
```

gives the following output:

```
3.334590E+004
3.3345897700E+004
3.3346e+004
```

Fixed-Point

The fixed-point format string converts the value to a string, with the number of places after the decimal point specified by the precision specifier. Two places are used if the precision specifier is omitted. This example:

```
Console.WriteLine("{0:F}", 33345.8977);
Console.WriteLine("{0:F0}", 33345.8977);
Console.WriteLine("{0:F5}", 33345.8977);
```

gives the following output:

```
33345.90
33346
33345.89770
```

General

The general format string converts the value to either a fixed-point or scientific format, whichever one gives a more compact format. This example:

```
Console.WriteLine("{0:G}", 33345.8977);
Console.WriteLine("{0:G7}", 33345.8977);
Console.WriteLine("{0:G4}", 33345.8977);
```

gives the following output:

```
33345.8977
33345.9
3.335E+04
```

Number

The number format string converts the value to a number that has embedded commas, such as the following:

```
12,345.11
```

By default, the number is formatted with two digits to the right of the decimal point. This can be controlled by specifying the number of digits after the format specifier. This example:

```
Console.WriteLine("{0:N}", 33345.8977);
Console.WriteLine("{0:N4}", 33345.8977);
```

gives the following output:

```
33,345.90
33,345.8977
```

It's possible to control the character used for the decimal point by passing a NumberFormatInfo object to the Format() function.

Round-Trip

Consider the following code:

```
class RoundTrip
{
    public static void Main()
    {
        Random random = new Random();
        while (true)
        {
            double value = random.NextDouble();

            if (value != ToStringAndBack(value))
            {
                Console.WriteLine("Different: {0}", value);
            }
        }
    }
    public static double ToStringAndBack(double value)
    {
        string valueAsString = value.ToString();

        return Double.Parse(valueAsString);
    }
}
```

The ToStringAndBack() method converts a double to a text value and then converts it back to a double. This is the same operation that might be occur when writing a double value to a file and then reading it back in again. Does this code write anything to the console?

The surprising answer is yes. The double type uses the IEEE 754 floating-point representation,[1] and that representation stores nearly (but not quite) 16 decimal digits. When you convert a double to a string, the conversion routine will return only the 15 digits of precision that it is sure are correct, and the extra bits get lost.

If you need to preserve the exact number, you can use the R format.

```
string valueAsString = value.ToString("R");
```

This ensures that the value read back will be identical[2] to the one that is saved.

■ **Note**   If you are doing numerical calculations, this loss of precision can be important. For more information about this and other properties of floating-point numbers, search for *what every computer scientist should know about floating-point arithmetic* online.

---

[1] Actually, pretty much everything uses IEEE 754.
[2] *Identical* means "has exactly the same bit pattern."

Hexadecimal

The hexadecimal format string converts the value to hexadecimal format. The minimum number of digits is set by the precision specifier; the number will be zero-padded to that width.

Using X will result in uppercase letters in the converted value; x will result in lowercase letters. This example:

```
Console.WriteLine("{0:X}", 255);
Console.WriteLine("{0:x8}", 1456);
```

gives the following output:

```
FF
000005b0
```

NumberFormatInfo

The NumberFormatInfo class is used to control the formatting of numbers. By setting the properties in this class, the programmer can control the currency symbol, decimal separator, and other formatting properties.

Custom Format Strings

Custom format strings are used to obtain more control over the conversion than is available through the standard format strings. In custom format strings, special characters form a template that the number is formatted into. Any characters that do not have a special meaning in the format string are copied verbatim to the output. Table 38-2 describes the custom strings available.

Table 38-2. *Custom Format Strings*

Character	Description	Result
0	Display zero placeholder	Displays leading zero if a number has fewer digits than there are zeroes in the format.
#	Display digit placeholder	Replaces # with the digit only for significant digits.
.	Decimal point	Displays the decimal point.
,	Group separator and multiplier	Separates number groups, such as 1,000. When used after a number, divides it by 1,000.
%	Display % notation	Displays the percent character.
;	Section separator	Uses different formats for positive, negative, and zero values.

Digit or Zero Placeholder

The zero (0) character is used as a digit or zero placeholder. If the numeric value has a digit in the position at which the 0 appears in the format string, the digit will appear in the result. If not, a zero appears in that position. This example:

```
Console.WriteLine("{0:000}", 55);
Console.WriteLine("{0:000}", 1456);
```

gives the following output:

```
055
1456
```

Digit or Space Placeholder

The pound (#) character is used as the digit or space placeholder. It works exactly the same as the 0 placeholder, except that the character is omitted if there is no digit in that position. This example:

```
Console.WriteLine("{0:#####}", 255);
Console.WriteLine("{0:#####}", 1456);
Console.WriteLine("{0:###}", 32767);
```

gives the following output:

```
255
1456
32767
```

Decimal Point

The first period (.) character that appears in the format string determines the location of the decimal separator in the result. The character used as the decimal separator in the formatted string is controlled by a NumberFormatInfo instance. This example:

```
Console.WriteLine("{0:#####.000}", 75928.3);
Console.WriteLine("{0:##.000}", 1456.456456);
```

gives the following output:

```
75928.300
1456.456
```

Group Separator

The comma (,) character is used as a group separator. If a comma appears in the middle of a display digit placeholder and to the left of the decimal point (if present), a group separator will be inserted in the string. The character used in the formatted string and the number of numbers to group together is controlled by a NumberFormatInfo instance. This example:

```
Console.WriteLine("{0:##,###}", 2555634323);
Console.WriteLine("{0:##,000.000}", 14563553.593993);
Console.WriteLine("{0:#,#.000}", 14563553.593993);
```

gives the following output:

```
2,555,634,323
14,563,553.594
14,563,553.594
```

Number Prescaler

The comma (,) character can also be used to indicate that the number should be prescaled. In this usage, the comma must come directly before the decimal point or at the end of the format string.

For each comma present in this location, the number is divided by 1,000 before it is formatted. This example:

```
Console.WriteLine("{0:000,.##}", 158847);
Console.WriteLine("{0:000,,,.###}", 1593833);
```

gives the following output:

```
158.85
000.002
```

Percent Notation

The percent (%) character is used to indicate that the number to be displayed should be displayed as a percentage. The number is multiplied by 100 before it is formatted. This example:

```
Console.WriteLine("{0:##.000 %}", 0.89144);
Console.WriteLine("{0:00 %}", 0.01285);
```

gives the following output:

```
89.144 %
01 %
```

Exponential Notation

When E+0, E-0, e+0, or e-0 appears in the format string directly after a # or 0 placeholder, the number will be formatted in exponential notation. The number of digits in the exponent is controlled by the number of 0 placeholders that appear in the exponent specifier. The E or e is copied directly into the formatted string, and a + means that there will be a plus or minus sign in that position, while a minus sign means there is a character there only if the number is negative. This example:

```
Console.WriteLine("{0:###.000E-00}", 3.1415533E+04);
Console.WriteLine("{0:#.0000000E+000}", 2.553939939E+101);
```

gives the following output:

```
314.155E-02
2.5539399E+101
```

Section Separator

The semicolon (;) character is used to specify different format strings for a number, depending on whether the number is positive, negative, or zero. If there are only two sections, the first section applies to positive and zero values, and the second applies to negative values. If there are three sections, they apply to positive values, negative values, and the zero value. This example:

```
Console.WriteLine("{0:###.00;0;(###.00)}", -456.55);
Console.WriteLine("{0:###.00;0;(###.00)}", 0);
Console.WriteLine("{0:###.00;0;(###.00)}", 456.55);
```

gives the following output:

```
457
(.00)
456.55
```

Escapes and Literals

The slash (\) character can be used to escape characters so they aren't interpreted as formatting characters. Because the slash already has meaning within C# literals, it will be easier to specify the string using the verbatim literal syntax; otherwise, a double slash (\\) is required to generate a single slash in the output string.

A string of uninterpreted characters can be specified by enclosing them in single quotes; this may be more convenient than using the slash character. This example:

```
Console.WriteLine("{0:###\\#}", 255);
Console.WriteLine(@"{0:###\#}", 255);
Console.WriteLine("{0:###'#0 %;'}", 1456);
```

gives the following output:

```
255#
255#
1456#0 %;
```

Date and Time Formatting

The DateTime class provides flexible formatting options. Several single-character formats can be specified, and custom formatting is also supported. Table 38-3 specifies the standard DateTime formats.

Table 38-3. *Date and Time Formats*

Character	Pattern	Description
D	MM/dd/yyyy	ShortDatePattern
D	dddd, MMMM dd, yyy	LongDatePattern
F	dddd, MMMM dd, YYYY HH:mm	Full (long date + short time)
F	dddd, MMMM dd, yyyy HH:mm:ss	FullDateTimePattern (long date + long time)
G	MM/dd/yyyy HH:mm	General (short date + short time)

(continued)

Table 38-3. (*continued*)

Character	Pattern	Description
G	MM/dd/yyyy HH:mm:ss	General (short date + long time)
m, M	MMMM dd	MonthDayPattern
r, R	ddd, dd MMM yy HH':'mm':'ss 'GMT'	RFC1123Pattern
s	yyyy-MM-dd HH:mm:ss	SortableDateTimePattern (ISO 8601)
s	YYYY-mm-DD hh:MM:SS GMT	Sortable with time zone information
t	HH:mm	ShortTimePattern
T	HH:mm:ss	LongTimePattern
u	yyyy-MM-dd HH:mm:ss	Same as s, but with universal instead of local time
U	dddd, MMMM dd, yyyy HH:mm:ss	UniversalSortableDateTimePattern

Custom DateTime Format

Table 38-4 lists the patterns that can be used to build a custom format.

Table 38-4. *Custom Date Formats*

Pattern	Description
D	Day of month as digits with no leading zero for single-digit days
Dd	Day of month as digits with leading zero for single-digit days
Ddd	Day of week as a three-letter abbreviation
dddd	Day of week as its full name
M	Month as digits with no leading zero for single-digit months
MM	Month as digits with leading zero
MMM	Month as three-letter abbreviation
MMMM	Month as its full name
Y	Year as last two digits, no leading zero
Yy	Year as last two digits, with leading zero
Yyyy	Year represented by four digits

The day and month names are determined by the appropriate field in the DateTimeFormatInfo class.

Custom Object Formatting

Earlier examples have overridden the ToString() function to provide a string representation of a function. An object can supply different formats by defining the IFormattable interface and then changing the representation based upon the string of the function.

For example, an employee class could add additional information with a different format string. This example:

```
using System;
class Employee: IFormattable
{
    public Employee(int id, string firstName, string lastName)
    {
        m_id = id;
        m_firstName = firstName;
        m_lastName = lastName;
    }
    public string ToString (string format, IFormatProvider fp)
    {
        if ((format != null) && (format.Equals("F")))
        {
            return String.Format("{0}: {1}, {2}",
                m_id, m_lastName, m_firstName);
        }
        else
        {
            return(m_id.ToString(format, fp));
        }
    }
    int m_id;
    string m_firstName;
    string m_lastName;
}
class Test
{
    public static void Main()
    {
        Employee fred=new Employee(123, "Fred", "Morthwaite");
        Console.WriteLine("No format: {0}", fred);
        Console.WriteLine("Full format: {0:F}", fred);
    }
}
```

produces the following output:

```
No format: 123
Full format: 123: Morthwaite, Fred
```

The ToString() function looks for the F format. If it finds it, it writes out the full information. If it doesn't find it, it uses the default format for the object.

The Main() function passes the format flag in the second WriteLine() call.

Numeric Parsing

Numbers are parsed using the Parse() method provided by the numeric data types. Flags from the NumberStyles class can be passed to specify which styles are allowed, and a NumberFormatInfo instance can be passed to control parsing.

A numeric string produced by any of the standard format specifiers (excluding hexadecimal) is guaranteed to be correctly parsed if the NumberStyles.Any style is specified. This example:

```
using System;
class Test
{
    public static void Main()
    {
        int value = Int32.Parse("99953");
        double dval = Double.Parse("1.3433E+35");
        Console.WriteLine("{0}", value);
        Console.WriteLine("{0}", dval);
    }
}
```

produces the following output:

```
99953
1.3433E35
```

Using TryParse to Avoid Exceptions

If there is a reasonable chance that the input string contains invalid characters, which means that Parse() will be unable to convert to the appropriate type and throw an exception, the TryParse() method should be used instead. Rather than throwing an exception if the input cannot be successfully converted, TryParse() instead returns a boolean that indicates the success of the conversion, with the result of the conversion returned as an out parameter.

```
Console.WriteLine("Please enter an integer and press Enter");
int numberEntered;
while(!int.TryParse(Console.ReadLine(), out numberEntered))
{
    Console.WriteLine("Please try again");
}
Console.WriteLine("You entered " + numberEntered.ToString());
```

Input and Output

The .NET Common Language Runtime provides I/O functions in the System.IO namespace. This namespace contains classes for doing I/O and for other I/O-related functions, such as directory traversal, file watching, and so on.

Reading and writing are done using the Stream class, which merely describes how bytes can be read and written to some sort of backing store. Stream is an abstract class, so in practice classes derived from Stream will be used. Table 38-5 lists the available stream classes.

Table 38-5. *Basic .NET Stream Classes*

Class	Description
FileStream	A stream on a disk file
MemoryStream	A stream that is stored in memory
NetworkStream	A stream on a network connection
BufferedStream	Implements a buffer on top of another stream
GZipStream	A stream that can compress or decompress data passing through it using GZip (RFC 1952)
DeflateStream	A stream that can compress or decompress data passing through it using LZW77 (RFC 1951)

With the exception of BufferedStream, GZipStream, and DeflateStream, which sit on top of another stream, each stream defines where the written data will go.

The Stream class provides raw functions to read and write at a byte level, both synchronously and asynchronously. Usually, however, it's nice to have a higher-level interface on top of a stream, and there are several supplied ones that can be selected depending on what final format is desired.

Binary

The BinaryReader and BinaryWriter classes are used to read and write values in binary (or raw) format. For example, a BinaryWriter can be used to write an int, followed by a float, followed by another int. These classes operate on a stream.

Text

The TextReader and TextWriter abstract classes define how text is read and written. They allow operations on characters, lines, blocks, and so on. Two different implementations of TextReader are available.

The somewhat strangely named StreamWriter class is the one used for "normal" I/O (open a file, read the lines out) and operates on a Stream.

The StringReader and StringWriter classes can be used to read and write from a string.

XML

The XmlTextReader and XmlTextWriter classes are used to read and write XML. They are similar to TextReader and TextWriter in design, but they do not derive from those classes because they deal with XML entities rather than text. They are low-level classes used to create or decode XML from scratch. See Chapter 29 for more information on dealing with XML.

Serial Ports

The serial ports on a machine can be accessed using the SerialPort class in the System.IO.Ports namespace. The SerialPort class allows properties such as baud rate, parity, and timeouts to be set. SerialPort has methods that provide direct access to the data that is flowing through the port, and it also supports stream-based access so helper streams like BufferedStream or asynchronous operations can be used.

This sample shows both the direct and stream-based approaches:

```
using System.IO.Ports;
...
byte[] buffer = new byte[256];
using (SerialPort sp = new SerialPort("COM1", 19200))
{
    sp.Open();
    //read directly
    sp.Read(buffer, 0, (int)buffer.Length);
    //read using a Stream
    sp.BaseStream.Read(buffer, 0, (int)buffer.Length);}
```

Writing Files

It is simple to create a file using the File and StreamWriter[3] classes.

```
using (StreamWriter writer = File.CreateText("output.txt"))
{
    writer.WriteLine("{0} {1}", "test", 55);
}
```

Reading Files

It is simple to read a file; this time you will use the File and StreamReader classes.

```
using (StreamReader reader = File.OpenText("output.txt"))
{
    string line = reader.ReadLine();
    Console.WriteLine(line);
}
```

Traversing Directories

This example shows how to traverse a directory structure. It defines both a DirectoryWalker class that takes delegates to be called for each directory and file and a path to traverse.

```
public static class DirectoryWalker
{
    public static void DoWalk(
        Action<DirectoryInfo, int> directoryCallback,
        Action<FileInfo, int> fileCallback,
        string rootDirectory)
```

---

[3]At this point, you may be asking, "Why do I read and write text files using the StreamWriter class? Why don't I use the TextWriter class?" Many people have asked that question, and the answer is that it's just one of the few unfortunate naming choices in the framework.

```csharp
    {
        DoWalk(
            directoryCallback,
            fileCallback,
            new DirectoryInfo(rootDirectory),
            0);
    }
    static void DoWalk(
        Action<DirectoryInfo, int> directoryCallback,
        Action<FileInfo, int> fileCallback,
        DirectoryInfo dir,
        int level)
    {
        foreach (FileInfo file in dir.EnumerateFiles())
        {
            if (fileCallback != null)
            {
                fileCallback(file, level);
            }
        }
        foreach (DirectoryInfo directory in dir.EnumerateDirectories())
        {
            if (directoryCallback != null)
            {
                directoryCallback(directory, level);
            }
            DoWalk(directoryCallback, fileCallback, directory, level + 1);
        }
    }
}
public class DirectoryWalkerTest
{
    public static void PrintDir(DirectoryInfo d, int level)
    {
        Console.WriteLine(new string(' ', level * 2));
        Console.WriteLine("Dir: {0}", d.FullName);
    }
    public static void PrintFile(FileInfo f, int level)
    {
        Console.WriteLine(new string(' ', level * 2));
        Console.WriteLine("File: {0}", f.FullName);
    }
    public static void Main()
    {
        DirectoryWalker.DoWalk(
            PrintDir,
            PrintFile,
            "..");
    }
}
```

Starting Processes

The .NET BCL provides the Process class, which is used to start processes. The following example shows how to start Notepad:

```
using System.Diagnostics;
class Test
{
    public static void Main()
    {
        ProcessStartInfo startInfo = new ProcessStartInfo();
        startInfo.FileName = "notepad.exe";
        startInfo.Arguments = "process.cs";

        Process.Start(startInfo);
    }
}
```

The arguments used in starting the process are contained in the ProcessStartInfo object.

Redirecting Process Output

Sometimes it's useful to get the output from a process. This can be done with the following code:

```
using System;
using System.Diagnostics;
class Test
{
    public static void Main()
    {
        Process process = new Process();
        process.StartInfo.FileName = "cmd.exe";
        process.StartInfo.Arguments = "/c dir *.cs";
        process.StartInfo.UseShellExecute = false;
        process.StartInfo.RedirectStandardOutput = true;
        process.Start();

        string output = process.StandardOutput.ReadToEnd();

        Console.WriteLine("Output:");
        Console.WriteLine(output);
    }
}
```

Detecting Process Completion

It's also possible to detect when a process exits.

```
using System;
using System.Diagnostics;
class Test
{
    static void ProcessDone(object sender, EventArgs e)
    {
        Console.WriteLine("Process Exited");
    }

    public static void Main()
    {
        Process process = new Process();
        process.StartInfo.FileName = "notepad.exe";
        process.StartInfo.Arguments = "process3.cs";
        process.EnableRaisingEvents = true;
        process.Exited += ProcessDone;
        process.Start();
        process.WaitForExit();
        Console.WriteLine("Back from WaitForExit()");
    }
}
```

This example shows two different ways of detecting process completion. The ProcessDone() function is called when the Exited event is fired, and the WaitForExit() function also returns when the process is done.

Serialization

Serialization is the process used by the runtime to persist objects in some sort of storage or to transfer them from one location to another.

The metadata information on an object contains sufficient information for the runtime to serialize the fields, but the runtime needs a little help to do the right thing.

This help is provided through two attributes. The [Serializable] attribute is used to mark an object as OK to serialize. The [NonSerialized] attribute can be applied to a field or property to indicate that it shouldn't be serialized. This is useful if it is a cache or derived value.

The following example has a container class named MyRow that has elements of the MyElement class. The cacheValue field in MyElement is marked with the [NonSerialized] attribute to prevent it from being serialized.

In this example, the MyRow object is serialized and deserialized to a binary format:

```
using System;
using System.IO;
using System.Collections.Generic;
using System.Linq;
using System.Runtime.Serialization;
using System.Runtime.Serialization.Formatters.Binary;

[Serializable]
public class MyElement
```

```csharp
{
    public MyElement(string name)
    {
        m_name = name;
        m_cacheValue = 15;
    }
    public override string ToString()
    {
        return String.Format("{0}: {1}", m_name, m_cacheValue);
    }
    string m_name;
    // this field isn't persisted.
    [NonSerialized]
    int m_cacheValue;
}
[Serializable]
public class MyRow
{
    public void Add(MyElement myElement)
    {
        m_elements.Add(myElement);
    }
    public override string ToString()
    {
        return String.Join(
            "\n",
            m_elements
                .Select(element => element.ToString())
                .ToList());
    }
    List<MyElement> m_elements = new List<MyElement>();
}
public class SerializationTest
{
    public static void Main()
    {
        MyRow row = new MyRow();
        row.Add(new MyElement("Gumby"));
        row.Add(new MyElement("Pokey"));

        Console.WriteLine("Initial value");
        Console.WriteLine("{0}", row);

        // write to binary, read it back
        using (Stream streamWriter=File.Create("MyRow.bin"))
        {
            BinaryFormatter binaryWriter=new BinaryFormatter();
            binaryWriter.Serialize(streamWriter, row);
        }

        MyRow rowBinary = null;
        using (Stream streamReader = File.OpenRead("MyRow.bin"))
```

```
        {
            BinaryFormatter binaryReader = new BinaryFormatter();
            rowBinary = (MyRow)binaryReader.Deserialize(streamReader);
        }

        Console.WriteLine("Values after binary serialization");
        Console.WriteLine("{0}", rowBinary);
    }
}
```

The example produces the following output:

```
Initial value
Gumby: 15
Pokey: 15

Values after binary serialization
Gumby: 0
Pokey: 0
```

The field cacheValue is not preserved since it was marked as [NonSerialized]. The file MyRow.Bin will contain the binary serialization. To serialize to XML, use the XmlSerializer class.

Custom Serialization

If the standard serialization doesn't do exactly what is desired or doesn't give sufficient control, a class can define exactly how it wants to be serialized,[4] like in this example:

```
using System;
using System.IO;
using System.Runtime.Serialization;
using System.Runtime.Serialization.Formatters.Binary;

[Serializable]
class Employee : ISerializable
{
    int m_id;
    string m_name;
    string m_address;

    public Employee(int id, string name, string address)
    {
        m_id = id;
        m_name = name;
        m_address = address;
    }
```

---

[4]If you're familiar with how MFC serialization worked in Visual C++, this approach will seem fairly familiar.

```csharp
    public override string ToString()
    {
        return (String.Format("{0} {1} {2}", m_id, m_name, m_address));
    }

    Employee(SerializationInfo info, StreamingContext content)
    {
        m_id = info.GetInt32("id");
        m_name = info.GetString("name");
        m_address = info.GetString("address");
    }

    // called to save the object data...
    public void GetObjectData(SerializationInfo info, StreamingContext content)
    {
        info.AddValue("id", m_id);
        info.AddValue("name", m_name);
        info.AddValue("address", m_address);
    }
}

class CustomSerializationTest
{
    public static void Serialize(Employee employee, string filename)
    {
        using (Stream streamWrite = File.Create(filename))
        {
            IFormatter writer = new BinaryFormatter();
            writer.Serialize(streamWrite, employee);
        }
    }

    public static Employee Deserialize(string filename)
    {
        Employee employee = null;
        using (Stream streamRead = File.OpenRead(filename))
        {
            IFormatter reader = new BinaryFormatter();
            employee = (Employee)reader.Deserialize(streamRead);
        }
        return (employee);
    }

    public static void Main()
    {
        Employee employee = new Employee(15, "Fred", "Bedrock");

        Serialize(employee, "emp.dat");
        Employee employeeBack = Deserialize("emp.dat");
        Console.WriteLine("Employee: {0}", employeeBack);
    }
}
```

To perform custom serialization, an object must implement the ISerializable interface. The GetObjectData() method is the only method on that interface. The implementation of that method stores each value by calling AddValue() on each value and passing in a name for the field and the field value.

To deserialize an object, the runtime relies on a special constructor. This constructor will call the appropriate get function to fetch a value based on the name.

Although this approach does take some extra space to store the names—and a bit of time to look them up—it versions very well, allowing new values to be added without invalidating existing stored files.

XML Serialization

The XmlSerializer class can be used to serialize an object to an XML representation. Here's an example:

```
public class Employee
{
    public string Name { get; set; }
    public Decimal Salary { get; set; }
    public DateTime DateOfBirth { get; set; }
}
public static void SaveEmployee()
{
    Employee employee = new Employee();
    employee.Name = "Peter";
    employee.Salary = 15123M;
    employee.DateOfBirth = DateTime.Parse("12/31/1994");

    XmlSerializer serializer = new XmlSerializer(typeof(Employee));

    using (Stream writeStream = File.OpenWrite("Employee.xml"))
    {
        serializer.Serialize(writeStream, employee);
    }
}
```

This code will generate the following output:

```
<?xml version="1.0"?>
<Employee xmlns:xsi="http://www.w3.org/2001/XMLSchema-instance
" xmlns:xsd="http://www.w3.org/2001/XMLSchema">
  <Name>Peter</Name>
  <Salary>15123</Salary>
  <DateOfBirth>1994-12-31T00:00:00</DateOfBirth>
</Employee>
```

Reading the object back in is equally simple.

```
public static Employee LoadEmployee()
{
    XmlSerializer serializer = new XmlSerializer(typeof(Employee));
```

```
    using (Stream readStream = File.OpenRead("Employee.xml"))
    {
        return (Employee) serializer.Deserialize(readStream);
    }
}
```

The `XmlSerializer` class provides a considerable amount of control over the format of the XML representation. Here's an example:

```
[XmlType(TypeName = "Employee2005")]
public class Employee
{
    [XmlElement("FullName")]
    public string Name { get; set; }

    [XmlAttribute("Salary")]
    public Decimal Salary { get; set; }

    public DateTime DateOfBirth { get; set; }

    [XmlIgnore]
    public int Weight { get; set; }
}
```

The attributes have the following effects:

- The `XmlType` attribute changes the name of the `Employee` element to `Employee2005`.

- The `XmlElement` attribute changes the name of the `Name` property to `FullName`.

- The `XmlAttribute` attribute saves the salary as an attribute instead of an element.

- The `XmlIgnore` attribute skips the weight value during serialization.

Here is the generated XML:

```
<?xml version="1.0"?>
<Employee2005 xmlns:xsi="http://www.w3.org/2001/XMLSchema-instance"
xmlns:xsd="http://www.w3.org/2001/XMLSchema" Salary="15123">
  <FullName>Peter</FullName>
  <DateOfBirth>1994-12-31T00:00:00</DateOfBirth>
</Employee2005>
```

XmlSerializer or XElement?

Reading and writing XML can be done through using the `XmlSerializer` class or using the `XElement` class discussed in Chapter 29. Using `XmlSerializer` is generally a bit easier but may be harder to understand than the same code written using `XElement`. My recommendation is to use `XmlSerializer` if the destination of the data is a class that is easily expressed using the serialization attributes and to use `XElement` for the remainder of the scenarios.

Reading Web Pages

The following example demonstrates how to fetch a web page using C#[5]:

```csharp
using System;
using System.Net;
using System.IO;
using System.Text;
using System.Text.RegularExpressions;

static class PageFetcher
{
    public static string Fetch(string url)
    {
        WebRequest req = WebRequest.Create(new Uri(url));
        WebResponse resp = req.GetResponse();

        string contents = null;
        using (Stream stream = resp.GetResponseStream())
        using (StreamReader reader = new StreamReader(stream))
        {
            contents = reader.ReadToEnd();
        }

        return (contents);
    }
}
class WebPageTest
{
    public static void Main()
    {
        string page = PageFetcher.Fetch("http://www.microsoft.com");
        Console.WriteLine(page);
    }
}
```

Accessing Environment Settings

The System.Environment class can be used to obtain information about the machine and environment, as the following example demonstrates:

```csharp
using System;
using System.Collections;

class EnvironmentTest
{
    public static void Main()
    {
```

---

[5]See Chapter 35 for more information on this subject.

```csharp
        Console.WriteLine("Command Line: {0}", Environment.CommandLine);
        Console.WriteLine("Current Directory: {0}", Environment.CurrentDirectory);
        Console.WriteLine("Machine Name: {0}", Environment.MachineName);

        Console.WriteLine("Environment Variables");
        foreach (DictionaryEntry var in Environment.GetEnvironmentVariables())
        {
            Console.WriteLine("    {0}={1}", var.Key, var.Value);
        }
    }
}
```

CHAPTER 39

■ ■ ■

Deeper into C#

This chapter will delve deeper into some issues you might encounter using C#. It covers some topics of interest to the library/framework author, such as style guidelines and XML documentation, and it also discusses how to write unsafe code and how the .NET Runtime's garbage collector works.

C# Style

Most languages develop an expected idiom for expression. When dealing with C character strings, for example, the usual idiom involves pointer arithmetic rather than array references. There are a number of different C# guidelines around, and a popular one is the "Class Library Design Guidelines" section in the .NET documentation.

■ **Note** The published guidelines are designed for those who write class libraries that are used by other teams and/or customers. If you are not doing that, some of the guidelines do not apply.

The examples in this book conform to the guidelines, so they should be fairly familiar already. The .NET Common Language Runtime classes and samples also have many examples.

Naming

Two naming conventions are used.

- PascalCasing capitalizes the first character of each word.
- camelCasing is the same as PascalCasing, except the first character of the first word isn't capitalized.

In general, PascalCasing is used for anything that would be visible externally from a class, such as classes, enums, methods, and so on. The exception to this is method parameters, which are defined using camelCasing.

Private members of classes, such as fields, are defined using camelCasing.

There are a few other conventions in naming.

- Avoid common keywords in naming to decrease the chance of collisions in other languages.
- Event classes should end with EventArgs.
- Exception classes should end with Exception.

- Interfaces should start with I.

- Attribute classes should end in `Attribute`.

Hungarian naming (prefixing the name of the variable with the type of the variable) is discouraged for C# code because the added information about the variable isn't as important as making the code easier to read. For example, `strEmployeeName` is tougher to read than `employeeName`.[1]

Conventions such as adding `m_` or `_` at the beginning of fields to denote that the field belongs to an instance is a matter of personal choice.

Guidelines for the Library Author

The following guidelines are useful to programmers who are writing libraries that will be used by others.

Class Naming

To help prevent collisions between namespaces and classes provided by different companies, namespaces should be named using the `CompanyName.TechnologyName` convention. For example, the full name of a class to control an X-ray laser would be something like this:

```
AppliedEnergy.XRayLaser.Controller
```

Unsafe Context

There are many benefits of code verification in the .NET Runtime. Being able to verify that code is typesafe not only enables download scenarios but also prevents many common programming errors.

When dealing with binary structures or talking to COM objects that take structures containing pointers or when performance is critical, more control is needed. In these situations, unsafe code can be used.

Unsafe simply means that the runtime cannot verify that the code is safe to execute. It therefore can be executed only if the assembly has full trust, which means it cannot be used in download scenarios or any other scenario lacking full trust.

The following is an example of using unsafe code to copy arrays of structures quickly. The structure being copied is a point structure consisting of x and y values.

There are three versions of the function that clone arrays of points. `ClonePointArray()` is written without using unsafe features and merely copies the array entries over. The second version, `ClonePointArrayUnsafe()`, uses pointers to iterate through the memory and copy it over. The final version, `ClonePointArrayMemcpy()`, calls the system function `CopyMemory()` to perform the copy.

To give some time comparisons, the following code is instrumented:

```
public struct Point
{
    public Point(int x, int y)
    {
        m_x = x;
        m_y = y;
    }
```

---

[1]My one exception is to use "p" in front of any pointer variables if I am writing unsafe code. That makes it very clear that the variable is something out of the ordinary.

```csharp
// safe version
public static Point[] ClonePointArray(Point[] sourceArray)
{
    Point[] result = new Point[sourceArray.Length];

    for (int index = 0; index < sourceArray.Length; index++)
    {
        result[index] = sourceArray[index];
    }

    return (result);
}

// unsafe version using pointer arithmetic
unsafe public static Point[] ClonePointArrayUnsafe(Point[] sourceArray)
{
    Point[] result = new Point[sourceArray.Length];

    // sourceArray and result are pinned; they cannot be moved by
    // the garbage collector inside the fixed block.
    fixed (Point* src = sourceArray, dest = result)
    {
        Point* pSrc = src;
        Point* pDest = dest;
        for (int index = 0; index < sourceArray.Length; index++)
        {
            *pDest = *pSrc;
            pSrc++;
            pDest++;
        }
    }

    return (result);
}
// import CopyMemory from kernel32
[DllImport("kernel32.dll")]
unsafe public static extern void
CopyMemory(void* dest, void* src, int length);

// unsafe version calling CopyMemory()
unsafe public static Point[] ClonePointArrayCopyMemory(Point[] sourceArray)
{
    Point[] result = new Point[sourceArray.Length];

    fixed (Point* src = sourceArray, dest = result)
    {
        CopyMemory(dest, src, sourceArray.Length * sizeof(Point));
    }

    return (result);
}
```

```csharp
    public override string ToString()
    {
        return (String.Format("({0}, {1})", m_x, m_y));
    }

    int m_x;
    int m_y;
}

class Test
{
    const int Iterations = 20000;    // # to do copy
    const int Points = 1000;         // # of points in array
    const int TimeCount = 5;         // # of times to time

    public delegate Point[] CloneFunction(Point[] sourceArray);

    public static void TimeFunction(Point[] sourceArray,
        CloneFunction cloneFunction, string label)
    {
        Point[] result = null;
        TimeSpan minimumElapsedTime = TimeSpan.MaxValue;

        Stopwatch stopwatch = new Stopwatch();

        // do the whole copy TimeCount times, find fastest time
        for (int retry = 0; retry < TimeCount; retry++)
        {
            stopwatch.Start();
            for (int iteration = 0; iteration < Iterations; iteration++)
            {
                result = cloneFunction(sourceArray);
            }
            stopwatch.Stop();
            if (stopwatch.Elapsed < minimumElapsedTime)
            {
                minimumElapsedTime = stopwatch.Elapsed;
            }
        }
        Console.WriteLine("{0}: {1} seconds", label, minimumElapsedTime);
    }

    public static void Main()
    {
        Console.WriteLine("Points, Iterations: {0} {1}", Points, Iterations);
        Point[] sourceArray = new Point[Points];
        for (int index = 0; index < Points; index++)
        {
            sourceArray[index] = new Point(3, 5);
        }
```

```
        TimeFunction(sourceArray, Point.ClonePointArrayCopyMemory, "Memcpy");
        TimeFunction(sourceArray, Point.ClonePointArrayUnsafe, "Unsafe");
        TimeFunction(sourceArray, Point.ClonePointArray, "Baseline");
    }
}
```

The timer function uses a delegate to describe the clone function so that it can use any of the clone functions.

As with any benchmarking, the initial state of memory is very important. To help control for this, TimeFunction() does each method five times and prints out only the shortest time. Typically, the first iteration is slower, because the CPU cache isn't ready yet, and subsequent times get faster.

The program was run with several different values for points and iterations. Table 39-1 summarizes the results.

Table 39-1. *Copy Array Timings*

Method	p=10, i=2,000,000	p=1,000, i=20,000	p=100,000, i=200
Baseline	0.12	0.09	0.11
Unsafe	0.11	0.08	0.13
CopyMemory()	0.15	0.04	0.10

For small arrays, the overhead of calling CopyMemory() (which involves an interop transition) makes it slower. It is faster for medium-sized arrays, and for large arrays, it's a dead heat.

The point here is that unsafe isn't always faster, so if you are thinking of using it, make sure you measure the performance. It will vary across scenarios, and it will also vary across machines.

XML Documentation

Keeping documentation synchronized with the actual implementation is always a challenge. One way of keeping it up-to-date is to write the documentation as part of the source and then extract it into a separate file.

C# supports an XML-based documentation format. The compiler verifies that the XML is well-formed, does some context-based validation, adds some information that only a compiler can get consistently correct, and writes it out to a separate file.

C# XML support can be divided into two sections: compiler support and documentation convention. In the compiler support section, there are tags that are specially processed by the compiler, for verification of contents or symbol lookup. The remaining tags define the .NET documentation convention and are passed through unchanged by the compiler.

Compiler Support Tags

The compiler support tags are a good example of compiler magic; they are processed using information that is known only to the compiler. The following example illustrates the use of the support tags:

```
// file: employee.cs
using System;
namespace Payroll
{
```

```
/// <summary>
/// The Employee class holds data about an employee.
/// This class class contains a <see cref="String">string</see>
/// </summary>
public class Employee
{
    /// <summary>
    /// Constructor for an Employee instance. Note that
    /// <paramref name="name">name2</paramref> is a string.
    /// </summary>
    /// <param name="id">Employee id number</param>
    /// <param name="name">Employee Name</param>
    public Employee(int id, string name)
    {
        m_id = id;
        m_name = name;
    }

    /// <summary>
    /// Parameterless constructor for an employee instance
    /// </summary>
    /// <remarks>
    /// <seealso cref="Employee(int, string)">Employee(int, string)</seealso>
    /// </remarks>
    public Employee()
    {
        m_id = -1;
        m_name = null;
    }
    int m_id;
    string m_name;
}
}
```

The compiler performs special processing on four of the documentation tags. For the param and paramref tags, it validates that the name referred to inside the tag is the name of a parameter to the function.

For the see and seealso tags, it takes the name passed in the cref attribute and looks it up using the identifier lookup rules so that the name can be resolved to a fully qualified name. It then places a code at the front of the name to tell what the name refers to. For example, the following:

```
<see cref="String">
```

becomes the following:

```
<see cref="T:System.String">
```

String resolved to the System.String class, and T: means that it's a type.

The seealso tag is handled in a similar manner. The following:

```
<seealso cref="Employee(int, string)">
```

becomes the following:

```
<seealso cref="M:Payroll.Employee.#ctor(System.Int32,System.String)">
```

The reference was to a constructor method that had an int as the first parameter and a string as the second parameter.

In addition to the preceding translations, the compiler wraps the XML information about each code element in a member tag that specifies the name of the member using the same encoding. This allows a postprocessing tool to easily match up members and references to members.

The generated XML file from the preceding example is as follows (with a few word wraps):

```
<?xml version="1.0"?>
<doc>
    <assembly>
        <name>employee</name>
    </assembly>
    <members>
        <member name="T:Payroll.Employee">
            <summary>
            The Employee class holds data about an employee.
            This class class contains a <see cref="T:System.String">string</see>
            </summary>
        </member>
        <member name="M:Payroll.Employee.#ctor(System.Int32,System.String)">
            <summary>
            Constructor for an Employee instance. Note that
            <paramref name="name2">name</paramref> is a string.
            </summary>
            <param name="id">Employee id number</param>
            <param name="name">Employee Name</param>
        </member>
        <member name="M:Payroll.Employee.#ctor">
            <summary>
            Parameterless constructor for an employee instance
            </summary>
            <remarks>
            <seealso cref="M:Payroll.Employee.#ctor(System.Int32,System.String)">
Employee(int, string)</seealso>
            </remarks>
        </member>
    </members>
</doc>
```

Generating Real Documentation

The best way to generate documentation from the XML output of the compiler is by using SandCastle,[2] a free tool supported by Microsoft. It can generate documentation that looks like the MSDN documentation.

---

[2]Find it at http://www.sandcastledocs.com. Use it with Sandcastle Help File Builder, at http://shfb.codeplex.com.

XML Documentation Tags

The remaining XML documentation tags describe the .NET documentation conventions. The tags are listed in Table 39-2.

Table 39-2. *XML Documentation Tags*

Tag	Description
<c>	Formats characters as code within other text
<code>	Multiline section of code—usually used in an <example> section
<example>	An example of using a class or method
<exception>	The exceptions a class throws
<include>	Includes XML from an external file
<list>	A list of items
<para>	Adds paragraph to the text
<param>	Describes a parameter to a member function
<paramref>	A reference to a parameter in other text
<permission>	The permission applied to a member
<remarks>	A long description of an item
<returns>	The return value of a function
<see cref="member">	A link to a member or field in the current compilation environment
<seealso cref="member">	A link in the "see also" section of the documentation
<summary>	A short description of the item
<value>	Describes the value of a property
<typeparam>	Describes a generic type parameter
<typeparamref>	Identifies a word that is a generic type parameter

The compiler does not enforce a specific schema on the XML tags that are used in the XML comments; it requires only that the XML be well-formed. This allows it to be extended at will; a team could add an 272103_1_En tag or a <version> tag if desired, and it will be passed into the resulting XML file.

XML Include Files

In a project that has a separate technical-writing team, it may be more convenient to keep the XML text outside of the code. To support this, C# provides an include syntax for XML documentation. Instead of having all the documentation before a function, the following include statement can be used:

```
/// <include file='Foo.csx' path='doc/member[@name="Foo.Comp"]' />
```

This will open the `Foo.csx` file and look for a `<doc>` tag. Inside the doc section, it will then look for a `<member>` tag that has the name `Foo.Comp` specified as an attribute. Here's an example:

```
<doc>
    <member name="Foo.Comp">
        <summary>A description of the routine</summary>
        <param name="obj1">the first object</param>
    </member>
    ...
</doc>
```

Once the compiler has identified the matching section from the include file, it proceeds as if the XML were contained in the source file.

Garbage Collection in the .NET Runtime

Garbage collection has a bad reputation in a few areas of the software world. Some programmers feel they can do a better job at memory allocation than a garbage collector (GC) can.

They're correct; they can do a better job, but only with a custom allocator for each program and possibly for each class. Custom allocators are a lot of work to write, to understand, and to maintain.

In the vast majority of cases, a well-tuned garbage collector will give similar or better performance to an unmanaged heap allocator.

This section will explain a bit about how the garbage collector works, how it can be controlled, and what can't be controlled in a garbage-collected world. The information presented here describes the situation for platforms such as the PC. Systems with more constrained resources are likely to have simpler GC systems.

Note also that there are optimizations performed for multiproc and server machines, which will be covered later in this section.

Allocation

Heap allocation in the .NET Runtime world is very fast; all the system has to do is make sure that there's enough room in the managed heap for the requested object, return a pointer to that memory, and increment the pointer to the end of the object.

Garbage collectors trade simplicity at allocation time for complexity at cleanup time. Allocations are really, really fast in most cases, though if there isn't enough room, a garbage collection might be required to obtain enough room for object allocation.

Of course, to make sure that there's enough room, the system might have to perform a garbage collection.

To improve performance, large objects (greater than 85KB in size, though this number is subject to change) are allocated from a large object heap.

Mark and Compact

The .NET garbage collector uses a "Mark and Compact" algorithm. When a collection is performed, the garbage collector starts at root objects (including globals, statics, locals, and CPU registers) and finds all the objects that are referenced from those root objects. This collection of objects denotes the objects that are in use at the time of the collection, and therefore all other objects in the system are no longer needed.

To finish the collection process, all the referenced objects are copied down in the managed heap, and the pointers to those objects are all fixed up. Then, the pointer for the next available spot is moved to the end of the referenced objects.

Since the garbage collector is moving objects and object references, there can't be any other operations going on in the system. In other words, all useful work must be stopped while the GC takes place.

■ **Note**   This discussion refers to the behavior of the garbage collector that runs on desktop computers. The behavior in other variants of the runtime—the server version, the compact version, and the micro version—may differ in significant ways.

Generations

It's costly to walk through all the objects that are currently referenced. Much of the work in doing this will be wasted work, since the older an object is, the more likely it is to stay around. Conversely, the younger an object is, the more likely it is to be unreferenced.

The runtime capitalizes on this behavior by implementing generations in the garbage collector. It divides the objects in the heap into three generations.

Generation 0 objects are newly allocated objects that have never been considered for collection. Generation 1 objects have survived a single garbage collection, and generation 2 objects have survived multiple garbage collections. In design terms, generation 2 tends to contain long-lived objects such as applications, generation 1 tends to contain objects with medium lifetimes such as forms or lists, and generation 0 tends to contain short-lived objects such as local variables.

When the runtime needs to perform a collection, it first performs a generation 0 collection. This generation contains the largest percentage of unreferenced objects and will therefore yield the most memory for the least work. If collecting that generation doesn't generate enough memory, generation 1 will then be collected and finally, if required, generation 2.

Figure 39-1 illustrates some objects allocated on the heap before a garbage collection takes place. The numerical suffix indicates the generation of the object; initially, all objects will be of generation 0. Active objects are the only ones shown on the heap, but there is space for additional objects to be allocated.

| A0 | B0 | C0 | D0 | E0 |

Figure 39-1. *Initial memory state before any garbage collection*

At the time of the first garbage collection, B and D are the only objects that are still in use. The heap looks like Figure 39-2 after collection.

| B1 | D1 |

Figure 39-2. *Memory state after first garbage collection*

Since B and D survived a collection, their generation is incremented to 1. New objects are then allocated, as shown in Figure 39-3.

| B1 | D1 | F0 | G0 | H0 | J0 |

Figure 39-3. *New objects are allocated*

Time passes. When another garbage collection occurs, D, G, and H are the live objects. The garbage collector tries a generation 0 collection, which leads to the layout shown in Figure 39-4.

B1	D1	F0	G0	H0	J0

B1	D1	G1	H1

Figure 39-4. *Memory state after a generation 0 collection*

Even though B is no longer live, it doesn't get collected because the collection was only for generation 0. After a few new objects are allocated, the heap looks like Figure 39-5.

B1	D1	G1	H1	K0	L0	M0	N0

Figure 39-5. *More new objects are allocated*

Time passes, and the live objects are D, G, and L. The next garbage collection does both generation 0 and generation 1 and leads to the layout shown in Figure 39-6.

B1	D1	G1	H1	K0	L0	M0	N0

D2	G2	L1

Figure 39-6. *Memory state after a generation 0 and generation 1 garbage collection*

Finalization

The garbage collector supports a concept known as *finalization*, which is somewhat analogous to destructors in C++. In the C# spec, they are known as destructors and are declared with the same syntax as C++ destructors (with the ~ClassName syntax), but from the runtime perspective, they are known as *finalizers*,[3] and that is the name that I will use.

Finalizers allow the opportunity to perform some cleanup before an object is garbage collected. They are useful in cases where the class owns a resource that the garbage collector doesn't know something about; perhaps it created an unmanaged resource to perform interop.

When an object with a finalizer is allocated, the runtime adds the object reference to a list of objects that will need finalization. When a garbage collection occurs, if an object has no references but is contained on the finalization list, it is marked as ready for finalization.

After the garbage collection has completed, the finalizer thread wakes up and calls the finalizer for all objects that are ready for finalization. After the finalizer is called for an object, it is removed from the list of objects that need finalizers, which will make it available for collection the next time garbage collection occurs.

This scheme results in the following limitations regarding finalizers:

- Objects that have finalizers have more overhead in the system, and they hang around longer; an object that could be collected has to wait until the next collection. This also means that the object is promoted to the next generation, so you have to wait that much longer for the object to be collected.

---

[3]Since their behavior is so different from C++ destructors, re-using the term was probably a bad choice.

- Finalization takes place on a separate thread from execution, which makes the timing of collection unspecified.

- There is no guaranteed order for finalization. If object a has a reference to object b and both objects have finalizers, the object b finalizer might run before the object a finalizer, and therefore object a might not have a valid object b to use during finalization.

- While finalizers are usually called on normal program exit, there are times where this will not occur. If a process is terminated aggressively (for example, if the Win32 `TerminateProcess` function is called), finalizers will not run. Finalizers can also fail to run if the finalization queue gets stuck running finalizers for a long time on process exit. In this case, attempts to run the finalizers will time out.

Finalizers should be used only in the following situations:

- A class holds an unmanaged resource and needs to dispose of it when an instance of the class is no longer being used. If at all possible, the class should use a `SafeHandle` instance to hold the unmanaged resource instead of creating a finalizer. If the class does declare a finalizer, it should also implement the `Dispose()` pattern.

- A singleton class needs to perform a shutdown operation.

- While a program is under development, a finalizer can identify cases where `Dispose()` is not being called.

Controlling GC Behavior

At times, it may be useful to control the GC behavior. This should be done in moderation; the whole point of a managed environment is that it controls what's going on, and controlling it tightly can lead to problems elsewhere.

Forcing a Collection

The function `System.GC.Collect()` can be called to force a collection. There are two reasonable times to force a collection.

- If you know more than the garbage collector does. If, for example, you have just closed a big document and you know that there are tons of free objects around, you *might* choose to force a collection.

- If you are chasing a bug and want to be sure it isn't because of a collection issue. If you forget to save a delegate that is passed to a native routine, it may cause a bug that shows up sporadically. If you force a collection, that may make it show up consistently.

Suppressing Finalization

As mentioned earlier, an instance of an object is placed on the finalization list when it is created. If it turns out that an object doesn't need to be finalized (because the cleanup function has been called, for example), the `System.GC.SupressFinalize()` function can be used to remove the object from the finalization list.

Deeper Reflection

Examples in the attributes section showed how to use reflection to determine the attributes that were attached to a class. Reflection can also be used to find all the types in an assembly or dynamically locate and call functions in an assembly. It can even be used to emit the .NET Intermediate Language on the fly to generate code that can be executed directly.

The documentation for the .NET Common Language Runtime contains more details on using reflection.

Listing All the Types in an Assembly

This example looks through an assembly and locates all the types in that assembly.

```
using System;
using System.Reflection;
enum MyEnum
{
    Val1,
    Val2,
    Val3
}
class MyClass
{
}
struct MyStruct
{
}
class Test
{
    public static void Main(String[] args)
    {
            // list all types in the assembly that is passed
            // in as a parameter
        Assembly assembly = Assembly.LoadFrom (args[0]);
        Type[] types = assembly.GetTypes();

            // look through each type, and write out some information
            // about them.
        foreach (Type type in types)
        {
            Console.WriteLine ("Name: {0}", type .FullName);
            Console.WriteLine ("Namespace: {0}", type .Namespace);
            Console.WriteLine ("Base Class: {0}", type .BaseType.FullName);
        }
    }
}
```

If this example is run, passing the name of the .exe in, it will generate the following output:

```
Name: MyEnum
Namespace:
Base Class: System.Enum
Name: MyClass
Namespace:
Base Class: System.Object
Name: MyStruct
Namespace:
Base Class: System.ValueType
Name: Test
Namespace:
Base Class: System.Object
```

Finding Members

This example will list the members of a type.

```
using System;
using System.Reflection;
class MyClass
{
    MyClass() {}
    static void Process()
    {
    }
    public int DoThatThing(int i, Decimal d, string[] args)
    {
        return(55);
    }
    public int m_value = 0;
    public float m_log = 1.0f;
    public static int m_value2 = 44;
}
class Test
{
    public static void Main(String[] args)
    {
            // Iterate through the fields of the class
        Console.WriteLine("Fields of MyClass");
        Type type = typeof (MyClass);
        foreach (MemberInfo member in type.GetFields())
        {
            Console.WriteLine("{0}", member);
        }

            // and iterate through the methods of the class
        Console.WriteLine("Methods of MyClass");
        foreach (MethodInfo method in type.GetMethods())
```

```
    {
        Console.WriteLine("{0}", method);
        foreach (ParameterInfo parameter in method.GetParameters())
        {
            Console.WriteLine("  Param: {0} {1}",
                parameter.ParameterType, parameter.Name);
        }
    }
}
}
```

This example produces the following output:

```
Fields of MyClass
Int32 value
Single log
Int32 value2
Methods of MyClass
Void Finalize ()
Int32 GetHashCode ()
Boolean Equals (System.Object)
  Param: System.Object obj
System.String ToString ()
Void Process ()
Int32 DoThatThing (Int32, System.Decimal, System.String[])
  Param: Int32 i
  Param: System.Decimal d
  Param: System.String[] args
System.Type GetType ()
System.Object MemberwiseClone ()
```

For information on how to reflect over an enum, see Chapter 21.

When iterating over the methods in MyClass, the standard methods from object also show up.

Invoking Functions

In this example, reflection will be used to open the names of all the assemblies on the command lines, to search for the classes in them that implement a specific interface, and then to create an instance of those classes and invoke a function on the instance.

This is useful to provide a very late-bound architecture, where a component can be integrated with other components' runtime.

This example consists of four files. The first one defines the IProcess interface that will be searched for. The second and third files contain classes that implement this interface, and each is compiled to a separate assembly. The last file is the driver file; it opens the assemblies passed on the command line and searches for classes that implement IProcess. When it finds one, it instantiates an instance of the class and calls the Process() function.

File IProcess.cs
```
namespace MamaSoft
{
    interface IProcess // the interface we will search for.
    {
        string Process(int param);
    }
}
```

File Process1.cs

```
using System;
namespace MamaSoft
{
    class Processor1: IProcess
    {
        public Processor1() {}

        public string Process(int param)
        {
            Console.WriteLine("In Processor1.Process(): {0}", param);
            return("Raise the mainsail! ");
        }
    }
}
```

File Process2.cs

```
using System;
namespace MamaSoft
{
    class Processor2: IProcess
    {
        public Processor2() {}

        public string Process(int param)
        {
            Console.WriteLine("In Processor2.Process(): {0}", param);
            return("Shiver me timbers! ");
        }
    }
}
class Unrelated
{
}
```

File Driver.cs

```
using System;
using System.Reflection;
using MamaSoft;
class Test
```

```
{
    public static void ProcessAssembly(string aName)
    {
        Console.WriteLine("Loading: {0}", aName);
        Assembly assembly = Assembly.LoadFrom (aName);

            // walk through each type in the assembly
        foreach (Type type in assembly .GetTypes())
        {
                // if it's a class, it might be one that we want.
            if (type.IsClass)
            {
                Console.WriteLine(" Found Class: {0}", type.FullName);

                    // check to see if it implements IProcess
                if (type.GetInterface("IProcess") == null)
                    continue;

                    // it implements IProcess. Create an instance
                        // of the object.
                object o = Activator.CreateInstance(type);

                    // create the parameter list, call it,
                    // and print out the return value.
                Console.WriteLine("    Calling Process() on {0}",
                            type.FullName);
                object[] args = new object[] {55};
                object result;
                result = type.InvokeMember("Process",
                    BindingFlags.Default |
                    BindingFlags.InvokeMethod,
                    null, o, args);
                Console.WriteLine("    Result: {0}", result);
            }
        }
    }
    public static void Main(String[] args)
    {
        foreach (string arg in args)
            ProcessAssembly(arg);
    }
}
```

After all the files have been compiled, it can be run with the following:

```
process process1.dll process2.dll
```

which will generate the following output:

```
Loading: process1.dll
  Found Class: MamaSoft.Processor1
    Calling Process() on MamaSoft.Processor1
In Processor1.Process(): 55
    Result: Raise the mainsail!
Loading: process2.dll
  Found Class: MamaSoft.Processor2
    Calling Process() on MamaSoft.Processor2
In Processor2.Process(): 55
    Result: Shiver me timbers!
  Found Class: MamaSoft.Unrelated
```

For more information on generating code at execution time, see Chapter 32.

When calling functions with MemberInvoke(), any exceptions thrown will be wrapped in a TargetInvocationException, so the actual exception is accessed through the inner exception.

Dealing with Generics

Reflection can also be used with generic types. The simplest way to determine whether a particular type is generic is the new property of Type called IsGenericTypeDefinition. This property will return true only if the type is generic and the generic types have not been bound to a nongeneric type.

```
class Program
{
    static void Main(string[] args)
    {
        List<int> list = new List<int>();

        //will be false
        bool b1 = list.GetType().IsGenericTypeDefinition;

        //will be true
        bool b2 = list.GetType().GetGenericTypeDefinition().IsGenericTypeDefinition;
    }
}
```

In this case, the IsGenericTypeDefinition returns false for the type List<int>, which is a type that does not have any generic parameters. The method GetGenericTypeDefinition() can be used to get a reference from the constructed type List<int> back to the unbound generic type List<T>. The IsGenericTypeDefinition property returns true for this unbound generic type.

The generic arguments for a type or method can be accessed via the GetGenericArguments() method. Consider the following generic type:

```
class MyGenericClass<T> { }
```

The generic parameter can be displayed by the following code:

```
static void DumpGenericTypeParams(Type type)
{
    if (type.IsGenericTypeDefinition)
    {
        foreach (Type genericType in type.GetGenericArguments())
        {
            Console.WriteLine(genericType.Name);
        }
    }
}
```

The output from this code when run against typeof (MyGenericClass<>) is simply as follows:

```
T
```

While simply dumping out the type name may not be overly useful, various reflection methods exist to access information such as the constraints that apply to the generic parameters (Type.GetGenericParameterConstraints()) and to bind generic parameters to nongeneric types (Type. BindGenericParameters()).

Optimizations

The majority of the code optimizations performed in .NET are done by the runtime, but the C# compiler does perform a few optimizations when the /optimize+ flag is used.

- Local variables that are never read are eliminated, even if they are assigned to.

- Unreachable code (code after a return, for example) is eliminated.

- A try-catch with an empty try block is eliminated.

- A try-finally with an empty try is converted to normal code.

- A try-finally with an empty finally is converted to normal code.

- Branch optimization is performed.

- Field initializers that set a member variable to its default value are removed.

Additionally, when optimization is turned on, it enables optimizations by the JIT compiler.

CHAPTER 40

■ ■ ■

Logging and Debugging Techniques

The .NET Runtime provides a few facilities to make programming less dangerous. Conditional methods and tracing can be used to add checks and log code to an application, to catch errors during development, and to diagnose errors in released code.

Conditional Methods

Conditional methods are typically used to write code that performs operations only when compiled in a certain way. This is often used to add code that is called only when a debug build is made and is not called in other builds, usually because the additional check is too slow.

In C++, you would do this by using a macro in the `include` file that changes a function call to nothing if the debug symbol isn't defined. This doesn't work in C#, however, because there is no `include` file or macro.

In C#, a method can be marked with the `conditional` attribute, which indicates when calls to it should be generated. Here's an example:

```
using System;
using System.Diagnostics;

class MyClass
{
    public MyClass(int i)
    {
        m_i = i;
    }

    [Conditional("DEBUG")]
    public void VerifyState()
    {
        if (m_i != 0)
        {
            Console.WriteLine("Bad State");
        }
    }

    int m_i = 0;
}
```

```
class Test
{
    public static void Main()
    {
        MyClass myClass = new MyClass(1);

        myClass.VerifyState();
    }
}
```

The VerifyState() function has the Conditional attribute applied to it, with DEBUG as the conditional string. When the compiler comes across a function call to such a function, it looks to see whether the conditional string has been defined. If it hasn't been defined, the call to the function is eliminated.

If this code is compiled using /D:DEBUG on the command line, it will print out Bad State when it is run. If compiled without DEBUG defined, the function won't be called, and there will be no output.

■ **Note** Because conditional methods are sometimes missing, they cannot be used in any situation where their absence would be missed. This includes returning a value, overriding a virtual method, or implementing an interface method.

Asserts

An *assert* is simply a statement of a condition that should be true, followed by some text to output if it is false. The preceding code example would be written better as this:

```
using System;
using System.Diagnostics;

class MyClass
{
    public MyClass(int i)
    {
        m_i = i;
    }

    public void VerifyState()
    {
        Debug.Assert(m_i == 0, "Bad State");
    }

    int m_i = 0;
}

class AssertExample
{
    public static void Test()
    {
        MyClass myClass = new MyClass(1);

        myClass.VerifyState();
    }
}
```

The call to Debug.Assert() validates that the specified condition is true. If it is not true and the program was built with a debug build, the runtime will show a message box with the specified text.

If the same behavior is desired in all builds, Trace.Assert() should be used instead of Debug.Assert().

TO DEBUG OR TO TRACE?

The traditional view has been that using Debug.Assert() is a good thing to do; it improves the quality of the code and doesn't cause any performance degradation in the actual software.

This is true. There are two other things that are also true, however.

- The cost of most assertions is small enough that it has no measurable impact on the performance of programs.

- The kind of information that is produced by assertions is hugely valuable when you are trying to debug a problem in your program after it has been released.

If an assertion is important enough to write, it's likely to be useful in both debug and release builds. For release builds, however, it's usually more useful to write the information to a file instead of showing the user an ugly dialog. The next section shows how to do this.

Changing the Assert Behavior

The previous example showed the default behavior of calling Assert(). This may not be the desired behavior for some programs; a web page or service is unable to show a message box, and even on programs with UI, it may be desirable not to interrupt the user with the information.

```
class AssertToFileExample
{
    public static void Test()
    {
        Debug.Listeners.Clear();
        Debug.Listeners.Add(new ConsoleTraceListener());

        MyClass myClass = new MyClass(1);

        myClass.VerifyState();
    }
}
```

Both the Debug and Trace classes expose a collection of TraceListener instances, and when an Assert() message needs to be sent, the class will send the assert message to each of them. There are a wide variety of predefined listeners, which can send output to the event log, to a file, to a web page, or to other destinations. If those are sufficient, a custom trace listener can be created.

Adding Other Messages to Debug or Trace Output

In addition to asserts, the Debug and Trace classes can be used to send useful information to the current debug or trace listeners. This is a useful adjunct to running in the debugger, in that it is less intrusive and can be enabled in release builds to generate log files.

The Write() and WriteLine() functions send output to the current listeners. These are useful in debugging but not really useful in released software, since it's rare to want to log something all the time.

The WriteIf() and WriteLineIf() functions send output only if the first parameter is true. This allows the behavior to be controlled by a static variable in the class, which could be changed at runtime to control the amount of logging that is performed.

```
using System;
using System.Diagnostics;
class MyClass
{
    public MyClass(int i)
    {
        m_i = i;
    }

    public void VerifyState()
    {
        Debug.WriteLineIf(debugOutput, "In VerifyState");
        Debug.Assert(m_i == 0, "Bad State");
    }

    static public bool DebugOutput {get; set;}

    int m_i = 0;
}

class Test
{
    public static void Main()
    {
        Debug.Listeners.Clear();
        Debug.Listeners.Add(new TextWriterTraceListener(Console.Out));
        MyClass myClass = new MyClass(1);

        myClass.VerifyState();
        MyClass.DebugOutput = true;
        myClass.VerifyState();
    }
}
```

This code produces the following output:

```
Fail: Bad State
In VerifyState
Fail: Bad State
```

Using Switches to Control Debug and Trace

The previous example showed how to control logging based upon a bool variable. The drawback of this approach is that there must be a way to set that variable within the program. What would be more useful is a way to set the value of such a variable externally.

The BooleanSwitch and TraceSwitch classes provide this feature. Their behavior can be controlled at runtime by setting either an environment variable or a registry entry.

BooleanSwitch

The BooleanSwitch class encapsulates a simple boolean variable, which is then used to control logging.

```
using System;
using System.Diagnostics;

class MyClass
{
    public MyClass(int i)
    {
        m_i = i;
    }

    [Conditional("DEBUG")]
    public void VerifyState()
    {
        Debug.WriteLineIf(m_debugOutput.Enabled, "VerifyState Start");

        if (m_debugOutput.Enabled)
        {
            Debug.WriteLine("VerifyState End");
        }
    }

    BooleanSwitch m_debugOutput =
            new BooleanSwitch("MyClassDebugOutput", "Control debug output");
    int m_i = 0;
}

class Test
{
    public static void Main()
    {
        Debug.Listeners.Clear();
        Debug.Listeners.Add(new TextWriterTraceListener(Console.Out));
        MyClass myClass = new MyClass(1);

        myClass.VerifyState();
    }
}
```

In this example, an instance of BooleanSwitch is created as a static member of the class, and this variable is used to control whether output happens. If this code is run, it produces no output, but the debugOutput variable can be controlled by setting the value in the configuration file for the assembly. This file is named <assembly-name>.config, which for this example means it's called boolean.exe.config, and it has to be in the same directory as the assembly. Not surprisingly, the config file uses XML to store its values. Here's the config file for the example:

```
<configuration>
    <system.diagnostics>
        <switches>
            <add name="MyClassDebugOutput" value="1" />
        </switches>
    </system.diagnostics>
 </configuration>
```

Running the code using this file produces the following result:

```
VerifyState Start
VerifyState End
```

The code in VerifyState shows two ways of using the variable to control output. The first usage passes the flag off to the WriteLineIf() function and is the simpler one to write. It's a bit less efficient, however, since the function call to WriteLineIf() is made even if the variable is false. The second version, which tests the variable before the call, avoids the function call and is therefore slightly more efficient.

TraceSwitch

It is sometimes useful to use something other than a boolean to control logging. It's common to have different logging levels, each of which writes a different amount of information to the log.

The TraceSwitch class defines four levels of information logging. They are defined in the TraceLevel enum (see Table 40-1).

Table 40-1. *Levels of Logging Defined by TraceSwitch*

Level	Numeric Value
Off	0
Error	1
Warning	2
Info	3
Verbose	4

Each of the higher levels implies the lower level; if the level is set to Info, Error and Warning will also be set. The numeric values are used when setting the flag via an environment variable or Registry setting.

The TraceSwitch class exposes properties that tell whether a specific trace level has been set, and a typical logging statement would check to see whether the appropriate property was set. Here's the previous example, modified to use different logging levels:

```
using System;
using System.Diagnostics;

class MyClass
{
    public MyClass(int i)
    {
        m_i = i;
    }
```

```
    [Conditional("DEBUG")]
    public void VerifyState()
    {
        Debug.WriteLineIf(m_debugOutput.TraceInfo, "VerifyState Start");

        Debug.WriteLineIf(m_debugOutput.TraceVerbose,
            "Starting field verification");

        if (m_debugOutput.TraceInfo)
        {
            Debug.WriteLine("VerifyState End");
        }
    }

    static TraceSwitch m_debugOutput =
        new TraceSwitch("MyClassDebugOutput", "Control debug output");
    int m_i = 0;
}

class Test
{
    public static void Main()
    {
        Debug.Listeners.Clear();
        Debug.Listeners.Add(new TextWriterTraceListener(Console.Out));
        MyClass c = new MyClass(1);

        c.VerifyState();
    }
}
```

User-Defined Switch

The Switch class nicely encapsulates getting the switch value from the Registry, so it's easy to derive a custom switch if the values of TraceSwitch don't work well.

The following example implements SpecialSwitch, which implements the Mute, Terse, Verbose, and Chatty logging levels:

```
using System;
using System.Diagnostics;

enum SpecialSwitchLevel
{
    Mute = 0,
    Terse = 1,
    Verbose = 2,
    Chatty = 3
}
```

```csharp
class SpecialSwitch: Switch
{
    public SpecialSwitch(string displayName, string description) :
        base(displayName, description)
    {
    }

    public SpecialSwitchLevel Level
    {
        get
        {
            return((SpecialSwitchLevel) base.SwitchSetting);
        }
        set
        {
            base.SwitchSetting = (int) value;
        }
    }
    public bool Mute
    {
        get { return(base.SwitchSetting == 0); }
    }

    public bool Terse
    {
        get
        {
            return(base.SwitchSetting  >= (int) (SpecialSwitchLevel.Terse));
        }
    }
    public bool Verbose
    {
        get
        {
            return(base.SwitchSetting  >= (int) SpecialSwitchLevel.Verbose);
        }
    }
    public bool Chatty
    {
        get
        {
            return(base.SwitchSetting  >=(int) SpecialSwitchLevel.Chatty);
        }
    }

     protected new int SwitchSetting
    {
        get
        {
            return((int) base.SwitchSetting);
        }
```

```
        set
        {
            if (value < 0)
            {
                value = 0;
            }
            else if (value > 4)
            {
                value = 4;
            }

            base.SwitchSetting = value;
        }
    }
}

class MyClass
{
    public MyClass(int i)
    {
        m_i = i;
    }

    [Conditional("DEBUG")]
    public void VerifyState()
    {
        Console.WriteLine("VerifyState");
        Debug.WriteLineIf(m_debugOutput.Terse, "VerifyState Start");

        Debug.WriteLineIf(m_debugOutput.Chatty,
            "Starting field verification");

        if (m_debugOutput.Verbose)
        {
            Debug.WriteLine("VerifyState End");
        }
    }

    static SpecialSwitch m_debugOutput =
        new SpecialSwitch("MyClassDebugOutput", "application");
    int m_i = 0;
}
```

```
class Test
{
    public static void Main()
    {
        Debug.Listeners.Clear();
        Debug.Listeners.Add(new TextWriterTraceListener(Console.Out));
        MyClass myClass = new MyClass(1);

        myClass.VerifyState();
    }
}
```

This switch can be controlled with the same config file as the other example.

Capturing Process Metadata

The simple information written in a typical trace call may not be sufficient to track down an issue in a complex situation; it may be important know what thread and process created the trace. To allow this information to be captured without forcing the developer to manually code its retrieval, the Trace class includes a method called TraceInformation().

This method can provide the following information:

- The callstack
- The date and time the Trace statement was made
- The logical operation stack (which is the chain of calls in the current call context and may span multiple threads)
- The process ID
- The thread ID
- A timestamp, containing the number of ticks in the system timer.

The user of the trace decides which information to use. To output all the available information, you could use the following code:

```
ConsoleTraceListener ctl = new ConsoleTraceListener();

ctl.TraceOutputOptions =
    TraceOptions.Callstack | TraceOptions.DateTime |
    TraceOptions.LogicalOperationStack | TraceOptions.ProcessId |
    TraceOptions.ThreadId | TraceOptions.Timestamp;

    System.Diagnostics.Trace.Listeners.Add(ctl);
    Trace.TraceInformation("An error occured ");
```

This code produces the following output:

```
Trace.exe Information: 0 : An error occured    ProcessId=2324
    LogicalOperationStack=
    ThreadId=1
    DateTime=2005-01-25T10:52:56.4135000Z
    Timestamp=15259908099
Callstack=    at System.Environment.GetStackTrace(Exception e,
Boolean needFileInfo)
    at System.Environment.get_StackTrace()
    at System.Diagnostics.TraceEventCache.get_Callstack()
    at System.Diagnostics.TraceListener.WriteFooter(TraceEventCache eventCache)
    at System.Diagnostics.TraceListener.TraceEvent(TraceEventCache eventCache,
     String source, TraceEventType severity, Int32 id, String message)
    at System.Diagnostics.TraceInternal.TraceEvent(TraceEventType severity,
    Int32 id, String format, Object[] args)
    at System.Diagnostics.Trace.TraceInformation(String message)
    at Trace1.Program.Main(String[] args) in
z:\code\trace\trace\program.cs:line 17
```

Collecting all of this information is an expensive process, and programs should collect only the information that is necessary.

Improving Your Debugger Experience

The Visual Studio debugger has some nice facilities that allow you to inspect the values of variables as you debug; you can drill down into the values of variables and even view the contents of XML or text variables in a nice pop-up window. What is often overlooked is that it is possible to customize and extend this behavior, using a set of features known collectively as *debugger visualizations*.

Consider the following class:

```
class CommaSeparatedValues
{
    public CommaSeparatedValues(string valuesAsString)
    {
        m_values = valuesAsString.Split(',');
    }

    string[] m_values;
}
```

This class takes in a simple, comma-separated string and breaks it apart into separate values. If you are using this class in code and you look at a variable of this type, the debugger will show the following value:

```
CommaSeparatedValues
```

This is, of course, just the result of the call to ToString(). You can add an override.

```
public override string ToString()
{
    return String.Format("({0}) {1}", m_values.Length, String.Join(",", m_values));
}
```

The output is now the following:

(5) a,b,c,d,efg

That displays both the count of items and the actual string, both of which are useful for debugging. But it also introduces another issue; you can't use ToString() to get the actual comma-separated string out of the class. What you need is a way to specify a different string to use during debugging.

The DebuggerDisplay Attribute

The DebuggerDisplay attribute allows you to do just that: to specify how an item should be displayed in the debugger.

```
[DebuggerDisplay("({m_values.Length}) {ToString()}")]
class CommaSeparatedValues
{
    public CommaSeparatedValues(string valuesAsString)
    {
        m_values = valuesAsString.Split(',');
    }
    public override string ToString()
    {
        return String.Join(",", m_values);
    }
    string[] m_values;
}
```

The DebuggerDisplay attribute declares a single string that will be used by the debugger to display the value of the instance. The values you want to show are listed inside curly braces ({}). In the debugger, the value will now be shown as follows:

(5) "a,b,c,d,efg"

Note that the count is obtained from the private m_values field; the attribute is evaluated by the debugger, which can access all fields.

The debugger display format is a mix of a String.Format-like approach and a C# expression approach; this makes it hard to read, and if you use C#-specific syntax (such as the ? or ?? operator), it will fail when used in other languages. There is a better approach.

```
[DebuggerDisplay("{DebuggerDisplay,nq}")]
class CommaSeparatedValues
{
    public CommaSeparatedValues(string valuesAsString)
    {
        m_values = valuesAsString.Split(',');
    }
```

```csharp
    public override string ToString()
    {
        return String.Join(",", m_values);
    }
    public string DebuggerDisplay
    {
        get
        {
            return String.Format(@"({0}) ""{1}""",
                m_values.Length,
                ToString());
        }
    }
    string[] m_values;
}
```

The class now exposes a DebuggerDisplay property, and the attribute merely refers to the property. The nq in the attribute specifies that the value should not be displayed inside quotes.

Changing the Display of Existing Types

If you don't own a type that has a poor display in the debugger, you can still change the way in which the type displays. You can find an autoexp.cs file in the <user>\Documents\Visual Studio XXXX\Visualizers directory. In it, you will find a series of lines that look like this:

```csharp
[assembly: DebuggerDisplay(@"\{X = {x} Y = {y}}", Target = typeof(Point))]
```

This defines a DebuggerDisplay attribute for the System.Drawing.Point type.

Changing the Detail Display for a Type

When the user clicks the + icon for a display, the debugger will show all fields for that instance. You can control the visibility and default state of each member by adding the DebuggerBrowsable attribute.

```csharp
[DebuggerBrowsable(DebuggerBrowsableState.Never)]
string[] m_values;
```

The array of values will no longer show up in the detail view for the instance. If, on the other hand, you want to always show all of the values in that array, you can use the following:

```csharp
[DebuggerBrowsable(DebuggerBrowsableState.RootHidden)]
string[] m_values;
```

This will remove the m_values line from the display and instead show the contents of the array; the display will look something like this:

```
[0]     a
[1]     b
[2]     c
[3]     d
[4]     efg
```

This capability is very useful to hide implementation details from the users of a class.

Full Customization of the Detail Display

When the user clicks the + icon for a display, the debugger will show all public properties and fields for that instance. It is sometimes desirable to substitute a modified view. This is done by defining a debugger type proxy for the type.

```
[DebuggerTypeProxy(typeof(CommaSeparatedValuesDebuggerProxy))]
class CommaSeparatedValues
{
    public CommaSeparatedValues(string valuesAsString)
    {
        m_values = valuesAsString.Split(',');
    }
    string[] m_values;

    class CommaSeparatedValuesDebuggerProxy
    {
        CommaSeparatedValues m_commaSeparatedValues;
        public CommaSeparatedValuesDebuggerProxy(CommaSeparatedValues commaSeparatedValues)
        {
            m_commaSeparatedValues = commaSeparatedValues;
        }
        public int Count
        {
            get { return m_commaSeparatedValues.m_values.Length; }
        }
        public string FirstItem
        {
            get
            {
                return m_commaSeparatedValues.m_values.Length != 0 ?
                    m_commaSeparatedValues.m_values[0] : null;
            }
        }
        public string[] Items { get { return m_commaSeparatedValues.m_values; } }
    }
}
```

The DebuggerTypeProxy attribute instructs the debugger that when it needs to display the details of a CommaSeparatedValues instance, it should instead construct a CommaSeparatedValuesDebuggerProxy instance and pretend that the user asked for that instance's values to be displayed. This allows the format of the debugger display to be customized; members can be renamed, hidden lists can be promoted to the top level, and so on. In this case, the debugger will now display the following:

Count	5
FirstItem	"a"
Items	{string[5]}

Debugger Visualizers

The default debugger detail view is limited to a grid-based approach, with a single line for each element. There are many types for which that is not a useful way to view data. The debugger provides a way to write visualizers, which can provide whatever view you want on an instance (the text, XML, and HTML views for `string` are implemented as visualizers). Visualizers can also be written that allow editing of the current instance.

For more information, see "How to: Write a Visualizer" in the MSDN documentation.

Debugging into the .NET Framework

The Visual Studio debugger makes it very simple to debug the code you write, but there are some scenarios where it would be useful to be able to debug into the .NET Framework source.

The Visual Studio debugger supports this. See the "How To: Debugging .NET Framework Source" topic in the MSDN documentation.

CHAPTER 41

■ ■ ■

IDEs and Utilities

Many resources may be helpful when developing C# programs; this chapter lists some of the most useful ones.

IDEs

If you are running on Windows, you can use Visual Studio Pro, Visual Studio Express (a free version of Visual Studio), or SharpDevelop (a free open source IDE).

If you are running on other systems using the Mono runtime, you can use the MonoDevelop IDE, and there is some support for Mono in SharpDevelop.

Unit Testing and TDD

If you are using TDD or want to do unit testing, three libraries have been popular.[1]

- NUnit, a basic unit-testing library and tools for TDD

- xUnit.net, written by the authors of NUnit to address some of the lessons they learned from NUnit

- MSTest, which ships with Visual Studio

Test Utilities/Runners

A number of utilities can make test execution quicker and easier. I recommend you look at each of them and figure out which one (or ones) works best for your situation.

- TestDriven.net is a unit-testing add-in that runs in Visual Studio.

- Gallio is a system that sits on top of various testing libraries and provides a common object model.

- Resharper and CodeRush provide an improved test-running experience in Visual Studio.

- NCrunch is an automated parallel continuous testing tool for Visual Studio.

- Visual Studio provides support for running unit tests.

---

[1]There are, of course, other libraries. It's been said that a good unit test library is simple enough that you should write your own, though it's more expensive to come up with a good test runner, and I don't believe in reinventing the wheel.

Disassemblers and Decompilers

Disassemblers and decompilers can be useful to understand how library code works or what the C# compiler is doing when you use features such as Linq or lambdas.

.NET ships with the ILDASM disassembler, which lets you explore an assembly and view the IL for all the methods.

I've used Red Gate's Reflector and JetBrains' dotPeek decompilers, and both have worked well for me. Other decompilers are available as well.

Obfuscators

Obfuscators make the generated IL more obscure, that is, harder to understand when it is disassembled or decompiled. I haven't used any of them and therefore can't recommend any, but they are available.

General Productivity

If you use Visual Studio, take a look at Resharper from JetBrains or CodeRush from DevExpress. They do a ton of things to make your Visual Studio experience nicer. CodeRush offers a free edition for the non-Express versions of Visual Studio.

Regular Expressions

A good regular expression utility makes developing regular expressions much easier, and there are a number of good free ones.

If you can't find one, there's a somewhat ancient one named Regex Workbench that I wrote.

Profilers

Visual Studio Professional (and above) ships with an excellent execution and memory profiler. The memory profiler is available separately; search for *CLR profiler*. There are also third-party solutions offered by Red Gate, SciTech, and JetBrains.

Answering Your Questions

If you have a C# question, you can ask a question on the MSDN C# forum. I have also found StackOverflow (http://stackoverflow.com/) to be very useful.

Index

Printed by Publishers' Graphics LLC